Colony, Nation, and Globalisation

Colony, Nation, and Globalisation
Not at Home in Singaporean and Malaysian Literature

Eddie Tay

香港大學出版社
HONG KONG UNIVERSITY PRESS

Hong Kong University Press
14/F Hing Wai Centre
7 Tin Wan Praya Road
Aberdeen
Hong Kong
www.hkupress.org

© Hong Kong University Press 2011

ISBN   978-988-8028-74-0

All rights reserved. No portion of this publication may be reproduced or transmitted in any form or by any means, electronic or mechanical, including photocopy, recording, or any information storage or retrieval system, without permission in writing from the publisher.

British Library Cataloguing-in-Publication Data
A catalogue record for this book is available from the British Library.

This digitally printed version 2011.

Contents

Acknowledgements		vii
Introduction		1
I. Colony: British Malaya		13
Chapter 1	Amok and Arrogation: Frank Swettenham's 'Real Malay'	15
Chapter 2	Discourses of Difference: Isabella Bird, Emily Innes, and Florence Caddy	31
Chapter 3	The Exhaustion of Colonial Romance: W. Somerset Maugham and Anthony Burgess	45
II. Nations: Malaya, Singapore, and Malaysia		61
Chapter 4	'There is no way out but through': Lee Kok Liang and the Malayan Nation	63
Chapter 5	Nationalism and Literature: Two Poems Concerning the Merlion and Karim Raslan's "Heroes"	77
Chapter 6	Irresponsibility and Commitment: Philip Jeyaretnam's *Abraham's Promise* and Gopal Baratham's *A Candle or the Sun*	93

III. Globalisation: Home is Elsewhere   107

Chapter 7   The Post-Diasporic Imagination: The Novels of K. S. Maniam   109

Chapter 8   Two Singaporeans in America: Hwee Hwee Tan's *Mammon Inc.* and Simon Tay's *Alien Asian*   121

Chapter 9   Writing Back Home: Tash Aw's *The Harmony Silk Factory*, Vyvyane Loh's *Breaking the Tongue*, and Lau Siew Mei's *Playing Madame Mao*   133

Conclusion   151

Works Cited   153

Index   163

Acknowledgements

This book evolved from a Ph.D. dissertation written at the University of Hong Kong. I would like to thank my thesis supervisor, Elaine Ho, for her guidance. I owe her an intellectual debt.

I would like to thank my examiners: Bill Ashcroft, Otto Heim and Philip Holden. Their comments and advice persuaded me to develop a doctoral dissertation into a book intended for a larger readership.

Kudos to Michael Duckworth at Hong Kong University Press.

I am grateful to David Huddart, Julian Lamb, Michael O'Sullivan, Li Ou, and David Parker for their support and for wonderful conversations over coffee. I am fortunate in having colleagues who are also friends. To the folks at the University of Hong Kong from my location at the Chinese University of Hong Kong in Sha Tin, I would like to say "Hands across the Harbour".

My research assistants, Kristy Chan and Lily Liu, are indefatigable.

Early versions and portions of several chapters were previously published as follows. I would like to acknowledge my gratitude to the editors and anonymous reviewers at these publications:

- "Discourses of Difference: Isabella Bird, Emily Innes and Florence Caddy". *Asian Crossings: Travel Writing on China, Japan and Southeast Asia*. Eds. Steve Clark and Paul Smethurst. Hong Kong: Hong Kong University Press, 2008. 99–112.
- "'A Construction from Spare Parts': Inventing National Identity in Singapore". *The Nation across the World: Postcolonial Literary Representations*. Eds. Harish Trivedi, Meenakshi Mukherjee, C. Vijayasree, and T. Vijay Kumar. New Delhi: Oxford University Press, 2007. 213–229.
- "'There is no way out but through': Alienation and Interpolation in Lee Kok Liang's *London Does Not Belong to Me* and 'Return to Malaya'". *New Literatures Review*. No. 44. October 2005. 63–75.

- "Hegemony, National Allegory, Exile: The Poetry of Shirley Lim". *Textual Practice*. 19 (3): 289–308.
- "In America: The Alien Asian and the Cosmopolitan Chic". *Southeast Asian Review of English*. No. 46. April 2005. 123–142.

This book is dedicated to May Lyn, Titus, Tabitha, and Peggy.

Introduction

This book is about the condition of anxiety. It explores literary works that articulate a pervasive uneasiness that attends to the notion of home. It concerns the condition of being deracinated, deculturalised, and displaced, of being neither here nor there—not at home where one should be. We are interested in the realisation that identity markers and cultural signs are perpetually under contestation even within a defined geographical terrain. This book seeks to give a name to these conditions and a history one can trace in Anglophone literary works of Malaya and those of post-independence Singapore and Malaysia.

Home is a physical space; it is also the location of the self, a symbolic terrain invested with social, political, and cultural meanings. To be at home is to identify an image of the self in prevalent ideological discourses; hence, if one is not at home, one is at odds with prevailing social and political conditions. By engaging with debates pertaining to colonialism, nation formation, and globalisation, I argue that Anglophone literary works about colonial Malaya and independent Singapore and Malaysia are projects that invariably narrate a condition wherein one is not at home.

There are five permutations to the condition of not being at home as narrated through the works considered in this book. The first involves geographical dislocation. This condition applied to many, of course, but we are interested in its effect upon British colonial administrators and women who wrote of Malaya in the nineteenth century. In their colonial narratives about Malaya, there is an attempt to create an environment hospitable to the colonial enterprise. This was a response to the condition of not being at home. The second sense of this condition is found in portrayals of Malaya during its period of rapid decolonisation after the Second World War. As nationalist thought and sentiment emerged, Malaya was no longer tenable as a site of mystery, exoticism, and colonial adventure; it could no longer be cast as a home away from home for the British who were stationed there. We find the third sense of not being at home during the post-independence era. It involves writers at odds with the political landscapes of their own countries, as in the case of writers in contemporary Malaysia and Singapore whose work overtly criticises their national ideologies. The fourth sense of not being at home involves expatriates who are or have been temporarily away from their countries of birth or long-term residence. In response, they often seek to recreate Malaya, Malaysia, and Singapore through novelistic experiments. The fifth sense of not being at home, finally, has to do with globalisation. Given transnational flows of capital, labour, and media images, the boundaries of home and one's sense of belonging may need to be redefined, and this, too, is articulated in literary work.

An historical trajectory runs through these five iterations of not-at-homeness, beginning with the Pangkor Treaty in 1874, whereby British Residents were appointed to various states in what is now Peninsular Malaysia. This residential system in British Malaya was based on the policy of indirect rule devised after the Indian "Mutiny". While Residents were officially advisors to the Sultans, their advice was seldom unheeded. As T. N. Harper argues, "strictly speaking, the British presence was not a state at all, or rather it worked on the pretence that it was not a state" (18). With the subtle installation of colonial institutions, combined with literary portrayals of the inhabitants of Malaya by colonial administrators and authors such as Frank Athelstane Swettenham (1850–1946) and Hugh Charles Clifford (1866–1941) as well as by travel writers such as Isabella Lucy Bird (1831–1904), Malaya was transformed politically and depicted in writing as a quasi-domestic space within the British Empire. The arrival of the British is often narrated in tandem with the humanist ideals of European Enlightenment. The rule of law and the attendant institutions of colonialism were often mapped onto a Malaya portrayed as pre-modern. Inhabitants were hence rendered as unhomely and backward figures who needed to be brought forward into a colonial modernity. In this respect, while Malaya was rendered homely for British administrators and for readers back in England, the inhabitants of Malaya were depicted as figures alienated from their immediate surroundings.

The dismantling of the empire, naturally enough, caused considerable uncertainty among colonial administrators. After the British surrender to the Japanese during the Second World War, the prevailing sentiment in Malaya was that they were no longer legitimate rulers. Subsequently, the anti-colonial battle cry of "*Merdeka*", meaning "freedom" or "independence", led to a new chapter in the history of Malaya. Malaya no longer seemed like the home it once had been to the British sailors, soldiers, policemen, teachers, administrators, and their *memsahibs* stationed there. This sentiment is captured poignantly in Anthony Burgess' novels *Time for a Tiger* (1956), *The Enemy in the Blanket* (1958) and *Beds in the East* (1959), works known together as *The Malayan Trilogy*. For the author and lawyer Lee Kok Liang (1927–92), who was studying law in London in the 1950s, the centre would no longer hold, we may say. The eloquent title of his posthumously published novel *London Does Not Belong to Me* (2003) signalled a sense of disaffection with the imperial centre as well as hope for the postcolonial future of Malaya.

With the separation of Singapore and Malaysia in 1965, the two nations diverged, each pursuing a variant form of nationalism. Nationalism, broadly speaking, is a set of statist discourses that seeks to create a sense of allegiance and belonging, so turning the nation-state into a home for its citizens. In the case of Singapore, the government pursued what may be called a pragmatic mode of nationalism that privileged economic and capitalist considerations above all else. Various labels have been used to describe Singapore's political economy, ranging from "communitarian" (Chua Beng-Huat) to "authoritarian" (Garry Rodan). Debates pertaining to democracy, political freedom, and civil society were often regarded by the government to be of secondary importance compared with the state of the economy. Not surprisingly, literary works have emerged to show that there are those who are not at home within the government's paternal and quasi-authoritarian approach to governance. Not-at-homeness takes the form of political critique and resistance in these works. Lau Siew Mei's *Playing Madame Mao* (2000), which makes comparisons between Lee Kuan Yew and Mao, is a case in point. Given that Lau has emigrated to Australia; one may speculate that, like the protagonist in her novel, she was not at home with Singapore's mode of governance.

Malaysia's nationalism has been said to privilege a major ethnicity at the expense of others. The New Economic Policy, implemented in 1970, sought to address the economic disparity between the new nation's Chinese minority and Malay majority. While, as a policy, it has officially ended in 1990, it remains the dominant state ideology. Shirley Geok-lin Lim (1944–) and Ee Tiang Hong (1933–90), both Malaysian Chinese, were the most prominent authors who left as a result of what they perceived as discriminatory policies. In this respect, the Malaysian nation is no longer home for those who are not regarded as *bumiputeras*, "sons of the soil", a term that underscores the Malay claim to be the indigenous ethnic group. There are those, among them the lawyer, journalist and author Karim Raslan (1963–) who sought to articulate in their work—short stories in Karim's case—their uneasiness with Malaysia as their national home. The novels of K. S. Maniam (1942–) narrate a post-diasporic condition as a response to being marginalised by the prevailing nationalist discourse in Malaysia.

If globalisation implies the interpenetration of cultures facilitated by rapid transnational flows of capital, labour, and commodities, then the boundaries of home and one's sense of belonging to a specific locality and national home may need to be redefined. Can one still consider the nation and its associated locality as determinants of home? This question is particularly relevant when we consider work by authors whose readerships (or who themselves) traverse national boundaries. Hwee Hwee Tan (1974–) is a case in point. She was born in Singapore, lived for a period in the Netherlands, and was educated in the United Kingdom and America. Her novel,

Mammon Inc. (2001), narrates the experience of a young Singaporean faced with various career opportunities in Oxford and New York. Given that authors such as Tan may identify with more than one locality and nation, can one say that work devoted to narrating these experiences are re-imagining the idea of what constitutes home? Or is home to be recast in a reflexive manner, to be recalled even as one admits that memory is fallible? Perhaps such is the case with Tash Aw's (1971–) *The Harmony Silk Factory* (2005), a novel that presents three overlapping (and at times incompatible) points of view of 1940s Malaya.

The central concern of this book resonates with other recent works on the cultures and literatures of Singapore and Malaysia. In *Occidentalism in Novels of Malaysia and Singapore* (2005), Tamara S. Wagner examines how Anglophone literatures of Singapore and Malaysia continually "reimagin[e] 'the West' … vis-à-vis the impact of its imported literary traditions on English literature" (25). There is a need, then, to acknowledge that the "local" literary traditions of Singapore and Malaysia are always influenced, if they are not engendered, by English literary traditions. Robbie B. H. Goh's *Contours of Culture* (2005) analyses spatial, social, and cultural demarcations in Singapore. Goh makes the salient point that in modern Singapore, "[p]ostcolonial voices … are [undermined] by global communications, which often pose threats of neo-colonial influences and cultural imperialisms" (22). The implication here is that the processes of globalisation may bring about a return of colonial ideological structures. C. J. W.-L. Wee's *The Asian Modern* (2007), which examines Singapore's cultural modernity, hypothesises that as part of Singapore's nation-building project, immigrant culture was "deterritorialise[d]" so as to "further the loss of culture in relation to social and geographical territory". He argues that there was subsequently an "attempt at *reterritorialising* the city-state" so as to inscribe "Confucian" and "Asian" values onto the dominant social discourse during the 1980s and mid-1990s [emphasis in original] (8–9). Wee is arguing that as part of nation building, organic and indigenous culture may have already been eradicated and replaced with cultural values consonant with nationalist ideology.

One common point between these recent critical works and mine lies in the acknowledgement that in the case of Singapore, one can no longer speak of such a thing as an "authentic" or "pure" culture. Indeed, among Wee's crucial points is that "Singapore is a case study of original authenticity being given up and of various versions of both the 'West' and 'Asia' being used to reterritorialise the cultural space" (11). There is no "outside" then. To encounter the unhomely is to encounter the difference within the self. I extend this point by mapping in literary works the topoi of colony, nation, and globalisation and their attendant motifs, so as to bring into relief the impossibility of envisioning a home that is free from incursions from the "outside".

Postcolonialism and Commonwealth literary studies

Much of the critical vocabulary of this book derives from the fields of Commonwealth literary studies as well as postcolonialism, though it has to be said that the final portion of the book extends its critical reach so as to explore issues pertaining to the transnational and the global. As we may recall, Commonwealth literary studies was inaugurated in 1964 at the School of English at the University of Leeds, where the first Conference on Commonwealth Literature was held; the proceedings were subsequently collected in John Press's *Commonwealth Literature: Unity and Diversity in a Common Culture* (1965).

The label "Commonwealth literature" has drawn criticism from various quarters. As Meenakshi Mukherjee argues, the term reinstates the centrality of the English literary canon ("Interrogating Post-colonialism" 6). Salman Rushdie in his 1983 polemical essay "'Commonwealth Literature' Does Not Exist" makes the point that the label is indicative of the formation of an "exclusive ghetto" (63). Yet we must recognise that Rushdie's success may be due in part to the endeavours of scholars working in the field of Commonwealth literature (as well as postcolonial literary studies). Furthermore, Rushdie may have overstated his point, since those working in Commonwealth literature are acutely aware of the potential problems of identifying too readily with the label, as Mukherjee's argument makes plain.

The heterogeneity of the field of Commonwealth literary studies is also evident in the way its scholars respond to postcolonial theory and criticism. Indeed, the essay collections *Postcolonizing the Commonwealth* (2000) edited by Roland Smith and *Interrogating Post-colonialism* (1996) edited by Harish Trivedi and Meenakshi Mukherjee provide a measure of the extent of exchanges between scholars in these two fields. Arun P. Mukherjee, in particular, is sceptical of subsuming Commonwealth literary studies under the aegis of postcolonialism. He argues that the danger of postcolonial theory is that "homegrown oppressors" might be misconstrued as "'the oppressed' who get all the postcolonialist's sympathy for their suffering at the hands of the colonizer" ("Some Uneasy Conjectures" 17).

While Frantz Fanon and Aimé Césaire anticipated the scope of postcolonial studies even before the term "postcolonialism" gained currency, it was Edward Said, Gayatri Spivak, Homi Bhabha, and other postcolonial critics and theorists who re-conceptualised the discourses of colonialism, ethnicity, nationality, and culture through their affiliations with French cultural theory. The emergence of postcolonial studies in the late 1970s may be traced to Edward Said's *Orientalism* (1978), which argued that European scholarship consistently represents cultures of the Middle East as inferior, backward, and unsophisticated, while Europe is cast as the centre of enlightenment, progress, and civilisation. Said extended this argument in *Culture and Imperialism* (1993) through its examination of a variety of European texts to uncover the binary oppositions between the centre and the periphery, First World and Third World, coloniser and colonised. Theorists such as Spivak and Bhabha have extended Said's inauguration of the field. Spivak's concerns, including the status of the subaltern, the relationship between Third World and First World feminism, and caste identities in India broaden the scope of postcolonial studies in her insistence that there are various conditions of oppression that demand acknowledgement. Bhabha's *The Location of Culture* (1994) and *Nation and Narration* (1990) explore cultural issues raised by race, migration, and the relationship between the discourses of postcolonialism and postmodernism. Together, Said, Bhabha, and Spivak form what Robert J. C. Young calls "the Holy Trinity of colonial-discourse analysis" (*Colonial Desire* 163).

Postcolonial theory and criticism initiated by critics working within metropolitan academies tend to privilege contrapuntal texts such as Jean Rhys's *Wide Sargasso Sea* (1966) and J. M. Coetzee's *Foe* (1986). The former is read as a contrapuntal narrative to *Jane Eyre* and the latter as a subversive re-visioning of *Robinson Crusoe*. While *Wide Sargasso Sea* and *Foe* are works that challenge their respective literary predecessors, paradoxically, what occurs is that the prominence and centrality of colonial writing tend to be reinforced and revisited under the aegis of postcolonial theory and criticism. Aijaz Ahmad draws our attention to this polarised dynamic when he observes that "It is in the metropolitan country ... that a literary text is first designated a Third World text ... and then globally redistributed with that aura attached to it" (45). As he points out, there is a certain kind of text favoured by critics in metropolitan institutions, specifically those amenable to "critical positions [that] are framed by the cultural dominance of postmodernism" (125). He points to the work of Fredric Jameson as symptomatic, with its resulting tendency of "identification of 'Third World literature' with 'naive' realism" (125–126).

The overlapping fields of postcolonial studies and Commonwealth literature are fraught with contestations and consist of a variety of critical positions and methodologies. While they are not the primary focus of this book, I draw attention to them as they form the theoretical setting for my discussions of literary texts. Despite the caveats just noted, the critical concepts and theoretical insights developed in the fields of postcolonial studies and Commonwealth literary studies are relevant for a study that seeks to address the trajectories of literary narratives extending from British Malaya to contemporary Malaysia and Singapore. This is because much of postcolonial studies involves reading against the grain of colonial ideology, and this is particularly important in the case of colonial-era writings. The work of Frantz Fanon is crucial to our reading of Swettenham, just as Bill Ashcroft's elaboration of dis-identification is relevant to our understanding of how Lee Kok Liang's writings represent an expression of resistance against the metropolitan discourse. Likewise, the thematics of nationhood and nationalism are informed by debates pertaining to decolonisation within Commonwealth literary studies. This is especially so when we are considering how the contours of national life are shaped by political elites in contemporary Singapore and Malaysia. When we take up works written under the aegis of diaspora, globalisation and transnationalism, we reference notions of cultural displacement that have also developed within postcolonial studies.

Also, one may argue that there is a transactional and transnational representation at work in Anglophone literature by writers born in Singapore and Malaysia and who live and work in these two countries. This is evidenced especially in the bibliographic classifications of Singapore and Malaysian literatures. Ismail S. Talib has made the point that while Anglophone literatures in Singapore and Malaysia have taken on distinctive trajectories after Singapore's separation from Malaysia in 1965, "a discussion of either Singapore or Malaysian literature quite often depends on knowledge of the other, and it may be useful to discuss the two literatures together" (72).

Given the history and geographic proximity of the two countries, some writers elude classification by way of national categories. Talib cites several instances wherein authors such as Marie Gerrina Louise, who are more suitably identified as Malaysian, have been included in bibliographies of Singaporean literature (73). The reverse is true in the case of Colin Cheong and Stella Kon (Talib 73). One may also cite the case of Suchen Christine Lim, the first winner of the Singapore Literature Prize for her novel, *Fistful of Colours* (1993). Born in Malaysia and currently based in Singapore, her novels make important statements about the social and political conditions of Singapore, as in *Fistful of Colours,* and the recent history of Peninsula Malaysia, as in *A Bit of Earth* (2001). It is not surprising, therefore, to find her name listed in the bibliographic categories of both Singapore and Malaysia.

Due to the ease with which authors and the themes of their work are able to cross over into each other's national space, Malaysian writers are in some ways already living abroad with respect to Singapore, and the reverse is also true. Just as Malaysian literature is always already transnational with respect to Singapore, the same is true of Singapore literature. Thus, the categories "Singapore Literature" and "Malaysian Literature", while useful as geographical and national markers, sometimes conceal rather than reveal the complexities of literary production and reception, such that an absolute insistence on these labels becomes problematic. In the case of colonial writings this problem of demarcation is retrospective, rendering exclusivist national markers problematic: Should the Malayan works of Frank Swettenham, Hugh Clifford, W. Somerset Maugham, and Anthony Burgess now be studied under the category of "English Literature" or "Singapore and Malaysian Literature"? In this respect, I find it useful to examine the literatures of Malaya, Singapore, and Malaysia alongside one another.

Choice of texts

I have selected texts that are useful in engaging the themes of home and belonging as these relate to a broader range of debates taking place within the fields of Commonwealth literary studies, postcolonialism, and transnational cultural studies. The order in which they are discussed is chronological so as to trace the two themes through history. The first group of texts were written during the colonial period of Malaya, the second group arose out of the nationalist period in Singapore and Malaysia, and the final group have diasporic and transnational settings.

The texts to be discussed were chosen for a number of reasons. First, some are of historical significance. The works of Frank Swettenham, Isabella Bird, Emily Innes, and Florence Caddy are important literary representations of Malaya. Swettenham's writings, especially their deployment of the trope of natives running amok, are informed by the colonial will to govern, while we find in the works of the women writers the ways in which the colonial landscape of Malaya is constructed through gendered writing. The works of Bird, Innes, and Caddy will be considered alongside Sara Mill's argument in her book *Discourses of Difference* (1991) that the colonial voice is a masculine voice which female writers cannot adopt easily. In contrast, the works of W. Somerset Maugham and Anthony Burgess represent a significant turn in colonial narratives in that they allow us to explore the exhaustion of colonial romance.

Second, some of these texts were chosen because their themes are of political significance to contemporary Singapore and Malaysia. They allow us to examine literary responses to nation and nationalism. With Lee Kok Liang's less frequently studied novel, *London Does Not Belong to Me,* and his short story "Return to Malaya", we can continue to examine the themes of home and belonging by way of work that is contrapuntal to colonial narratives. Lee's work is important in that it documents the postcolonial hope of a Malayan nation. It has been said that Edwin Thumboo (1933–) "is the closest Singapore has to a poet laureate" (Shirley Lim *Against the Grain* 22). His poem, "Ulysses by the Merlion", cannot be ignored when we consider the relationship between literature and the nation-building project. Likewise, Alfian bin Sa'at (1977–) is regarded as an anti-establishment poet, short-story writer, and playwright whose work engages directly with Singapore's national ideology. A reading of Thumboo's poem and Alfian's poem "The Merlion" provides a starting point from which one is able to critique the state's ideological construction of the Singaporean nation as home. While Lee Tzu Pheng's (1946–) poem "My Country and My People" is certainly a useful counterfoil to Thumboo's poem (Goh "Imagining the Nation" 31), a comparison of poems by Thumboo and Sa'at allows one to foreground the iconography of the Merlion as a national symbol. In a similar vein, Philip Jeyaretnam's *Abraham's Promise* (1995) and Gopal Baratham's *A Candle or the Sun* (1991) are significant because they offer overt critiques of Singapore's state ideology.

Third, certain other texts are chosen because they are narratives that feature various forms of dislocation. Contemporary post-diasporic novels such as those written by K. S. Maniam are examined in relation to nation building in Malaysia. These novels offer alternative narratives that constitute a reaction against Malaysia's ethnic-based state ideology as it turns the nation into an unhomely space for non-Malays. The choice of Karim Raslan's short story "Hero" exemplifies my argument that those who are narrated by Malaysia's nationalist ideology as being at home within the nation are in fact not at home with the dominant state ideology.

Fourth, certain texts are chosen because they enable us to examine the trope of home and belonging in transnational and diasporic settings. Simon Tay's travelogue, *Alien Asian: A Singaporean in America* (1997) and Tan's novel *Mammon Inc.*, both set in America, are two very different narratives that seek to negotiate between the social and cultural spaces of Singapore and America. They are valuable in helping us understand how one's sense of home and belonging is affected by globalisation as the latter induces increased mobility and interconnections between different national and cultural spaces.

Finally, I have chosen certain texts because they are by a relatively younger group of writers whose non-realist mode of writing is a consequence of their different responses to the exigencies of nation building. Tash Aw's *The Harmony Silk Factory*, Vyvyane Loh's *Breaking the Tongue* (2004) and Lau's *Playing Madame Mao* are narratives of home written outside the space of the nation in that the authors are based outside of Singapore and Malaysia and are writing back to their home countries. The first two novels recuperate the sense of home by reworking the history of colonialism and national independence, while the last centres on political events in Singapore in the late 1980s and distances itself from its national home as an act of political critique. Reading these three novels together allows us to examine the act of reconstituting home from memory and history.

The ethnicity of some of the authors mentioned above examined cannot be overlooked, especially when considered in the context of nationhood in Malaysia and Singapore. The ethnic-nationalist climate of Malaysia in the 1960s and 1970s was such that Chinese Malaysian writers such as Shirley Lim and Ee Tiang Hong opted to emigrate. As I have argued elsewhere, there is a tendency for anthologists to assume that Malaysian literary works of merit are written only in the Malay language (Tay 294). The Anglophone writer Karim Raslan, as we shall see in Chapter 5, recognises that his privileged position as a Malay lawyer, business owner and writer is due in part to the 1970s and 1980s economic and political climate of Malaysia, which brought about the rise of a Malay middle-class while marginalising other ethnic communities. In this respect, the multicultural Malayan nationhood envisioned in Lee's "Return to Malaya" was interrupted from the 1960s onward by a nationalism that privileges a single ethnic group. Maniam's novels, considered in Chapter 7, attest to the difficulties faced by those of South Asian descent as they lay claim to a Malaysia shaped by Malay nationalism.

In the case of Singapore, multicultural as well as meritocratic policies supposedly ensure that the concerns of its minorities are represented, to the extent that Thumboo, who is of South Asian and Chinese parentage, is able to fuse the theme of multicultural harmony with a narrative of Singapore's modernity in poems such as "Ulysses by the Merlion" and "Conversation with My Friend Kwang Min at Loong Kwang of Outram Park". There are indeed authors in Singapore who write in Tamil, Malay, and Chinese and who are highly regarded within their ethnic communities. Yet it is the Anglophone writers who are more prominently featured by the English-language media as well as in highly regarded online Anglophone literary journals such as the *Quarterly Literary Review Singapore*. Poets such as Alvin Pang, Toh Hsien Min, and Cyril Wong, among others, have been invited to showcase their works at international literary festivals. Nonetheless, there are moments when ethnic anxieties are made manifest in literary works. For instance, in Alfian's poem "The Last Kampung", from the collection *One Fierce Hour* (1998), the poetic persona laments that the traditional Malay way of life has been written out of Singapore's modern landscape. Also, in poems such as "A Visit to a Relative's House in Malaysia" and "Train Ride to Malaysia", we detect the fissuring of Malay ethnicities by the nationalist discourses of Singapore and Malaysia.

A reader may perhaps point to omissions of certain texts and authors. But this book makes no claim to engaging with the entire canon of Malayan, Singaporean, and Malaysian literature. Rather, it positions itself alongside a considerable body of studies of literary works of the region. The works chosen here engage with the themes of home and belonging, or the lack thereof. These are themes germane to colonial and postcolonial narratives of displacement, nationhood, and diaspora. Discussions of certain texts and authors are omitted because they have been thoroughly explored by others working in postcolonial and Commonwealth literary studies. With regard to the colonial period, the works of Joseph Conrad are omitted, though we consider his influence on writers such as Maugham and Burgess in Chapter 3. Those interested in Conrad's Malaya might wish to consult J. H. Stape's "Conrad's 'Unreal City': Singapore in 'The End of the Tether'" in the volume *Conrad's Cities*, edited by Gene M. Moore and published in 1992. Important discussions of racial politics in Conrad's Malayan novels may be found in Agnes Yeow's "'Here comes the Nazarene': Conrad's Treatment of the Serani and the Racial Politics of Empire" in the journal *Conradiana* as well as "Conrad and the Straits Chinese: The Politics of Chinese Enterprise and Identity in the Colonial State" in the journal *The Conradian*. For a discussion of early university writings in Malaya which brought together writers such as Edwin Thumboo, Wong Phui Nam, Ee Tiang Hong and Wang Gungwu, see Anne Brewster's *Towards a Semiotic of Postcolonial Discourse: University Writing in Singapore and Malaysia* (1989) as well as Shirley Lim's "Finding a Native Voice: Singapore Literature in English" in *The Journal of Commonwealth Literature*. Kuo Pao Kun's play, *The Coffin is Too*

Big for the Hole (1984), is important as an allegory that investigates Singapore's political landscape. It is excluded from our discussion because many of the issues it raises overlap with the discussions of Baratham's and Jeyaretnam's novels.

Overview

This book is divided into three parts. Part I explores literature written during the colonial era. The first chapter begins with a discussion of colonialism as it was in British Malaya, and this is followed by an analysis of the theme of "amok" in the writings of Swettenham, who renders the phenomenon as unhomely—as external to the political economy of Malaya so as to legitimise the colonial presence. But amok is a trope that continues to trouble Swettenham's colonialist narrative. The image of the Malay running amok, I argue, represents the return of the repressed that haunts colonialist writings on Malaya.

In the second chapter, I examine representations of Malaya in the writings of Bird, Innes, and Caddy, who were in Malaya for different periods of time between 1879 and 1888. Following Sara Mills, I attempt to read their works as "discourses of differences" that nonetheless reinforce colonialist attitudes about Malaya and its people. The next chapter examines representations of Englishness and the empire in the writings of Maugham and Burgess. The former arrived in Malaya in the 1920s in search of material for his stories, while the latter arrived in the 1950s as a colonial education officer. Unlike the writings of those that came before him, Maugham's representation of Europeans in Malaya is troubled by a reservation expressed in the work as to the authority of Englishness. In the case of Burgess, his work, set in the period of imperial decline, harbours an anxiety as to the role of the Englishman in the tropics. In the productions of both of these authors, we see a Malaya that is gradually becoming socially and politically uninhabitable to its colonial occupants.

Part II of the book examines how literary works articulate a nation against colonialist and state-sponsored nationalist projects. Chapter 4 examines the postcolonial project of "writing back" against metropolitan representations of Malaya as evidenced in the works of Lee. In this respect, Lee narrates his disenchantment with London and reclaims Malaya as his home. The next two chapters address the question of whether nationalism in either its Singaporean or Malaysian variant gives the citizens of two new countries congenial national homes. Chapter 5 begins with a consideration of the discourses of nationalism in Singapore and Malaysia. The chapter examines Thumboo's "Ulysses by the Merlion", Alfian's "The Merlion" and Karim's short story "Heroes" so as to explore the consequences of nationalism on literary representations of Singapore and Malaysia. The notion of responsibility to the state is explored in the next chapter, which examines two novels by Singaporean authors. Given that the official version of nationalism in Singapore tilts towards economic pragmatism and the maintenance of the state, how does a writer then assume the responsibility of political critique if this critique amounts to opposition against the state itself? This question is addressed in the chapter with reference to Baratham's *A Candle or the Sun* and Jeyaretnam's *Abraham's Promise*.

The final part of this study engages debates pertaining to diaspora, globalisation, and transnationalism. Here our concern is with subjectivities outside of "home". Chapter 7 examines the novels of K. S. Maniam. It focuses his articulation of a post-diasporic consciousness against the ethnic nationalism expressed in the New Economic Policy. In Chapter 8, I examine representations of America and Singapore in Tan's *Mammon Inc.* and Tay's travelogue, *Alien Asian*. The chapter argues that in so far as globalisation fosters a subjectivity predicated on a dense network of interdependencies and connections with different localities, it also commodifies these subjectivities. The last chapter, with reference to Aw's *The Harmony Silk Factory*, Loh's *Breaking the Tongue* and Lau's *Playing Madame Mao*, explores how a reworking of cultural memory may provide a way out of this commodification.

This study is not an attempt at creating a canon out of Malayan, Singaporean, and Malaysian literary works. It offers a chronology, but not a teleology that presents the evolution of Singaporean and Malaysian subjectivities as emerging from the primordial soup of the pre-colonial era, passing through a troubled infancy with colonialism, reaching a rebellious adolescence with nationalism, and, finally, attaining an enlightened state in the present era of globalisation. I envision this project as a reminder that the topoi of colony, nation, and globalisation are not to be regarded as internally coherent discourses. Home, identity and one's sense of belonging are characterised not by continuity and constancy but by discontinuities and disruption. In this respect, one can never be completely at home. Given the changes in socio-political conditions through time, the contending claims of history, and the multiplicity of cultural localities and affiliations, the topoi of colony, nation, and globalisation are seen here as a series of projects, comprising acts of representation and counter-representation, erasures and appropriations, avowals and disavowals.

# I
Colony
British Malaya

1
Amok and Arrogation:
Frank Swettenham's 'Real Malay'

In *Charting the Shape of Early Modern Southeast Asia*, Anthony Reid draws attention to the efficacy of the term "early modern" as opposed to "such older terms as Renaissance, Reformation, or Age of Discovery" (6). He makes the point that "it has the advantage of being less culture-bound to a European schema, less laden with triumphalist values" (6). In doing so, he urges us to recognise that the work of history, in particular Southeast Asian history, has to be dissociated from colonialist historiography, as the latter conflates modernity with colonialism. In European historiography, colonial modernity is a signifier that distinguishes the pre-historical from the historical, the pre-modern from the modern, and so the pre-colonial from the colonial. In the writings of many colonial administrators, the histories of colonies were written in such a way as to collapse these three binary oppositions into a single Manichean dynamic, made manifest in colonialist representations of Malaya.

Such a conflation conveys the impression that before attaining political sovereignty as nation-states, the histories of Singapore and Malaysia began with the history of imperialism. This suppression of pre-colonial history creates the fallacious notion that the price of modernity in Singapore and Malaysia was colonial rule. As we will now establish, Frank Athelstane Swettenham and others who wrote of Malaya represented pre-colonial history in such a way as to allow it to be supplanted by colonial history. Through this process, indigenous subjectivity was construed as inferior to that of Europeans. This is the core of colonialist ideology, for a home without its own history, and which is portrayed without the benefit of its inhabitant's collective memories, is a home that can be easily appropriated by others.

The second part of this chapter draws inspiration from Philip Holden's "Love, Death and Nation: Representing Amok in British Malaya", a 1997 article that explores the significance of the trope of amok in British Malayan colonialist discourse with reference to Hugh Clifford's *Saleh: A Prince of Malaya* (1926) and Henri Fauconnier's *The Soul of Malaya* (1930). This chapter examines the unhomely image of Malay subjects who run amok. With reference to the writings of

Swettenham, it looks at how amok as a trope is deployed in his writings. Amok as a colonialist motif is a response to the condition of not being at home; it is a trope that seeks to create an environment hospitable to the colonial enterprise. However, as we shall see, this trope is often unstable in its range of signification, to the extent that it exceeds its colonialist framing of Malaya.

The significance of Swettenham to the colonialist historiography of Malaya cannot be overemphasised. Swettenham's career as a colonial administrator and his reputation as an expert on all matters related to British Malaya spanned a significant period of the British presence in Malaya. He arrived in Malaya as a cadet in 1871 and became assistant resident in Selangor (1874–76), assistant colonial secretary for native states (1876–82), resident in Selangor (1882–89), resident in Perak (1889–95), and resident-general to the federation (1896–1901). He was one of the key figures present at the signing of the Pangkor Treaty of 1874, which marked the formal beginning of British control over the administration and economy of the Malay States. Fluent in Malay, he possessed an intimate understanding of Malay culture and forged close relations with prominent members of the Malay ruling class. Apart from *British Malaya* (1906), a personal account of the history of the period, his other writings include essays and short stories in *Malay Sketches* (1895), *The Real Malay* (1900) and his memoirs, *Footprints in Malaya* (1942). As Susan Morgan points out, Swettenham was "the great hero of British imperial historiography about nineteenth-century British intervention in the Peninsula" (141–142). In the biography *Swettenham* (1995), H.S. Barlow likewise writes that Swettenham's *British Malaya* had been, until the 1960s, "the only authoritative account available of the period" (699). When one considers the range of Swettenham's output—consisting of short stories, sketches, memoirs, essays, a history of British Malaya and articles to British newspapers—alongside the roles he had played in the Pangkor Treaty, in the building of railway lines, and in various tin-mining and rubber enterprises, it is plain that his writing was among the many ways he contributed to the creation of British Malaya as a political entity, an extractive enterprise, and as an imagined community.

Arrogation: Colonialism and the beginning of history

Prior to the writing of colonial history, the earliest records of the geographic terrain that was to become modern Singapore and Malaysia were at best fragmentary. Historians have noted this lacuna in the history of Singapore. The history of Singapore before Stamford Raffles' arrival in 1819 is regarded as "incomplete, vague or contradictory, imprecise in dating and in description of events or locations … [It is] difficult to separate historical event from legend" (Arthur Lim 3). Albert Lau points out that "Practically nothing certain is known about the Singapore past before

1819 and the little that can be known must be based on textual references which are, unfortunately, difficult to interpret" (42). Indeed, historians of Singapore often discuss its pre-colonial history in terms of myth. C. M. Turnbull's *A History of Singapore, 1819–1988* alludes to a third century account by a Chinese envoy who wrote of the island as inhabited by "primitive cannibals with tails 5 or 6 inches long" (1).

The *Sejarah Melayu* (Malay Annals), the earliest account and a key text of Malay history in the region, is also mentioned by Turnbull in relation to two incidents (2–3). The first is an account of how the Indian prince Raja Chulan, encamped on the island while on his way to conquer China, encountered a ship manned by a crew of old men. The ship, with its cargo of rusty needles and trees, is purported to be a ruse concocted by the Chinese emperor so as to convey the impression that China is so far away as to be out of reach. The men have been instructed to tell Raja Chulan that they have started out on their trip as young men, with the ship carrying seeds and iron bars for trade, and that they have since aged, the seeds having matured into trees, and the iron bars having rusted away into needles. Raja Chulan is thus deceived into giving up his enterprise (Leyden *Malay Annals* 13–15). The second account concerned the prince Sang Nila Utama, the son of Raja Chulan, who sailed into a storm on his way to an island. It is only after discarding everything from the ship, including his crown, that the storm abated. On the island, he encounters a beast that is described as possessing a red body, a black head, and a white breast, which he mistakes for a lion, thus naming the island "Singa-pura", Lion City (Leyden 42–43).

Recent work focusing on pre-colonial Singapore, best represented by John N. Miksic and Cheryl-Ann Low Mei Gek's *Early Singapore, 1330s–1819: Evidence in Maps, Text and Artefacts* (2004), has uncovered a vibrant history dating from the fourteenth century. But for the colonials arriving in the nineteenth century, as a result of the scarcity of historical records, it was easy to conflate the historical beginnings of Singapore with a colonial imperative that relegated pre-colonial narratives to the vanishing horizon of history—into myth, hearsay, and legend. As myth and history in the *Malay Annals* are inseparable, the text is easily shifted onto the ground of the pre-modern, thus enabling the history of Singapore and of the region to be written over by historians sympathetic to the colonial cause. Swettenham's *British Malaya* is a case in point. Swettenham likens the *Malay Annals* to "the ramblings of the insane, who jumble up fact with fiction, [although] there is truth in this record" (*British Malaya* 12). Even though there is "small means of winnowing the wheat from the chaff", he proceeds to do so, taking it upon himself to separate truth from fiction in writing the history of British Malayan history (Swettenham *British Malaya* 12). After referring to various sources, Swettenham notes that there is a scarcity of records in the case of Singapore. Regarding this lacuna of six hundred years, Swettenham has this to say:

> So the ancient Singapura disappeared ... Now again, after six hundred years, Singapore rises from its ashes and draws to itself the trade of all rivals within a thousand miles ... What is strange is that, in those six hundred years, there should have been no Portuguese, no Hollander, no Englishman, with curiosity and application enough to make himself acquainted with the ancient history of Singapore, and prescience enough to realize that the existence, which had been suddenly and violently stifled, would revive in a new and far more vigorous life the moment it was carefully and intelligently treated. *The opportunity was there always, but the hand to seize it, to make the most of it, was wanting.* [emphasis added] (Swettenham *British Malaya* 31–32)

Colonialism does not take place on the material and economic plane alone. The colonisation of a physical terrain occurs alongside the colonisation of its history. In the above passage, the lacuna of six hundred years is written over with colonial desire; the absence of history is for Swettenham a point of lamentation not so much for the lack of history but for the lack of colonial history, thus laying bare the imperial will-to-power. We must bear in mind Nicholas Thomas's point in *Colonialism's Culture* that "[d]epiction and documentation ... did not merely create representations that were secondary to practices and realities, but constituted political actualities in themselves" (111–112). Having written of the lacuna of pre-modern history in the language of possession, trade and colonial power, one need only lament the lack of prescience, care and intelligence, and raise the need to rectify this through actual colonial enterprise—Singapore, as physical landscape and as historical entity, had to wait six hundred years for its history to arrive in 1819.

And so, colonial modernity arrived in Singapore in the figure of Stamford Raffles. The signing of the treaty between Raffles and the Temenggong Abdul Rahman was motivated by a combination of political ambition, commercial interest, and personal aspiration on the part of Raffles. Raffles was recalled in humiliation to England in 1816, when Java was ceded to the Dutch, the East India Company having sustained heavy financial losses as a result of ineffectual administration under his charge. As he puts it afterward, "I was not unconscious that errors in judgement might be found in the complicated and extensive administration with which I was entrusted" (Raffles 22). At that moment, Britain was in the process of resigning its interests in Southeast Asia; there were plans to restore Penang to the Netherlands, as well (Turnbull 6). In Java and later in Singapore, Raffles was motivated by a civilising mission. As he claims in the case of Singapore, "the interests of science and literature have been no less attended to than the moral improvement of the people" (Raffles 68). He was also apprehensive about Dutch expansion in Sumatra and its consequences for the British Empire and was therefore interested in establishing a port in the region so as to allow the British "the means of supporting and defending [their] commercial intercourse with the Malay States, and which, by its contiguity to the seat of the Dutch power, might enable [them] to watch the march of [Dutch] policy, and when necessary to counteract its influence" (Raffles 54).

Other scholars suggest that the publication of John Leyden's translation of the *Malay Annals* was initiated by Raffles as part of his strategy for convincing the directors of the Company of the viability of establishing a British station in Singapore, for it was depicted in the text that Singapore was the site of an ancient and flourishing trading emporium under the rule of Sang Nila Utama and his descendents (Hooker 43–46). Thus, pre-colonial history had been pressed into service of colonial modernity. Robert Young's statement that European imperialism appropriates the other into its history finds resonance in this instance, for the pre-colonial history of Singapore as presented in the *Malay Annals* was cited when it was convenient to do so (*White Mythologies* 35).

At points where pre-modern history draws attention to its incommensurability with colonial modernity, it would have to be removed. An instance of this occurred with the discovery of a stone at the mouth of Singapore River. An eyewitness account provided by Abdullah bin Abdul Kadir described it as follows:

> The rock was smooth, about six feet wide, square in shape, and its face was covered with a chiselled inscription. But although it had writing this was illegible because of extensive scouring by water. Allah alone knows how many thousands of years old it may have been. After its discovery crowds of all races came to see it. The Indians declared that the writing was Hindu but they were unable to read it. The Chinese claimed that it was in Chinese characters ... It was Mr. Raffles's opinion that the writing must be Hindu because the Hindus were the oldest of all immigrant races in the East ... It remained where it was until the time when Mr. Bonham was Governor of the three settlements of Singapore, Penang and Malacca. Mr. Coleman was then engineer in Singapore and it was he who broke up the stone ... He destroyed the rock because he did not realize its importance. (165–166)

The relic may be the only supporting evidence of the existence of an ancient civilisation presided over by Sang Nila Utama and his descendents from the eleventh to the thirteenth century. Or it might be a remnant of the Javanese empire of Majapahit, which attacked and claimed the island in the fourteenth century (Arthur Lim 9). It might be the only evidence substantiating in part the narrative of the *Malay Annals*. The artillery officer Peter James Begbie points out in his book *The Malayan Peninsula*, an early account of Malayan history, published in 1834, that there were three instances in the *Malay Annals* in which a stone of that size was mentioned (355–360). While the first two were mythical, involving human beings transformed into stone, the last instance had to do with the story of a Malay warrior who, as a test of strength, lifted the stone and hurled it onto the mouth of the river.

The inscriptions on the stone were made after his death as a record of his deeds and heroic exploits.

The stone was recognised by the populace as a relic bearing a link to ancient history. It was the lynchpin with which people projected their collective speculations regarding ethnic and ancestral claims to the land. The Hindus said the inscriptions on the rock were Hindu, the Chinese said they were Chinese, and Abdullah claimed them to be Arabic even though, as he mentions, no one could actually read it. As Ban Kah Choon points out, "The stone touches upon and raises at a critical moment in Singapore's founding those thorny questions of the hermeneutics of origin and tradition" (11). The stone bore evidence that there was an earlier claim on the island, thus suggesting that there was a history prior to colonial modernity. The matter came to an end when Robert Coleman, the colonial engineer, blew up the stone. As Ban points out, "what is extraneous and, therefore potentially unruly, is removed" (9). Only three pieces of the stone remain to this day, two of which are at a museum in Calcutta, and the third, referred to as the "Singapore Stone", is in the National Museum of Singapore (Arthur Lim 9).

Thus, even though there may be evidence that dates the pre-colonial history of Singapore back to the fourteenth century, most of the history of Singapore as we know it today is a history that begins with colonialism. In this sense, Singapore has no pre-colonial history to speak of. Kwa Chong Guan notes that this is indeed "the conventional and dominant view of Singapore's past" (137). Yet one may see this absence of pre-1819 history as arising out of a disregard of history so as to install colonial modernity as the only form of modernity. It has also often been consequently said that Singapore, both as a colony and later as a nation-state, is an invention and thus a testimony to the ingenuity of colonialism not only as a territorial enterprise but also as a capitalist enterprise, and this is an enterprise subsequently inherited by the government of Lee Kuan Yew. As Kwa points out, a perspective that casts Raffles as a "'great man' of history" who possessed prescience and foresight and who "founded" Singapore privileges a Eurocentric version of history, for it views "Southeast Asian history through the eyes of the European actors rather than the Asian actors" (137–138). This meta-narrative of Singapore having emerged *from nowhere* and *from nothing*, as something invented out of colonial governmental enterprise, is constitutive of modernity mapped from above.

As with the case of the pre-colonial history of Singapore, that of Malaya is likewise intertwined with colonial history. On the first page of *The Golden Chersonese and the Way Thither* (1883), the Victorian travel writer Isabella Bird characterises the Malay Peninsula as "somewhat of a *terra incognita*" with "no legitimate claim to an ancient history" (1). The characterisation of land *incognita* is a familiar colonialist strategy, whereby the claim of discovery is synonymous with the assertion of rights to a territorial claim. Having attributed the first mention of the peninsula as the Golden Chersonese to Ptolemy's *Aurea Chersonesus* and Milton's

Paradise Lost, Bird goes on to write of Malacca as having been "rediscovered in 1513 by the Portuguese" (*Chersonese* 2). The history of Malaya, then, cannot but begin with European colonialism. In Book XI of *Paradise Lost*, the archangel Michael shows Adam from "a hill / Of Paradise the highest" a panoramic view of "all earth's kingdoms and their glory" beginning with

> Cambalu, seat of Cathaian khan
> And Samarchand by Oxus, Temir's throne,
> To Paquin of Sinaean kings, and thence
> To Agra and Lahor of great mogul
> Down to the golden Chersonese, or where
> The Persian in Ecbatan sat, or since
> In Hispahan, or where the Russian czar
> In Mosco, or the sultan in Bizance,
> Turchestan-born ...
>
> (Milton 581–583)

The passage is part of a grand historical outline of the world as Milton knew it. As G. K. Hunter points out, the symmetrical structure of the epic is such that while the first two books of *Paradise Lost* deal with the establishment of the Kingdom of Hell in its fallen state, the last two deal with the future establishment of the kingdoms of the human world (151). Given that it provides Adam with a view of the future kingdoms of humankind, it is a divine prophecy, and Chersonese is the only kingdom without a ruler—and thus awaits colonial conquest. This is all the more significant when we consider that part of *Paradise Lost* was composed under the regime of Oliver Cromwell, whose interests in furthering the domain of the East India Company led to the first of three Anglo-Dutch Wars in 1652. As the second of three wars was fought based on issues related to colonies in West Africa, it would not have escaped the notice of the English that the Dutch had already established a presence in Asia by that time. The Dutch East India Company was founded in as early as 1602, and Batavia (now Jakarta) had, since 1619, become the central office from which the Dutch commandeered various outposts scattered in different port cities of Asia (Andaya 71–72).

Thus, from the beginning of the world as described in the narrative of *Paradise Lost*, the sovereignty of Malacca (and by extension the Malay Peninsula) was an absence, a political vacuum awaiting a colonial presence. When Isabella Bird wrote of the Malay Peninsula as having no claim to ancient history, she meant that there was no claim to history until the arrival of European colonialism. Just as Milton was reconstituting world history from his point of view during the period of the Glorious Revolution and of Cromwell's regime, Isabella Bird was reconstituting Malayan history from her point of view in the early period of colonial modernity. As such, Malaya has always been thought of as British Malaya and never was otherwise.

Running amok

In the economy of racial representation in colonialist portrayals of British Malaya, Malays are presented as lacking in cultural accomplishments. Swettenham described them as possessing "very few writings which can be dignified by the name of literature" (*British Malaya* 167). While he mentions classical Malay texts such as the *Sejarah Melayu* (Malay Annals), *Hikayat Hang Tuah* (The Adventures of Hang Tuah) and *Hikayat Abdullah* (The Story of Abdullah), he says of the last that the "style is far from classic, and his biography is not much read outside the Straits Settlements Colony" (Swettenham *British Malaya* 168). He provides an example of Malay literature by quoting Malay *pantuns*, which he calls "love ditties", explaining that Malays "are given to the writing of verses, like love-sick damsels and swains", thus implying that they are given to sentimental excess (*British Malaya* 168).

Equally, Swettenham portrays Malays as backward and unencumbered by the legacy of the European Enlightenment:

> It may seem curious that ... the ordinary Malay man should be extraordinarily sensitive in regard to any real or fancied affront, and yet that was, and is, characteristic of the people ... when the Malay feels that a slight or insult has been put upon him which, for any reason, he cannot resent, he broods over his trouble till, in a fit of madness, he suddenly seizes a weapon and strikes out blindly at every one he sees—man, woman, or child—often beginning with those of his own family. This is the *âmok*, the furious attack in which the madman hopes to find death and an end to his intolerable feeling of injury and dishonour. There can be little doubt that, except in rare instances, those who are suddenly seized by this fury to destroy are homicidal maniacs ... (*British Malaya* 143–144)

The depiction of the native who runs amok and attacks the members of his own family becomes a testimony to the native's irrationality; it is the psychological portrait of the Other of the European Enlightenment. It is the antithesis of European subjectivity, a condition by which familial and rational bonds find no hold on the individual. The above passage conveys implicitly the point that the colonisers are there to save the natives from themselves.

The real Malay, according to Swettenham, is a "good imitative learner", "makes a good mechanic", "lazy to a degree, is without method or order of any kind, knows no regularity ... and considers time as of no importance. His house is untidy, even dirty" (*Malay Sketches* 3). We are told that

> A Malay is intolerant of insult or slight; it is something that to him should be wiped out in blood. He will brood over a real or fancied stain on his honour until he is possessed by the desire for revenge. If he cannot wreck it on the offender, he will strike out at the first

human being that comes in his way, male or female, old or young. It
is this state of blind fury, this vision of blood, that produces the *âmok*.
(*Malay Sketches* 3–4)

As Homi Bhabha points out, "In the colonial discourse, that space of the other is always occupied by an *idée fixe*: despot, heathen, barbarian, chaos, violence" (*Location* 101). In the case of British Malaya, that *idée fixe* is the figure of the *pengamok*, the person who runs amok. Swettenham's sketch entitled "Âmok" exemplifies how the Manichean dynamic of European narrative form and non-European content, narrator and narrated, institutional order and native chaos is established. The sketch is drawn from a government report by J. W. Brewster, assistant superintendent at Lower Perak. This particular incident as narrated by Swettenham has the effect of affirming the relationship between mental deficiency and the Malay race. Its prescriptive authority is made evident in John C. Spores' *Running Amok: An Historical Inquiry*, a 1988 monograph that looks to historical data for a broader understanding of the mental disorder; the monograph reproduces the same government report on which Swettenham's narrative is based. To be sure, amok is not entirely a colonial invention. Spores made the point that in India as well as in Malaya, it was an acceptable and honoured practice for warriors (28). In *Hikayat Hang Tuah* (The Adventures of Hang Tuah), a work of Malay literature set in the fifteenth century, an outbreak of amok becomes an occasion for heroism on the part of several youths who subdued the *pengamok* (Sheppard 30–34). Amok as depicted in indigenous narrative is a functional phenomenon that can be contained by heroic members of Malay society.

For Swettenham, however, amok becomes a justification for colonial governance. In his writings, amok as depicted via colonial rationality becomes unhomely in the sense that it is a phenomenon that needs to be eradicated from Malaya. Swettenham's sketch begins with a hypothesis, to be followed by an exemplum, and ends with the certification of truth. At the beginning, the reader is told that the term "amok" is

> used to describe the action of an individual who, suddenly and without apparent cause, seizes a weapon and strikes out blindly, killing and wounding all who come in his way, regardless of age or sex, whether they be friends, strangers, or his own nearest relatives.
> (*Malay Sketches* 38–39)

This is followed by the tale of Imam Mamat, who seeks the pardon of his wife and brother-in-law before stabbing them with a spear and a knife and chasing after his sister-in-law and her children, eventually killing them.

It is not the cause but the consequence of amok that is elaborated. An official list is quoted and reproduced in the sketch, tabulated according to those killed and wounded (*Malay Sketches* 42). Eventually apprehended, Imam dies from the loss of blood. The surgeon's autopsy report quoted in the sketch certifies that the *pengamok* died "from haemorrhage from a wound" (*Malay Sketches* 43). Both the list and the autopsy report, as part of an institutionally sanctioned discourse, testify to the truth of amok. "In the colonial situation", writes Frantz Fanon in another context, "going to see the doctor [or] the administrator ... are identical moves" (*Dying Colonialism* 120). As a violent and destructive form of behaviour, amok signifies the native's failure at what we may call the government of the self. The implication is that if the Malays are unable to govern themselves, then others would have to do it for them.

What then, is the cause of amok? While the sketch is silent on the events that may have caused it, the explanations offered in Swettenham's other writings ascribe the cause of amok to the psychology of the Malays. In a sketch entitled "Faulty Composition" (a title intended to suggest the flawed make-up of the Malay psyche), Swettenham appeals to the writings of the ethnologist James Richardson Logan. Amok, Swettenham writes,

> consists in a proneness to chronic disease of feeling, resulting from a want of moral elasticity, which leaves the mind a prey to the pain of grief, until it is filled with a malignant gloom and despair, and the whole horizon of existence is overcast with blackness ... the great majority of *pĕng-âmoks* are monomaniacs ... it is clear that such a condition of mind is inconsistent with a regard for consequences. (*The Real Malay* 245–246)

Once defined as a psychological condition, amok becomes an ailment to be treated. It is noted also that since the arrival of the British, the number of incidences of Malays running amok has decreased. As Swettenham tells us,

> A simple explanation is that, with hospitals, lunatic asylums, and a certain familiarity with European methods of treatment, the signs of insanity are better understood, and those who show them are put under restraint before they do serious damage. (*The Real Malay* 253)

This tendency to run amok on the part of the Malays requires a different form of colonial governance; one may suggest that amok is represented in such a way so that it coheres with the residential system in Malaya. The terms of the Pangkor Treaty specified that those named as residents were to be advisors to individual states. Amok therefore has necessitated a colonial governance that is not based on force. James Wheeler Woodford Birch, the first resident appointed in Perak, is described by Swettenham as someone who "knew very little of Malays and almost nothing of their language", and Birch's aggressive behaviour, combined with his unrelenting attempts to enforce order and introduce reforms in the state, met with opposition, suspicion, and bitterness (*Malay Sketches* 229). Accompanied by a party equipped with a number of firearms and other weapons, Birch pasted the proclamations of the Pangkor Treaty in a number of villages before he was speared by the Malays in a fit of amok (Swettenham *Malay Sketches* 238–242). It was perhaps with this incident in mind that Swettenham wrote of the unique tasks of a colonial administrator in Malaya:

> The first requirement was to learn the language of the people to be ruled. I mean, to speak it and write it well. And the first use to make of this knowledge was to learn as much as possible about the people—their customs, traditions, characters, and idiosyncrasies. An officer who has his heart in his work will certainly gain the sympathies of those over whom he spends this trouble. (*The Real Malay* 32)

Particularly after the Indian "Mutiny", British Malaya was seen as an opportunity for the empire to redeem itself. Colonial rule in British Malaya was thus established not by military aggression but with compassion, not through force but through kindness and persuasion.

That the image of the colonised is constructed as inferior to the coloniser so as to justify imperialist ideology as a function of the Enlightenment project is a point many others have made. Chinua Achebe, in his reading of Conrad's *Heart of Darkness*, points out that "the image of Africa [is projected] as 'the other world,' the antithesis of Europe and therefore of civilization" (3). Likewise, Fanon argues thus in his characteristically strident terms:

> The feeling of the inferiority of the colonized is the correlative to the European's feeling of superiority. Let us have the courage to say it outright: *It is the racist who creates his inferior* [emphasis in original]. (*Black Skin, White Masks* 93)

Fanon provides a clue as to how Swettenham's treatment of amok may be read against the grain. In Fanon's work, amok is portrayed as an outbreak of anti-colonial resistance:

> The Algerian gave the isolated European the impression of being in permanent contact with the revolutionary high command. He showed a kind of amplified self-assurance which assumed rather extraordinary forms. There were cases of real "running amuck".
>
> Individuals in a fit of aberration would lose control of themselves. They would be seen dashing down a street or into an isolated farm, unarmed, or waving a miserable jagged knife, shouting, "Long live independent Algeria! We've won!" (*A Dying Colonialism* 62)

The above passage provides an alternative reading of amok. While characterised as a psychopathological condition on the part of the colonised subject, it can also be an expression of anti-colonial sentiment that is brewing among the native community. Here, the scene is rendered through the point of view of the isolated European. (Perhaps no European is more isolated and not at home than when he or she is in the empire—it is the ratio of the rulers to the ruled in the empire that renders the European vulnerable.) Here, amok is a source of anxiety for European colonisers:

> [The Europeans] would telephone to the nearest city, only to have it confirmed that nothing unusual had happened in the country. The European became aware of the fact that the life he had built on the agony of the colonized people was losing its assurance. (*A Dying Colonialism* 61–62)

What is interesting about this section of *A Dying Colonialism*, occurring in a chapter that examines the radio as an instrument of colonial rule and propaganda, is its suggestion that the psychopathology of the ruled engenders the psychopathology of their rulers:

> These hysterical cases were sometimes ... given over to the police for questioning. The pathological nature of their behaviour would not be recognized, and the accused would be tortured for days ... In the dominant group, likewise, there were cases of mental hysteria; people would be seized with a collective fear and panicky settlers were seen to seek an outlet in criminal acts. (*A Dying Colonialism* 62–63)

The amok of the colonised engenders the paranoia of the coloniser. Fanon is describing here the European paranoid reaction to amok. While he is not proposing a theory whereby the emergence of revolutionary consciousness may arise from amok, one may suggest nonetheless that this is a polemical moment in his writing whereby he dramatises amok as a possible nascent moment of anti-colonial revolution.

The appropriation of the other in colonialist writings is a function of the Manichean dynamic wherein binary oppositions were proposed between coloniser and colonised, administrators and natives, Europeans and non-Europeans. However, the colonisers as well as the colonised were both caught within this binary universe. If Fanon's writings concerning amok are brought to bear on Swettenham's, what emerges is the possibility of reading against the grain, such that the name of terror living in the heart of every colonial administrator in Malaya must be the *pengamok* who, with his jagged knife or *kris*, strikes at the walls of colonialism.

Amok is the return of the repressed; even as it dramatises the inferiority of indigenous subjectivity, it exceeds this colonialist portrayal, emerging as a phenomenon that engenders the coloniser's paranoia. One may also suggest that the dynamics of gender are at work in the representation of amok. Hence, amok becomes a trope that symbolises the violent and ungovernable manliness of the natives. The scene of amok almost invariably possesses a gendered economy. Those who run amok are always Malay men, armed with spears, or with *krisses* or knives ever ready at their belts. Birch, a victim of amok at Pâsir Sâlak, was in a bathhouse when he was killed. The scene of his death is described as an invasion of domestic privacy:

> Pandak Indut cried out, "Here is Mr. Birch in the bath-house, come, let us kill him," and, followed by three or four others shouting *âmok, âmok*, they leapt on to the floating timbers and thrust their spears through the open space in front of the house". (*Malay Sketches* 242)

Swettenham was due to meet Birch soon afterward on that day, and when it became clear that a trap was being set for him, Swettenham's Malay companion, in preparation for the coming amok, "seized his kris and tightened his belt in readiness for instant trouble" (*Footprints* 58). It is hard to miss the masculine physicality of amok. Of course, by describing the killing of Birch as an instance of amok, Swettenham's narrative avoids considering the possibility that the attack on Birch might be indicative of an anti-colonial agency.

If we recognise in the trope of amok the "appropriation of the other as a form of knowledge within a totalizing system", then we may retrieve the trope from its essentialist category so as to critique Swettenham's discourse of arrogation (Young *White Mythologies* 35). In Swettenham's writings, amok is an essentialist category justifying colonial rule. However, amok is in actuality an ambivalent trope; it is a colonialist stereotype created out of the disavowed elements of the European self. Amok, as Swettenham himself admits at one point, is a suppressed phenomenon in Europe and America:

> If the asylums of Europe and America were closed, and the inmates returned to their relatives, it is more than probable that cases of ... *âmok* ... would not be confined to the natives of the Peninsula ...
> (*The Real Malay* 253–254)

In Europe and America, amok is a symptom of insanity, and it is not to be found in ordinary people. However, in Malaya, it is represented as a general social phenomenon that occurs to ordinary Malays. Through disavowal and slippage, amok becomes an Orientalist projection that emerges as a colonialist stereotype. The ambivalent nature of amok can be located in an article by John Crawfurd, which Swettenham quoted at length:

> When the English infantry charged with the bayonet at Waterloo, a Malay might with propriety say the English ran a-muck; when the French charged over the bridge of Lodi, he might say the same thing.
> (Quoted in *The Real Malay* 233)

We may recall that the Battle of Lodi, on 10 May 1796, secured Napoleon's victory over Austrian forces, while the Battle of Waterloo, on 18 June 1815, marked the end of French ascendancy and brought an end to 750 years of Anglo-French conflict.

As Holden points out, this passage emphasises "the interchangeability of cultural systems, [it stresses] sameness, not difference, identity rather than alterity" ("Love, Death and Nation" 45). Amok is invested here with political agency in the European context, and it is by retrieving amok, as a form of political expression, from Swettenham's writings that we may call into question his discourse of arrogation.

It is no coincidence that Fanon, at a poignant moment in *A Dying Colonialism*, invokes amok as a function of anti-colonial agency. This is where amok is no longer a symptom of insanity but a signifier of political insurgency. In the slippage of the discourse of arrogation, we detect the colonial administrator's anxiety over the masculine ungovernability of Malaya. As soon as news of Birch's death spread, contingents from Hong Kong and India were sent, supported by a naval brigade, the force numbering, as Swettenham tells us, "about 1600 bayonets, with a battery and a half of Royal Artillery" (*Footprints* 64). That such a force was called upon to put down an uprising of fewer than 300 armed Malays testifies to the intensity of this colonial anxiety (Andaya 166). It is through the trope of amok that Swettenham established the inferiority of the Malays, and it is also through this trope that we are able to trace the coloniser's fear of their political and anti-colonial agency.

In the Malay-English dictionary they compiled, Hugh Clifford and Swettenham render the term as a signification of the Malay potential for violent revolt:

> To attack, to attack with fury, to make a charge, to assault furiously, to engage in furious conflict, to battle, to attack with desperate fury, to make an onslaught with the object of ruthless and indiscriminate slaughter, to run *âmok*, to dash against, to rush against; an attack, an assault, a charge. Âmok! Âmok! ... Attack! Attack! The war cry of the Malays. (*Dictionary* 47)

The accretion of clauses through the use of synonyms in this entry undermines the linguistic project of the dictionary: In the process of (dis)placing colonial subjects into a pre-modern past that needs to be translated (by the colonial administrators) into the present of colonial modernity, the word "amok" erupts into a vision of self-directed action on the part of the Malays. Perhaps that is why the following note is included at the end of the dictionary entry, as if to reassure readers (and the writers themselves) of the unlikelihood of such an event: "The advance of civilization has done much to repress this peculiarity of the Malays, and *âmok* running is becoming yearly more rare" (Clifford *Dictionary* 48). Such a statement is possible because another set of narratives about Malaya is in place, and these narratives will be examined in the next chapter.

The discourse of arrogation had been played out in the historiography of Malaya and in the representation of its inhabitants. The invoking of the image of Malays running amok occurs in tandem with colonial domination. However, it bears remembering that a discourse which seeks to dominate will contain fissures that will lead to its own undoing, for the colonialist trope of amok can be used against colonial empowerment. It is Fanon's incidental comments on amok that draw our attention to the possibility of reading the trope as representing the uncanny return of the repressed. In Swettenham's writings, even as amok is presented as testifying to the mental deficiencies of the Malays, rendering them into unhomely figures within the colonialist discourse and hence legitimising imperialism as a civilising mission, it exceeds this discursive frame, emerging as a trope that marks the coloniser's anxiety regarding the extent of control he has over the natives.

Amok is among the prominent tropes of British Malayan historiography. It has also to be said that British presence in Malaya also took form as a narrative of economic cooperation, wherein British capitalists, aided by enterprising Malay middlemen and diligent Chinese workers, were involved in the work of harnessing raw material from the land. This is a narrative one finds in Florence Caddy's travel writing, one of the three works about Malaya by women writers examined in the next chapter. Reconstituted as the enterprising intermediary between British capitalists and Chinese labour, the unhomely figure of the *pengamok* disappears.

2

Discourses of Difference:
Isabella Bird, Emily Innes, and Florence Caddy

Isabella Bird's *The Golden Chersonese and the Way Thither* (1883), Emily Innes' *The Chersonese with the Gilding Off* (1885), and Florence Caddy's *To Siam and Malaya in the Duke of Sutherland's Yacht 'Sans Peur'* (1889) are narratives by three very different women who were in Malaya under varied circumstances. By the time Bird embarked on her five-week visit to Malaya in 1879, she was already the renowned author of *The Englishwoman in America* (1856) and *The Hawaiian Archipelago* (1875); *Unbeaten Tracks in Japan* was to be published the following year. In contrast, Emily Innes would most likely have faded into obscurity if she had not written her book. She was the wife of James Innes, a junior colonial official who lived in distant parts of Malaya from 1876 to 1882. Florence Caddy, as her book title makes clear, set out in 1888 for Siam and Malaya as a guest on the Duke of Sutherland's yacht. While the ostensible purpose of the duke's journey was to recuperate from an illness, it was actually because he was invited by Prince Devavongse of Siam to submit a bid for a railway construction project (Gullick xi).

Bird and Caddy were on extended journeys when they reached Malaya. Bird's included visits to Japan, Hong Kong, Canton, Saigon, and Singapore. She was hosted by prominent colonial administrators, and it was during her stay in Singapore that she was invited to venture northward into the Malay Peninsula. Caddy's journey lasted four months and included stops in India, Singapore, and Siam; she returned to England via Malaya, Ceylon, and Egypt. Her host was in turn hosted by Thai and Malay aristocrats. In contrast to Bird and Caddy, Emily Innes lived in isolation (and misery, according to her narrative) in Malaya for close to six years. As Susan Morgan puts it, within the hierarchy of the British colonial administration, "the wife of a junior government servant is the lowest position in the imperial hierarchy, her husband occupying the second lowest" (168). A significant portion of Innes' *The Golden Chersonese with the Gilding Off* is devoted to the plight of her husband, who was forced to resign from the colonial service for having refused to issue warrants for the arrest of runaway slaves and for having accused his immediate superior,

William Bloomfield Douglas, of withholding income from the Sultan of Selangor. James Innes was denied a significant portion of his compensation:

> Everything was refused—the compensation for six years' service, the compensation for privilege leave, and the passage-money ... As, however, the passage-money had been paid, the Government ... did not ask for it back again. (Innes *Vol. II* 233)

Thus, much of the way Malaya is represented in Innes' text is filtered through the bitter experience with colonial administration that she and her husband shared.

In *Discourses of Difference*, Sara Mills makes the point that since imperialism is constituted by an investment in "constructing *masculine* British identity", women who wrote about their travels to colonised regions "were unable to adopt the imperialist voice with the ease with which male writers did" [emphasis in original] (3). Given this, "how was [colonialism] negotiated in texts by women who were conventionally seen not to be part of the colonial expansion?" (Mills 1). We shall engage this question in the writings of Bird, Innes, and Caddy on Malaya, exploring the extent to which their work conforms to the idea that travel writing by women might constitute "discourses of difference". I argue that, apart from gender, there are yet other differences to be found within the "discourses of difference". These include differences in terms of class, marital status, and the particular circumstances that brought women to Malaya. It is through the articulation of these differences that their narratives amount to a discourse that superimposes the domestic space of the metropole onto British Malaya. Like Swettenham's writings, the works of these women are a response to the condition of being not-at-home in that there is an attempt to create through their writings an environment that is hospitable to the colonial enterprise, even if the voices are different.

Isabella Bird: The worlding of Malaya

While Malacca, Singapore, and Penang formed an administrative unit called the Straits Settlements in 1826, it was the Pangkor Treaty in 1874 that marked the true beginning of British expansion in the Malay Peninsula. The years following the signing of the treaty were fraught with hostilities between appointed British residents and the Malay rulers due to differing interpretations of the treaty. James Birch, as already noted, was killed during his time as resident in Perak because he sought to implement a system of revenue collection and to abolish debt slavery through the "public humiliation" of Malay chiefs: The homes of the unrelenting chiefs were set on fire and their followers were made to surrender their weapons (Andaya 164–165). It was just four years after Birch's death that Bird arrived in Malaya, and the incident is described in her book:

> The Pangkor Treaty was signed in January 1874. On November 2d, 1875, Mr. Birch, the British Resident, who had arrived the evening before at the village of Passir Salah to post up orders and proclamations announcing that the whole kingdom of Pêrak was henceforth to be governed by English officers, was murdered as he was preparing for the bath. (*Chersonese* 270)

In "The Rani of Sirmur", Gayatri Spivak employs the term "worlding" to describe a process of transforming a physical terrain into colonised space (133). It is this process of worlding, as enacted by Birch, legitimised by the treaty, and implemented through posters and proclamations, that is depicted in the above passage. The worlding of Malaya is further consolidated in Bird's narrative in terms of causes and effects: (1) the treaty was signed, (2) Birch was the legitimate representative of the imperial order, and (3) he was murdered while engaged in the vulnerable act of preparing for a bath. Yet what the passage avoids noting is Birch's reputation for his ill-treatment of the Malays and his insensitivity to their laws and customs. Frank Swettenham was to describe Birch in a diplomatic manner as follows: "Unfortunately, he did not speak Malay, or understand the customs and prejudices of the people, and to this cause more than any other his death must be attributed" (*British Malaya* 197). In consolidating the worlding of Malaya, no political agency is ascribed to the Malays—this is to say, the possibility that Birch's murder was an instance of anti-colonial resistance is not raised.

There is no denying that Bird was reproducing the colonised world of Malaya for readers back home. As mentioned previously, the second sentence of the book makes the point that: "the Golden Chersonese is still somewhat of a *terra incognita*; there is no point on its mainland at which European steamers call" (Bird *Chersonese* 1). The narrative employs the familiar strategy of depicting pre-colonised land as a *tabula rasa* that awaits colonial intervention. In fact, Bird tells us, most people, like herself, were unaware of it (*Chersonese* 1). Yet to say that a place is little known to herself and others is not the same as to say, as she does, that the place 'has no legitimate claim to an ancient history' (*Chersonese* 1). Plainly enough, the Golden Chersonese was not *terra incognita* to its inhabitants, whom Bird describes as "a race of semi-civilised and treacherous Mohammedans" (*Chersonese* 1). The implication here is that the claim to history, ancient or otherwise, has to be legitimised via recognition from the metropolitan centre. Malaya is thus mapped onto the world as existing within a Eurocentric framework.

In her descriptions, Bird depicts Malaya as a resource, emphasising its pragmatic and economic value to the empire. The Straits Settlements, we are told, are "prized as among the most valuable of our possessions in the Far East" (*Chersonese* 3). She points out that the import-export figures amount to more than thirty-two million pounds (Bird *Chersonese* 3). "Iron ores are found everywhere", we learn, "and are so little regarded for their metallic contents that, though containing, according to Mr.

Logan, a skilful geologist, sixty per cent of pure metal, they are used in Singapore for macadamising the roads" (*Chersonese* 5). Even the subject of food caters to the European palate: "At European tables in the settlements the red mullet, a highly-prized fish, the pomfret, considered more delicious than the turbot, and the tungeree, with cray-fish, crabs, prawns, and shrimps, are usually seen" (*Chersonese* 12).

The chief trait of Bird's text regarding the people of Malaya lies in its shifts in tone. At first, she suggests that the Malays are, like the British, the colonisers of Malaya: 'The Malays are not the Aborigines of this singular spit of land, and they are its colonists rather than its conquerors' (*Chersonese* 12). However, one page later, she asserts that their colonisation of Malaya is only a point of conjecture: "The conquest or colonisation of the Malay Peninsula by the Malays is not, however, properly speaking, [a] matter of history, and the origin of the Malay race and its early history are only matters of more or less reasonable hypothesis" (*Chersonese* 13). Another change in emphasis occurs a few pages further:

> The Malays undoubtedly must be numbered among civilised peoples. They live in houses which are more or less tasteful and secluded ... they have possessed for centuries systems of government and codes of land and maritime laws which, in theory at least, show a considerable degree of enlightenment. (*Chersonese* 18)

However, four pages later, we are told that these civilised Malays "have no knowledge of geography, architecture, painting, sculpture, or even mechanics" (*Chersonese* 22). These acts of writing and rewriting, of vision and revision, of assertions and qualifications in her portrayal of the Malays are a function of ambivalence; they are perhaps a function of fluctuations between moments of complicity and resistance in relation to colonial rule.

Either way, Bird's narrative is certainly intended to depict the benevolence of British imperialism. This can be seen in the way she contrasts British imperialism to that of the Portuguese and the Dutch. Malacca in the sixteenth century was utilised by Portugal as a collection point for spices. This was after 1511, when Afonso de Albuquerque led a military expedition that ended in its seizure after more than a month of fighting (Andaya 58). In her chapter on Malacca, Bird has this to say: "my sober judgement is that Albuquerque and most of his Portuguese successors were little better than buccaneers" (*Chersonese* 150). The Dutch presence in the region can be traced to the amalgamation of small trading companies into the Dutch East India Company in 1602 (Andaya 40). Of the Dutch, Bird writes: "If the Portuguese were little better than buccaneers, the Dutch who drove them out were little better than hucksters—mean, mercenary traders, without redeeming qualities, content to suck the blood of their provinces and give nothing in return" (*Chersonese* 151).

These sweeping statements are in contrast to Bird's moving portraits of the British colonial administrators she met during her trip. In Singapore, she met Cecil

Clementi Smith, then the colonial secretary; in Malacca, she was hosted by Captain E. W. Shaw, the lieutenant-governor; in Sungei Ujong, she was met by the official resident, Patrick James Murray; in Penang, she had lunch with Hugh Low, the resident in Perak; W. E. Maxwell, the assistant resident, and William Robinson, the governor of the Straits Settlements. Her descriptions of these administrators reinforce the idea of the benevolence of British colonial rule. Of W. E. Maxwell, then assistant resident in Perak, Bird says:

> He is a man on whose word one may implicitly rely. Brought up among Malays, and speaking their language idiomatically, he not only likes them, but takes the trouble to understand them and enter into their ideas and feelings. He studies their literature, superstitions, and customs carefully, and has made some valuable notes upon them. I should think that few people understand the Malays better than he does ... I have the very pleasant feeling regarding him that he is the right man in the right place, and that his work is useful, conscientious, and admirable. As Assistant Resident he is virtually dictator of Larut, only subject to Mr. Low's interference. He is a judge, and can inflict the penalty of death, the regent's signature, however, being required for the death-warrant. (*Chersonese* 285–286)

In this passage, though we are told that Maxwell is "virtually dictator" because of his position, he is not so in person. Rather, he is a friend to the Malays: He understands them, likes them, speaks their language, enters into their thoughts and sentiments. Even though he has power over life and death, this is checked, as secondary authorisation is required. The passage at once testifies to the power of a colonial administrator while assuring readers that this power is restrained—first by the administrator's respect for Malay culture and, second, because of administrative checks put in place.

In the passage, the justification for British presence in Malaya is supplemented with affective qualities. The author confides to the reader her personal feelings for the man—her "right-man, right-place" intuition. Morgan identifies this narrative move as the "rhetoric of emotion", which "blends feminine domestic with colonial ideology" (159). She observes that in Bird's text, "colonial administrators are judged ... according to a British domestic ideology which values sympathy and tenderness over a more aggressive representation of manliness" (Morgan 153). Bird's depiction of Maxwell is congruent with liberal values in Victorian England, wherein we find an endorsement of personal qualities such as benevolence and kindness. At the same time, it is in keeping with the civilising mission of imperialism, whereby other cultures are brought into the ambit of civilisation and transformed—not by force but by compassion.

One feature of *The Golden Chersonese and the Way Thither* that requires mention is that the journey as narrated begins not in Malaya but in Hong Kong, Canton, and Saigon. "Why begin a book on British Malaya with chapters on Canton?" asks Morgan (150). The answer, she writes, is so that the "narrative order ... reiterate[s] the British trade route", beginning with China and ending with her departure for the Bay of Bengal, thus framing the chapters "within their primary imperial meaning" (Morgan 151). Travelling along this trade route, Bird was to compare the different governments of Hong Kong, Canton, and Saigon so as to bring to the forefront her argument about the benevolent nature of British colonialism, a theme elaborated in her chapters on Malaya.

After describing in detail the horrifying conditions of the Chinese prison in Canton, where the innocent and guilty alike are incarcerated and subjected to torture, Bird quotes the prisoners' words, implying that Hong Kong under the British is governed by compassion:

> "Would I were in your prison in Hongkong," and this was chorused by many voices saying, "In your prison at Hongkong they have fish and vegetables, and more rice than they can eat, and baths, and beds to sleep on; good, good is the prison of your Queen!" (*Chersonese* 71)

Of Saigon, Bird exclaims with some indignation that it "has the wild ambition to propose to itself to be a second Singapore!" (*Chersonese* 94). Of course, a statement such as this reflects the prevailing Anglo-French animosities at that point in time. After describing several scenes of extreme poverty, and after inspecting an army barracks she calls a "sickly station", where forty per cent of the soldiers are receiving hospital treatment for disease, Bird concludes that "The French don't appear to be successful colonists" (Bird *Chersonese* 103). The comparisons between the prison systems in Canton and Hong Kong, and between poverty-stricken Saigon and prospering Singapore, are intended, plainly enough, to legitimise the claims of British imperialism. Again, the implicit point is that British imperialism is guided not by economic interests but by compassion.

This repeated emphasis in *The Golden Chersonese and the Way Thither* has to be seen in the light of the Indian "Mutiny" of 1857. As Morgan puts it, in Malaya "the very notion of the glory of the British Empire [could be salvaged], tarnished as it had been by recent events in India" (147). Much of Bird's writing was based on her letters to her sister, Henrietta. In a letter to her publisher, John Murray, Bird describes Henrietta as her "best public, [her] home and fireside" (*Letters* 305). If Henrietta was to Bird the embodiment of her domestic reading public, then one of the key issues for Bird in her representation of Malaya was to write of it in such a way as to assure readers that it would not turn out to be another India. We must note in this connection that a section regarding William Bloomfield Douglas, the resident of Selangor, was excised from the final version of the book. In a letter to John Murray, Bird indicated that she planned to include the section; she wanted confirmation from Murray that Douglas had resigned from the colonial service to avoid an inquiry on charges of corruption. As Bird puts it, this would validate her descriptions of him as presiding over "a rule of fraud, hypocrisy, and violence"; at the same time, as Kay Chubbuck points out, Bird would also be protected from accusations of libel (*Letters* 267–268). In the end, Bird decided to exclude the section despite having received confirmation that Douglas had indeed resigned. The reason given was that she was abiding by the proverb, "Never kick a man when he's down" (*Letters* 268). One may suggest another reason for excluding the section on Douglas: It would have undermined her portrayal of the compassionate nature of British colonial rule in Malaya.

Bird's writing demonstrates that it is entirely possible to possess a *feminine* imperialist voice. At various moments in her writing, the emphasis on affect and the sympathetic portrayals of male colonial administrators are evidence that the feminine voice is an adjunct to masculine constructs of imperialism.

Emily Innes: Colonialism and its discontents

In *The Golden Chersonese with the Gilding Off*, Emily Innes has this to say of Bird:

> Miss Bird was a celebrated person, and wherever she went was well introduced to the highest officials in the land; Government vessels were placed at her disposal, and Government officers did their best to make themselves agreeable, knowing that she wielded in her right hand a little instrument that might chastise or reward them as they deserved of her. (*Vol. II* 242–243)

We can forgive Innes the touch of jealousy. Unlike Bird, whose visit lasted five weeks, Innes was in Malaya for almost six years. She accompanied her husband, James Innes, who was sent to Kuala Langat to take up the post of the revenue collector and magistrate. In *The Golden Chersonese with the Gilding Off*, she wrote of the difficulties of living in isolation. A dilapidated building served as office, courthouse, and living quarters. The only steam launch belonging to the Selangor government was not at their disposal. When her husband took a rowboat on inspection trips to tin mines and fishing villages, Innes was left on her own for days with no means of contact with the outside world.

Like Bird's text, that of Innes displays a certain measure of ambivalence in its depictions of the natives of Malaya. Some passages come close to paranoia and constitute instances of colonialist prejudice at its worst:

> The women who go out as ayahs [servants] in Malaya are the most degraded in the land. They are ready to steal, lie, drink, poison their master and mistress, or join in a plot for murdering them at any moment. (Innes *Vol. I* 24)

At other times, the text takes pains to vouch for the nobility of the Malay character:

> It seems to be the general impression in England that the Malay nature is 'treacherous, bloodthirsty, and cruel;' but I am so far from having found it so ... [the] country was far more peaceful than England, and life and property were more secure in it than in London ... and I know no 'civilized' country where it would be possible to leave your house perfectly open night and day for years as we did, without any serious loss of property. (Innes *Vol. I* 41–42)

The text moves between racist and empathetic portrayals of the local populace, between repulsion and acceptance, between loathing and approval. On the one hand, native women servants are depicted as deceitful, dangerous, and cunning; on the other, the racist image of Malays as "treacherous, bloodthirsty, and cruel" is to be challenged.

In a large portion of her book, Innes casts herself as a central character, laying bare her thoughts and reactions to her surroundings. While in a village shop, Innes is confronted with a crowd anxious to catch its first glimpse of a European lady. In response to this, she writes:

> It was no doubt flattering to find one's self looked on as the dove and olive-branch were on their return to the ark—a token that the troubled waters were abated; but I think if the original dove had been mobbed at the ark window by as motley and unpleasant a crowd of animals as the population of Klang, she would have flown away again very fast. (Innes *Vol. I* 8–9)

Here, her regard for the local populace is made clear. The affective quality that stands out is repulsion. There is an insistence on the differentiation of the self from the native: The local population is to Innes what a "motley and unpleasant ... crowd of animals" is to a dove, a symbol of innocence and purity. This depiction of the crowd as a threat, as an undifferentiated mass of Chinese, Indians, and Malays threatening to invade her innocent and vulnerable personal space, is metonymic of her encounters with the local populace.

The Chersonese with the Gilding Off is certainly a gendered text, gendered in the sense that it reproduces the Victorian roles of the woman as inhabiting the space of domestic economy circumscribed within the harsh landscape of Malaya. We are told, for instance, that Langat is no place for a woman. Langat, Innes writes,

> is nothing but a mud-swamp ... the house is an attap (palm-leaf) one, with no bath-room attached to it, the bathing-place being at some distance; there is no garden, not a tree, no flowers, scarcely even any grass ... and no society. The mere landing is an acrobatic feat, and the isolation is such that it would be sheer imprisonment to any Englishwoman ... remember, there is no European within a day's journey, man nor woman. (Innes *Vol. I* 3–4)

The landscape is presented as a colonial frontier, harsh and devoid of natural beauty. The relative isolation from a European community, the lack of an attached bathroom, and the fact that the house is made of attap would offer no security to a woman.

Innes writes of her considerable efforts to maintain a Victorian home in such an environment. She writes of saving eighty pounds a year by obtaining groceries from England instead of from Singapore (Innes *Vol. II* 25). She laments the difficulties of obtaining fresh food and supplies. At one point, an order for condensed milk and biscuits resulted in a delivery of milk biscuits (Innes *Vol. II* 32). She writes of having to prepare a meal for ten persons: She "arranged as fine a banquet as the combined resources of Singapore and Langat could be made to yield", only to be told at the last minute that the party was not coming (Innes *Vol. II* 35).

Given Innes' geographical isolation and the problems it entailed, it is no surprise that she describes her plight with resentment. In a discussion with Hugh Low, then the Perak resident, regarding her husband's refusal to issue warrants for the arrest of runaway slaves in his capacity as magistrate, Low, in an unguarded moment, remarked that since all married women are slaves, Emily is a slave herself (Innes *Vol. II* 139). "Just so", Innes retorted. "That is precisely why I can sympathize with other slaves" (*Vol. II* 139). It may seem that Innes, as a woman subjected to Victorian gender conventions, is at this point expressing sympathy for colonised subjects in Malaya. However, the book ends with a call for the annexation of the protected Malay States, so contradicting such a reading:

> I wish to point out that almost all the miseries from which we suffered in the Far East were a consequence, directly or indirectly, of the system of 'Protection.' Had the Malay Native States been annexed, how different would have been our position! ... the solitude and isolation which formed one of our greatest trials would have been modified, if not done away with altogether. (Innes *Vol. II* 245–246)

Annexation, as far as Innes is concerned, implies a change of colonial administration. That annexation is called for so as to protect junior colonial officials (and their wives) from being oppressed by their superiors indicates that Innes' experience of Malaya and her views on its people were shaped by her resentment of the colonial administration, an administration that had relegated her to being the wife of a minor official sent to an obscure outpost of the empire. Thus, Innes' call for annexation is motivated not by empathy with the colonised subject but by her envy of the positions of senior officers. Her narrative does not question the basic tenets of colonialism; rather, it draws attention to inequalities that exist among officers in the colonial administration.

What would happen to the Malays after annexation? "Whether Annexation would be good for the Malays is another question", Innes concludes (*Vol. II* 248). The final sentence of the book constitutes a dismissal of colonised subjects based on the assumption that they are unable to cope with modernity. Referring to what is for her the archetypal Malay, Innes remarks that "he cannot move with the times; and unless he moves out of the way ... he will certainly be crushed beneath the wheels of the car of progress" (*Vol. II* 250).

Passage after passage in Innes' writing runs contrary to Sara Mills' argument, noted earlier, that women travel writers could not assume "the imperialist voice" as male writers did. Innes' voice, indeed, cannot be separated from the male experience of colonialism; she was married to a junior colonial officer and subjected to the same tribulations.

Florence Caddy: 'High life in Asia'

Innes was jealous of the attentions afforded to Bird by senior colonial administrators, and we can assume she would have been bitter if she had known of Florence Caddy's associations with the British aristocracy and the way she had been hosted by members of the Thai and Malay aristocracies during her trip. Caddy embarked on her journey with the Duke of Sutherland in 1888. She was already the author of two novels, two books on how to manage a household, and two biographies (Gullick xii). While writing the biographies—of Linnaeus and Joan of Arc—Caddy had covered the routes traversed by her subjects, and she was thus already a seasoned traveller and writer (Gullick viii).

In *To Siam and Malaya in The Duke of Sutherland's Yacht 'Sans Peur'*, Caddy compares her work with that of Bird and Innes, declaring that she has "shown ... in how much comfort it is possible sometimes to leave the beaten tracks of travel":

> We had read the 'Golden Chersonese' by Miss Bird, and heard of the 'Chersonese with the Gilding off,' by a resident in Singapore ... but we found we must lay more gilding on, and deck our tale with jewels. (278)

Caddy wasted no opportunity in narrating the material ease and comfort of her travels. (One of the chapters in her book is entitled "High Life in Asia".) The yacht she sailed in is described as a luxurious vessel:

> The deck-house is lined with sofas; it has doors on each side and windows nearly all round, so that one can see the views while sitting at work or with a book. Above the wide, easy staircase that leads down to the saloon a folding table is spread, large enough to dine eight people, or a dozen at a pinch; the servants stand at the head of the staircase to wait, and the table does not impede their use of this short cut to the pantry, while the dishes are brought hot from the galley to the doors. (3)

"We have no privations on board the *Sans Peur*", writes Caddy (4). Indeed, the spaciousness of the yacht allows for space itself to be distinguished as for pleasure and for utility. From the pantry to the galley, from the head of the staircase to the staircase itself: These spaces are marked by differences of class, status, and privilege.

"We always speak of the yacht as home", writes Caddy, and this English domestic space outside of England is to be defended against possible intruders (18). Just as the ordering of space within the yacht distinguishes nobility from service, the ordering of space inside and outside of the yacht distinguishes the civilised from those construed as the barbaric Other. While the yacht moves from place to place, this ordering of space remains rigid and immobile. An array of weapons on board, including boarding pikes, personal revolvers, and a rifle, provides security for both passengers and crew. As the crew assures her, they are there "in case the savages come … In case those heathens think there is anything worth taking in a vessel of this sort, we'll give them a warm reception" (Caddy 6).

Such an ordering of space—distinguishing, on the one hand, between nobility and service and, on the other, between English domestic space and the world beyond—is metonymic of the text's collusion with the economic dimensions of colonialism. As Caddy points out, one of the reasons for the trip was that the duke was interested to see "if the application of English capital can benefit a colony or further British influence abroad … This is a thing that the workers cannot do for themselves. It requires leisure and capital" (77). The colonised subject is regarded as human labour just as colonies are regarded as sources of raw material. At one point in the narrative, Caddy remarks on the lush greenery and the easy availability of natural resources—lamenting, however, that because of the tropical climate, "we [the British] … cannot dig, but only direct the digging" (279).

The narrative draws a distinction between ruling and working classes among Malays, as well. Referring to those of the working class, Caddy laments that they refuse to work (279). In contrast, those of the ruling class are mentioned in a positive light, even though this might contradict colonial discourses as to the Malays' inability to govern themselves. They are regarded as enlightened in that they are willing middlemen for the British, amenable to the capitalist interests of the colonial regime:

> Sultan Abubeker is opening up the country energetically. He has attracted a multitude of Javanese, Chinese, and other settlers here; he has made Johore Baru a free port, with only small dues, and gives a free grant of land to settlers. He makes good roads, and villages spring up beside them as if by magic. By these and other enlightened measures the Sultan is yearly increasing his influence and his income. Instead of being crushed by the prosperity of Singapore, he is using the Lion City as a market, or rather a central depôt for the distribution of his native productions. (248)

If Caddy's admiration for the Sultan of Johore is undisguised, it is because the latter shares the same vision of Malaya: The Chinese, along with the Javanese and other settlers, are the workers of the land, transforming it and excavating it for raw material. It is the Chinese that are singled out as representatives of the ideal worker:

> Sultan Abubeker encourages the industrious Chinese; he says he finds them valuable as original settlers, as they are indefatigable labourers, clearing the jungle, cultivating the ground, and turning everything to account: then, as he sees openings,—and he is always looking for them,—he can set up companies for working mills, mines, &c., with Chinese labour under European direction. (265–266)

For Caddy, what is admirable about working-class Chinese is that, in contrast to their Malay counterparts, they labour willingly for British capital. They are diligent, and they further the commercial interests of the British. In Singapore, Caddy is fascinated by the spectacle of Chinese industry:

> This China town swarms like an ant-hill with the yellow race, who appear [sic] industrious to the last degree. Chinamen here are always carrying loads in their pairs of baskets, or pails, slung on a bamboo across the shoulders. Exception: when not busily carrying about something, they are being shaved.
> There are plenty of jinrickshas, or 'rickshas as they call them here ... these are all drawn by Chinamen, some of them extremely fine men, often admirable models for a worker in bronze. (80–81)

From the point of view of an outsider, the Chinese are first depicted as a mass of undifferentiated bodies at work, carrying loads, bearing bamboo poles, and pulling rickshaws. Their bodies are scrutinised so as to distil from them the quality of physical strength, a quality objectified as bronze metal. When her gaze rests on individual men, they are idealised as model workers.

As in the case of Bird's text, where comparisons are made between Canton, Hong Kong, and Saigon so as to extol the benefits of British influence, Caddy's text makes comparisons between the peoples of Malaya and Siam. The private secretary to the Sultan of Johore finds favour in Caddy's eyes because he displays outward signs of British influence: "[He is] a highly intelligent young man in European dress ... speaking English fluently" (233). In contrast, of the Siamese she writes, "It seems a grievous pity after the young Siamese have been educated in England to plunge them back into the semi-barbarism of the native habits" (126). At one point, Caddy goes so far as to remark, "In Siam civilization is potential; in Johore it is at work" (254). As mentioned earlier, the reason for the duke's trip to Siam was to bid for a railway project. As it turned out, the contract was awarded to Sir Andrew Clarke, the governor of the Straits Settlements (Gullick xi). As John Gullick suggests, it may be that the Thai aristocracy required the duke's competing presence so as to speed up their negotiations with Clarke (xi). One may surmise, then, that Caddy is displaying a measure of loyalty to the duke when she makes the above remarks in her book.

"A yacht", writes Caddy, "is something like the magic carpet of the Arabian Nights, that can transport its owner where he wishes, or, better still, like Hans Andersen's 'Flying Trunk,' for you pack up and get into it, and it carries you where you wish" (1). Caddy's narrative projects and superimposes the multiple discourses of class, capitalism, and colonialism onto Malaya. Her magic carpet allows her to see precisely what she wishes to see—a land where British capitalists, aided by enterprising Malay middlemen and diligent Chinese workers, are involved in the work of harnessing raw material to be imported back home.

Taken together, these three accounts of British presence in Malaya demonstrate the variety of ways in which colonialism was articulated by women writers in Malaya between 1879 and 1888. If Swettenham's trope of amok exceeds its colonialist frame, it is these narratives written by these women writers that restore Malaya as a homely space in the empire. In each of these three books, we witness attempts to refashion Malaya as a quasi-domestic space of the imperial nation. The women travel writers arrived in Malaya under different conditions. Bird was a celebrated writer and wrote of colonialism as a benevolent endeavour, Innes lived in isolation from the British community and wrote of what she perceived as unfair treatment, and Caddy took part in a business enterprise and laid bare the economic basis of colonialism—Malaya as a space of industry, a space of labour and natural resources that was an extension of the imperial nation and so sustained it.

Others have noted that travel allowed Victorian women to secure public positions as writers "with experience enough to write about the wider world" (Frawley 27). However, the three women authors we have considered secured public positions as writers whose narratives conformed to the domestic ideology prevalent in the imperial nation. They wrote of what they saw from the vantage point of their various social stations under the aegis of colonialism. If travel entails the act of leaving one's home and transcending one's immediate social and cultural surroundings to engage with other cultures, then it may be said that at many points in their journeys, these women writers had never truly left home.

3

The Exhaustion of Colonial Romance:
W. Somerset Maugham and Anthony Burgess

In the works of Swettenham, Bird, Innes, and Caddy, there is no doubt as to the hierarchical positioning of administrators and natives, coloniser and colonised, England and its Others. If their writings narrate Malaya as domestic space within the imperial nation, the works of W. Somerset Maugham and Anthony Burgess undermine the homeliness of their representation. Maugham and Burgess, unlike Swettenham and the women travel writers, portray the exhaustion of colonial romance. They also betray an awareness of their books as belated texts. The East, in many instances within their work, is no longer the site of mystery, exoticism, and adventure. Malaya can no longer be presented as a site of imperial mastery, but rather, as a land where imperialism had turned its colonialists into victims and anomic figures, a far cry from the monarchs of all that is surveyed, as portrayed in earlier narratives of imperialism.

Maugham arrived in Malaya in the 1920s in search of material for short stories. In his writings, Malaya refers largely to the Malay Archipelago, consisting of the Malay Peninsula, the island of Borneo (the northern part of which now constitutes the Malaysian states of Sabah and Sarawak), and the Dutch East Indies. In Maugham's writings, we see Malaya represented as a world where the lives of the Europeans depicted are out of place, devoid of romance, and caught within what has become the illusion of imperial conquest. Burgess arrived in Malaya as a colonial education officer three decades after Maugham. He taught at the Malay College in Kuala Kangsar in Perak before heading for Brunei. As his biographer, Andrew Biswell, points out, "The period of Burgess's stay [in Malaya] … coincided exactly with the final three years of … British presence" (152). Salient among the attributes of Burgess' characters is that they find their own positions as colonists to be troubling and increasingly untenable.

Belatedness is a function of what Harold Bloom identifies as the anxiety of influence. Bloom's point regarding a poet's relationship with a predecessor is that it is doubled and ambivalent: It is neither a straightforward rejection nor is it a disavowal; it constitutes not a rupturing of the predecessor's text but a "swerv[ing] away from [its] precursor" (14). We see in Maugham's and Burgess' work the anxiety of influence taking a postcolonial turn, wherein the familiar sign of Western hegemony is transformed in such a way as to call into question the premises of the imperial will to power. There are many Conradian moments in their works, and this is not surprising, for Joseph Conrad's writing career began and ended with the Malay Archipelago. Conrad acknowledged that his writing career began with the character of Almayer in Borneo: "If I had not got to know Almayer pretty well it is almost certain there would never have been a line of mine in print" (*Personal Record* 87). *Almayer's Folly* (1895) and *An Outcast of the Islands* (1896) were the novels with which Conrad launched his career, at the age of forty. The conception and writing of the third of the Lingard trilogy, *The Rescue* (1920), spanned the entirety of Conrad's writing career. As Heliéna Krenn points out, "It was the Malay Archipelago with its truths about human life dimmed by the mists of its jungles and waterways that started Conrad on his career as a novelist" (xiv). In the same way that these jungle mists and waterways haunt Conrad throughout his career, in the works of Maugham and Burgess, Conrad's texts return not only as a reminder of their belatedness, but also as a reminder of the ambivalence that attends to the critique of imperialism.

Like Conrad's writings, the works of Maugham and Burgess often foreground the prolonged isolation from their motherland of district officers, rubber planters, sailors, doctors, and lawyers, and the discovery of the English book signifies not the recuperation of the familiar sign of Englishness as the foundation of cultural superiority that propels the project of imperialism, but estrangement from that sign. In the empire, Englishness and texts that seek to uphold the authority of Englishness are plunged into crisis. For Bhabha, the "the English book" is the metonymy of authoritative texts such as the Bible; it is "an insignia of colonial authority" (*Location* 102). (Of course, the implicit irony of Bhabha's essay is that the Bible is originally not English at all.) Gauri Viswanathan has argued that the discovery of the English book, in this case English literature, "appeared as a subject in the curriculum of the colonies long before it was institutionalized in the home country" (3). English literature was the focal point around which the culture of the metropolitan centre was authorised, established and disseminated in the colonies. Yet interestingly, in the works of Maugham and Burgess, we encounter metonymic moments where the English book—in the form of English newspapers, Law Reports and novels—is read. In these moments, the lives of Europeans are at a disjunction from the hegemonic imperial superiority the book encodes.

Maugham's Malaya: The dissolution of European domestic space

> "There's no one who got atmosphere like Conrad," said Neil. "I can smell and see and feel the East when I read him."

> "Nonsense. What do you know about the East? Everyone will tell you that he made the grossest blunders. Ask Angus."
>
> "Of course he was not always accurate," said Munro, in his measured, reflective way. "The Borneo he described is not the Borneo we know. He saw it from the deck of a merchant-vessel and he was not an acute observer even of what he saw. But does it matter? I don't know why fiction should be hampered by fact. I don't think it's a mean achievement to have created a country, a dark, sinister, romantic, and heroic country of the soul." (Maugham 445)

The above passage, from Maugham's "Neil MacAdam", outlines three positions one may take in reading Conrad. Neil's notion of the East is derived from Conrad— "he knew his Conrad by heart and he was expecting a land of brooding mystery" (Maugham 439). Darya Munro dismisses this Conradian rhetoric of the East:

> He was all the superficiality of his countrymen. That stream of words, those involved sentences, the showy rhetoric, that affectation of profundity: when you get through all that to the thought at the bottom, what do you find but a trivial commonplace? (Maugham 445)

Angus Munro takes the middle position, pointing out that one need not expect the author to be faithful to the reality he purports to describe. The above passages dramatise a scene of reading, and one detects in this scene reservations as to Conrad's mode of writing. Conrad's representation of Borneo as an emblem of a romantic and exotic East fails to develop canonical authority even for his English readers, and in representing this failure Maugham is inscribing his own uncertainty and anxiety as to reading and writing about the East.

The characters in "Neil MacAdam" present different readings of Conrad, including both approbation and disapprobation, and this reflects Maugham's ambivalence about Conrad's legacy. Maugham's writing is permeated with anxiety about Conrad as an authoritative precursor whose influence is clearly visible even as it is simultaneously challenged. As Jeffrey Meyers, one of Maugham's biographers, points out, Conrad and Maugham, in their writings and lives, have much in common (141). Both were orphans, left their professions (Conrad a seaman, Maugham a doctor) to become writers and travelled to, among other places, Malaya and Borneo (Meyers 141–142). Many moments in Maugham's writings recall those of Conrad. As in *Heart of Darkness*, for instance, many of Maugham's Malayan works are stories within stories, with narrators seeking out Europans who, in turn, relate stories of other Europeans or of themselves. These Conradian echoes serve to underscore Maugham's ambivalence toward Conrad's influence. Maugham's narrators are like Marlow, a storyteller Conrad deployed more than once, a character in search of other Europeans so as to distil from them insights they have accumulated from their prolonged stay in remote outposts of the empire:

> Often in some lonely post in the jungle or in a stiff grand house …
> a man has told me stories about himself that I was sure he had never
> told a living soul. I was a stray acquaintance whom he had never seen
> before and would never see again, a wanderer for a moment through
> his monotonous life, and some starved impulse led him to bare his
> soul. (Maugham 270)

Yet their searches often end in anti-climaxes. For instance, the narrator of "German Harry" has this to say of the eponymous hero he finally meets:

> If what they tell us in books were true, his long communion with
> nature and the sea should have taught him many subtle secrets. It
> hadn't. He was a savage. He was nothing but a narrow, ignorant, and
> cantankerous sea-faring man. (Maugham 50)

In Maugham's stories of the East, Europeans are often depicted not as heroic empire-builders embarking on adventures in exotic landscapes, but as psychologically crippled victims of an imperialist ideology that creates the simulacrum of England as a metropolitan centre. In "Mirage", Grosely works as a customs inspector in China, saving his salary for a life of leisure in London:

> He lived in China as though in a dream … There was always before
> him the mirage of London, the Criterion Bar, himself standing with
> his foot on the rail, the promenade at the Empire and the Pavilion, the
> picked-up harlot, the serio-comic at the music-hall, and the musical
> comedy at the Gaeity. This was life and love and adventure. This was
> romance. This was what he yearned for with all his heart. (Maugham
> 309)

Yet when he finally returns to London, he is alienated by what it has become: "The old places were gone, the people were different … he was strangely lonely; he had never expected that in a great city like London" (Maugham 310). The irony of Grosely's situation is that just as he is not at home outside of England, neither is he at home in it.

Englishness, as it were, is constructed outside of England; as Simon Gikandi points out, it is "a product of the colonial culture" (x). The location of English culture, then, is found not within England, but without. The tragedy of Grosely's life is that he fails to recognise the (dis)location of Englishness. If the image of home is sustained by virtue of the fact that the individual is not at home, then he or she can never truly return. In "Masterson", the eponymous character admits that the only thing stopping him from marrying a native girl to whom he is devoted is his nostalgia for England:

> Sometimes I ask myself if it's worth while to sacrifice my happiness
> for a dream. It is only a dream, isn't it? It's funny, one of the things

that holds me back is the thought of a muddy lane I know, with great clay banks on both sides of it, and above, beech trees bending over. It's got a sort of cold, earthy smell that I can never quite get out of my nostrils. (Maugham 274–275)

The East in Maugham's writing is no European paradise; rather, it is the site of anomie. England is "only a dream", yet it is a dream that prevents Masterson from setting up a home away from home. In Maugham's stories, the English domestic idyll in Malaya is depicted as untenable: Notable in the Maugham stories we have just considered is the absence of domestic space. In one way or another, these are stories of the characters' failure to create a home in the empire because they are seduced by the romance of England as a signifier of home, belonging, and security.

The dissolution of the imperial narrative of conquest occurs in conjunction with the disruption of the ideal of English domesticity. In "The Outstation", Warburton, the British resident, has a nostalgia for an aristocratic English existence that is evident in his routines at home. His room is "neatly laid out as if he had an English valet" (Maugham 348). Every morning, he reads the daily edition of the six-week-old *Times* of London in the order they have arrived. Benedict Anderson has made the point that the daily act of reading the newspaper fosters an "imagined community" (3). In the case of Warburton, the act of reading an outdated newspaper is rendered farcical, for the imagined English community is characterised by temporal and spatial distance—and hence, incongruity.

Warburton, as an official representative of empire, is an anachronistic figure of the empire builder, his habits laughed at and scorned by other Europeans at the clubhouse. His solipsistic domestic arrangements are perpetually threatened by the fact that the outstation does not fit the English domestic ideal. Warburton's identification of himself with English aristocracy is made a point of irony: Even though he is of aristocratic lineage on his father's side, he is embarrassed by his mother's Liverpool-manufacturer background. Ironically, in his younger days in England, he was able to lead an aristocratic life of leisure because of an inheritance from his mother's family. Nonetheless, Warburton pines for an English aristocratic life that is no more:

> It seemed to him that the England of today had lost a good deal of what he had loved in the England of his youth … But these emotions he kept hidden from the eyes of men. (Maugham 356)

The irony of Warburton's position is that he is able to maintain this semblance of an aristocratic lifestyle only in the colonies. He has squandered his wealth and has no other option: "When a man in his set had run through his money, he went out to the colonies" (Maugham 354). The arrival of his new assistant, Allen Cooper, threatens his domestic idyll. As we have seen in the case of Florence Caddy, colonialism is portrayed as within the domain of aristocratic endeavours. Yet in Maugham's story, such a portrayal is being challenged. Cooper, born in a crown colony, scoffs at Warburton's notion of colonial rule as "the glory that was Greece and the grandeur that was Rome" (Maugham 359). "What we want is a business government by business men," he says (Maugham 360). This sentiment is underscored by the reply to Warburton's letter requesting that Cooper be transferred: "Of course it's a very good thing for a man to be a gentleman, but it's better that he should be competent and hardworking" (Maugham 369).

The outstation thus becomes a site of contestation—it is unhomely, not quite the English home of an aristocrat, just as colonialism is not quite an aristocratic, gentlemanly endeavour, but one motivated by commercial interests. Thus, if the replication of the domestic homestead represents an allegiance to the Enlightenment ideals that validate the project of imperialism, then the shattering of this domestic idyll represents the untenable condition of this allegiance. At the end of the story, the domestic idyll is restored when Cooper is found dead with a *kris* sticking out of his chest, a victim of an amok. Even as he resumes his English gentrified existence, Warburton is prepared to accommodate the perpetrator of the amok in his household: "Abas would make a very good house-boy" (Maugham 376). Ironically, Warburton's aristocratic way of life is restored through an unhomely act by a Malay.

The connection between the reading of English books and the narration of the lives of Europeans in Malaya is never more evident in Maugham's writings than in "The Book-Bag". In this story, the reading of an English book dramatises the instability of domestic values associated with England. The narrator is an avid reader who has the habit of carrying all his books with him wherever he goes: "like the dope-fiend who cannot move from place to place without taking with him a plentiful supply of his deadly balm I never venture far without a sufficiency of reading matter" (Maugham 9). But if the act of reading English books is an addiction, it is one that provides no comfort. It is while the narrator's host, Mark Featherstone, is reading *Life of Byron*, which he finds in the narrator's possession, that he begins to tell of the story of a pair of siblings in Malaya. The topic of the relationship between Byron and his half-sister, Augusta Leigh, leads Featherstone to tell the story of his friends, Tim and Olive Hardy. The English book in "The Book-Bag" is no longer an emblem of cultural superiority; instead, it becomes a departure point for a narrative about the unnameable conduct of a pair of English siblings in Malaya:

> People said they couldn't have been more united if they were married, and when you saw how some couples got on you couldn't help thinking they made most marriages look rather like a wash-out. (Maugham 23)

By the end of the story, we are told that the domestic idyll that Tim tries to create through his marriage with Sally is shattered by Olive's suicide: She has shot herself. Sally, shaken by this, says this to Featherstone: "He had no right to marry me. It was monstrous" (Maugham 42). "Did you know what she meant?" the narrator asks Featherstone (Maugham 42). "There was only one thing she could mean," Featherstone replies, "It was unspeakable. Yes, I knew all right. It explained everything." (Maugham 42). Featherstone's story hints at the possibility of incest, even though the word is never pronounced.

Just as the English book in "The Book-Bag" no longer assures its readers of England as a site from which English values of domestic order emanate, in "The Letter" it no longer assures its readers of the authority of the English rule of law. "The Letter" narrates the difficulty of policing the discursive boundary between Asia and Europe. At the beginning of the story, one detects the Manichean opposition of the chaotic street scene and the interior of a lawyer's office. As Holden points out, this passage "foregrounds an explicit contrast between Asian disorder and European order" (*Orienting Masculinity* 111). This contrast is further embodied in the gestures, habits, and physical appearance of the principle characters. Joyce, the lawyer, is the epitome of European rational order. His gestures often convey an impression of collected, meditative, and homely calm: "Mr Joyce leaned back again in his chair and once more placed the tips of his ten fingers together. The little construction he formed looked like the skeleton of a roof" (Maugham 316). When Joyce notices Crosbie's unkempt appearance, he "gave a slight frown" and reminds Crosbie to "pull [himself] together" and "keep [his] head" (Maugham 315). Joyce is impressed by Leslie's "self control" despite the fact that she has been detained for having killed a man (Maugham 317). The story places emphasis on Leslie's "good breeding" and on the fact that she "was a good hostess"; as such, she "was the last woman in the world to commit murder" (Maugham 318). In contrast, native characters are figures of suspicion. At one moment in the story, Joyce is in a shop "where three or four Chinese were standing behind the counter. It was one of those strange shops where nothing was on view, and you wondered what it was they sold there" (Maugham 341).

The discursive boundary between Asia and Europe in the story is troubled by the presence of Ong Chi Seng. Ong is trained in law at Gray's Inn. By virtue of his professional education, Ong's identity constitutes an authorised form of difference. Joyce, vaguely troubled by the fact that Ong speaks "beautiful English, accenting each word with precision", often wonders "at the extent of his vocabulary" (Maugham 315). The opening of the story resituates Ong's hybrid identity through a projection of deficiency. To employ a refrain from Bhabha, Ong's mastery of English is regarded as *almost the same* as that of Joyce, *but not quite*. This voice of the mimic man who addresses Joyce is not yet a troubling source of anxiety. At this point in the story, Ong is presented as Joyce's social inferior. He is employed in the office not because of his professional training, but rather because he is "industrious, obliging, and of exemplary character", qualities one looks for in a servant (Maugham 315). After all, the English book, which is here represented by the volumes of Law Reports on which Joyce's gaze is resting, is accessible to Joyce and not to Ong, even though the latter is by training capable of perusing them.

The boundary between Asia and Europe set up at the beginning of the story breaks down because the existence of the English book is no longer an assurance of the English rule of law. As the story progresses, it is Ong who commands the plot. The case to which Joyce is attending and on which Ong is assisting does not rest on Joyce's mastery over those Law Reports. Rather, it is Ong who submits a crucial piece of evidence: the letter from the accused, Mrs. Leslie Crosbie, to the deceased, Geoffrey Hammond, inviting the latter to the former's home on the night he was shot dead by her. The copy of the letter shown to Joyce, however, is "written in a flowing hand which the Chinese were taught at the foreign schools" (Maugham 326). Holden comments, "The letter itself is a double", and this mimic letter suffices to throw the whole case into doubt (*Orienting Masculinity* 112). Prior to the appearance of the letter, Joyce was confident of securing an acquittal. The case, as he says, is "comparatively plain sailing" (Maugham 332). Leslie's alibi never wavered: "The story she told [Joyce] the first time he saw her she had never varied in the smallest detail ... She told it connectedly, in a level, even voice" (Maugham 318). Her alibi was that Hammond had arrived at her home uninvited. When he tried to rape her, she shot him in self-defence. Yet now that there is a possibility of the original letter appearing as evidence in court, Joyce is no longer sure: "I don't know what they can prove ... But if their suspicions are aroused, if they begin to make inquiries, if the natives are questioned—what is it that can be discovered?" (Maugham 333).

If the truth is no longer in the hands of the defence lawyer and the accused, it must be bought and silenced. The original letter is in the hands of Hammond's Chinese mistress, and money is raised to purchase it. It is only after the letter is burnt that Leslie's acquittal is secured. In the final moments of the story, after having been acquitted, Leslie confesses the truth to Joyce. Leslie and Hammond were having an affair, and she killed him because he was about to leave her for the Chinese woman:

> "I seized the revolver and I fired. He gave a cry and I saw I'd hit him. He staggered and rushed for the veranda. I ran after him and fired again. He fell and then I stood over him and I fired till the revolver went click, click, and I knew there were no more cartridges."
>
> At last she stopped, panting. Her face was no longer human, it was distorted with cruelty, and rage and pain ... It was not a face, it was a gibbering, hideous mask. Then they heard a voice calling from another room, a loud, friendly, cheerful voice. It was Mrs Joyce.
>
> "Come along, Leslie darling, your room's ready. You must be dropping with sleep."
>
> Mrs Crosbie's features gradually composed themselves. Those passions, so clearly delineated, were smoothened away as with your hand you would smooth crumpled paper ... She was once more the well-bred and even distinguished woman. (Maugham 346)

The truth did not make its way into the courtroom, and neither will it find its way into the Law Reports. Like Leslie's face, what has been crumpled is later rendered smooth. The domestic tragedy at the heart of the story is written over with a return to domesticity. Leslie, guilty of murdering her lover, is found innocent by the court of law.

Maugham's short story is a palimpsest wherein one may locate moments when his own English book is rewritten so as to preserve the facade of domestic idyll. Truth resides in Ong, who is, in Bhabha's terms, the figure of colonial mimicry and sly civility. The moment he submits his letter is the moment that the British lawyer loses control over how the case is to be narrated. If Maugham's story is able to end with a scene that preserves the façade of domestic tranquillity so as to bring the narrative back within the ambit of the colonialist imperative, it does so at the expense of erasing native testimony. The lawyer is found by Maugham's narrator to be operating outside of the law, exemplifying Bhabha's point that colonial authority is articulated "through the figures of farce" (*Location* 85). In the final moments of the story, we see Maugham's narrative marked by anxiety, for the Law Reports on which Joyce rests his gaze in the earlier part of the story, the same reports Ong is not allowed to peruse and which are the basis of Joyce's authority over Ong, are no longer textual and legal guarantees of truth.

In Maugham's Malayan short stories, the metonymic reading of the English book, instead of providing affirmation of cultural superiority, becomes a troubling act. Reading *Life of Byron* leads a character to recall the incestuous relationship between brother and sister; the daily perusal of six-week-old newspapers dramatises the futility of Warburton's attempt to affirm his English identity; in the final story of those we have considered, the Law Reports cannot guarantee a true record of what actually happened, and thus, their emblematic status as the word of truth guaranteed by colonial institutional authority is thrown into doubt. In story after story, the European idyll of home as the domain of Enlightenment pursuits and pastimes is shattered by the discoveries, the reading, and the writing—and the rereading and rewriting—of the English book. Maugham's writing is invested with the discourse of Orientalism but also of Occidentalism in that they suggest how Europeans located in the empire look back at England. The irony is that Maugham's Europeans are disabled not because they are seduced by the romantic and exotic East but by the romance of England. Maugham's writings exemplify not just how the East ceases to look romantic and exotic to Western eyes, but also how the optic of representation is redirected towards nostalgic mirages, fantasies, and dreams of England.

Maugham has been accused of Eurocentrism because his writings dramatise the lives of Europeans while natives who appear, if at all, are often peripheral to the plot. As Klaus W. Jonas points out, "If natives appear at all in [Maugham's] writings, it is only as minor characters" (106). However, such comments, while justified, overlook the fact that Europeans in Maugham's writings are depicted in a very unflattering manner, to the extent that the work drew the ire of many members of the expatriate community during his time. As Burgess points out in his introduction to *Maugham's Malaysian Stories*, "there were ageing colonial expatriates who were angry and hurt and swore they would never forgive Maugham for placing them in his stories" (xvii). Burgess adds further that if Maugham had visited and written of Malaya in the 1950s, "his plots and main characters might have been very different" (xvi). One detects the anxiety of influence at work in the way Burgess directs the attention of Maugham's readers to his trilogy of Malayan novels. This anxiety is further underscored by the fact that prior to his arrival in Malaya, Burgess had never been to Asia. As Biswell points out, "most of what [he] knew of Asia and the British colonial territories came out of other people's books: George Orwell's novel, *Burmese Days* (1934); Somerset Maugham's Malayan short stories; Joseph Conrad's trilogy of Malayan novels ... ; and the works of Rudyard Kipling" (154). Even as Burgess is dissociating his writings from Maugham's, he is at the same time drawing attention to their similarities—specifically, their shared setting. After all, in his critique of Europeans, Maugham—and the same may be said of the rest of the authors so far considered—is a precursor to Burgess.

Burgess' Malaya: The jungle out there

By the time Burgess arrived in the 1950s, the social and political fabric of Malaya had undergone immense transformation since the days of Swettenham, Bird, and, later on, Maugham. A decade earlier, the British had surrendered Malaya and Singapore to the Japanese. After the departure of the Japanese at the end of the Pacific war, attitudes towards the returning British had changed. The inauguration in 1946 of the Malayan Union proposal, which sought to unite the different Malayan states on the peninsula under a single administration, was met with apprehension by the local populace, as it transferred political powers from traditional Malay rulers to a British governor. The indirect rule once derived from India would give way to direct rule. In the period immediately after Japanese occupation the Malayan Communist Party gained in prestige, its members regarded as anti-Japanese heroes (Turnbull 223). The party consolidated its control over labour by organising strikes that resulted in higher wages, thus attracting more people to join its unions (Turnbull 227). At the same time, political developments in China were such that the Chinese in Southeast Asia were encouraged to forge ties with the mainland, and this the British viewed with apprehension. These developments, along with MCP's policy of armed revolution, led to the declaration of the Malayan Emergency, under which regulations against and active resistance to militant left-wing activities began.

In 1949, the Malayan Forum, a discussion group consisting of Malayan students studying in British universities, was formed in London to further the Malayan independence movement. Among its members were Lee Kuan Yew, Goh Keng Swee, and Toh Chin Chye, all of whom returned to Singapore after their studies (and all of whom were prominent in Singaporean politics). Lee and Goh, along with Kenneth Michael Byrne, then a civil servant, formed a Council of Joint Action to stage a mass protest against excessive expatriation allowances for European officials, which resulted in an increase in the allowances paid to local employees (Turnbull 247). In 1953, a commission headed by Sir George Rendel developed a proposal by which Singapore might attain self-rule, and it was suggested that a new constitution be implemented in 1955, via elections. Both the creation of political parties fighting for self-rule and the communist insurgency are signs of emergent nationalism in Malaya. Burgess' three Malayan novels, *Time for a Tiger* (1956) *The Enemy in the Blanket* (1958), and *Beds in the East* (1959), are set in this period. It is worth recalling that the original title of the trilogy, *The Long Day Wanes*, is taken from Tennyson's "Ulysses", a poem that may be read in this context as an allegory of the decline of the British Empire: "We are not now that strength which in old days / Moved earth and heaven" (620).

The trilogy dramatises the lives of Europeans in Malaya: "That's what we're here for—to absorb the country ... Or be absorbed by it", says Victor Crabbe, the character who appears in all the three novels (Burgess *Malayan Trilogy* 57). Crabbe embodies the irony invested in his name: Apart from his disposition, he is by no means a victorious character. He is a teacher of history, who, even though he later rises to the rank of headmaster and then chief education officer, knows that history has passed him by: His real job is to prepare a native to take over his position. In the trilogy, Europeans and natives inhabit different worlds. Moments when Chinese, Malays, Indians, and Eurasians are discussing the impending independence of Malaya are contrasted with conversations among Europeans who are all too aware that the "Empire [is] now crashing about their ears" (Burgess *Malayan Trilogy* 192).

The anomic plight of the European characters is dramatised from the beginning. As Flaherty puts it in the opening paragraph of *Time for a Tiger*, "East? They wouldn't know the bloody East if they saw it. Not if you was to hand it to them on a plate would they know it was the East" (Burgess *Malayan Trilogy* 5). Their physical disabilities are symptomatic of their anomie, dislocation, and disorientation at a time when the empire is no longer a stable point of reference. In *Time for a Tiger*, nothing significant happens in the world of the Europeans; by contrast, everything that is significant occurs in the background. European characters are depicted as superfluous in a time marked by communist insurgency, emergent nationalism, and colonial dissolution. In the opening pages, Robin Hood, the contingent transport officer, is suffering from dysentery. Nabby Adams, a mechanic in the transport contingent, is an alcoholic heavily indebted to Chinese shopkeepers. His colleague Flaherty, having swallowed a cigarette and a glass tumbler, is now sick.

If much of English history happened outside of England during the era of imperial expansion, then the period of national independence, as it implies the withdrawal of the British presence, activates an anxiety pertaining to what constitutes Englishness. This is all the more so given that the period in which the novels are set also saw the decline of the British Raj. Malaya on the eve of national independence no longer functions as a familiar sign of the exotic; if the Other is at a moment of change, then it is this moment that brings the self into crisis. As Flaherty tells Nabby:

> And make up your mind about what bloody race you belong to. One minute it's all about being a farmer's boy in Northamptonshire and the next you're on about the old days in Calcutta and what the British have done to Mother India ... You're English right enough but you're forgetting how to speak the bloody language ... (*Malayan Trilogy* 7)

The familiar signs of Englishness, the empire, and the East are revisited in Burgess' trilogy through a rewriting of significant moments found in canonical English books. As in James Joyce's *A Portrait of the Artist as a Young Man*, the final moments of *The Enemy in the Blanket* are in the form of diary entries. Rupert Hardman is a failed lawyer who marries a wealthy Malay woman and converts to Islam out of financial desperation. At one moment in the novel, he persuades himself that his marriage to a Malay constitutes an adventure, with a line from Shakespeare's *Antony and Cleopatra* ringing in his mind: "The beds i' the East are soft." (Burgess *Malayan Trilogy* 245). Yet going native turns out not to be as pleasurable as Hardman has initially thought. The Orientalist fantasy of the Eastern woman as submissive and libidinous is overturned. Hardman is no Antony, as much as 'Che Normah is no Cleopatra. Unknown to his wife as she accompanies him on a pilgrim's trip to Mecca, he plans to leave her. "Gods of the soaring wing and steady engine, fail me not", Hardman writes in his diary (Burgess *Malayan Trilogy* 369). This echoes the final line of Joyce's novel, when Dedalus invokes in prayer the figure of Icarus: "Old father, old artificer, stand me now and ever in good stead" (218). As Hardman is unable to raise his fare back to England, he plans to slip away as soon as the ship he is on reaches Mecca. He has agreed to help a friend pilot a plane and help smuggle unspecified cargo into England.

The post-imperial dynamic already evident in Tennyson's "Ulysses", which finds a modernist turn in the writings of Joyce, is a legacy invested in Burgess' writings on Malaya. Dedalus' motto of silence, exile, and cunning is written over by Hardman's quiet desperation even as he schemes to return to England with cunning. As Hardman discovers of Malaya, "The silk girls bringing sherbet had gone, the beds i' the East were no longer soft" (Burgess *Malayan Trilogy* 317). While Dedalus' flight from Ireland constitutes an escape from conventional identity categories of nationalism and race, Hardman's flight from Malaya seems to constitute a return to these fixities. Yet it may not turn out to be so. As Crabbe puts it, "In the West we're shrivelling up. We're dried fruit" (Burgess *Malayan Trilogy* 371). The text deploys a cruel irony with regard to Hardman's flight. As he looks into a mirror, the readers are reminded that Hardman, as a combined result of a deficiency in skin pigmentation and burn scars due to a plane crash prior to his arrival in Malaya, is a "very white man" who had first left England because he was made to feel self-conscious about his appearance (Burgess *Malayan Trilogy* 213).

Just as the texts of Shakespeare and Joyce enter the *Malayan Trilogy* at moments when Englishness is made a point of interrogation, the events leading up to Crabbe's death (which make a statement about the superfluous presence of the British in Malaya) are replete with Conradian moments. Crabbe is tasked to investigate the murder of a headmaster at Durian Estate School, and on his journey to Durian Estate, which takes several days, he meets several people, including Moneypenny, an assistant protector of aborigines whom Crabbe regards as quite mad, and Temple Haynes, who calls himself a "linguistician" rather than a linguist. In reply to this, Crabbe remarks that when it comes to languages in Malaya, "It's a question of what patterns you can make emerge out of your inchoate experiences" (Burgess *Malayan Trilogy* 514). This line foreshadows Crabbe's encounter with Malaya, in contrapuntal relation to Marlow's "inconclusive experiences" (*Heart of Darkness* 52).

It may not be an exaggeration to say that Moneypenny is a very belated version of Kurtz. Subscribing to aboriginal taboos, he is horrified that Crabbe has laughed in the presence of a butterfly and warns him not to comb his hair when there is thunder (Burgess *Malayan Trilogy* 506). "Oh, would anybody believe it, would anybody believe it back home? They just don't know, they're all so, so innocent, sitting in their offices in Fleet Street and Holborn," Crabbe thinks to himself (Burgess *Malayan Trilogy* 506). Fleet Street, we recall, is where Marlow first saw the Congo River on a map, which gave him the idea of being the skipper of a steamboat. Moneypenny has spent six years with the aborigines, and, regarding anthropological classifications, he remarks: "You've got to get into the jungle. You've got to come face to face with the living reality ... There's no substitute for actual experience" (Burgess *Malayan Trilogy* 513). Later, Crabbe is seen to be embracing this living reality of the jungle: "There was nothing to believe in except the jungle. That was home, that was reality. Crabbe gazed in a kind of horror mixed with peace at the endless vista of soaring trunks, lianas, garish flowers" (Burgess *Malayan Trilogy* 537). Subsequently, he loses his footing and drowns while trying to board a launch. The death of Victor Crabbe may be read as an allegory of the end of the British presence in Malaya: "the twilight [is] here ... Malaya didn't want him" (Burgess *Malayan Trilogy* 325). Crabbe is Burgess' Marlow, yet, unlike Conrad's famous character, Crabbe did not survive to tell the tale of his journey.

In the Malaya Union proposal, which united the states under British sovereignty, the nation as an imagined community was rendered as yet untenable given existing racial tensions. Much in the same way, the trilogy dramatises the dissolution of colonial rule and at the same time takes a pessimistic perspective on Malaya's impending independence: It is cast in fictional narrative as an impending catastrophe where inter-ethnic hostility can no longer be contained. As Lim Cheng Po, an Anglicised Chinese who, for Crabbe, is "an unalloyed essence of Englishry", remarks,

> Perhaps a Malay shakes his fist at a Chettiar money-lender and, for some obscure reason, that sets off a brawl in a Chinese cabaret. Or a British tommy gets tight in K.L. and the Tamils start spitting at a Sikh policeman. The fact is that the component races of this exquisite and impossible country just don't get on. There was, it's true, a sort of illusion of getting on when the British were in full control. But self-determination's a ridiculous idea in a mixed-up place like this. There's no nation. There's no common culture, language, literature, religion. (Burgess *Malayan Trilogy* 414–415)

Crabbe's mission is to help usher in Malaya's moment of independence—this is his self-justification for his continued presence in Malaya. He organises a dinner party he hopes will bring people of different races together. Ironically, in doing so he is replicating the colonial system of multiculturalism, wherein different races co-exist under the supervision of the British. The party, however, ends in failure due to his guests' mutual suspicions and petty squabbles. In a line that foreshadows Crabbe's epiphany, an epiphany that dies with him, we are told that the "essential Malaya is jungle" (*Malayan Trilogy* 272).

He next places his hopes on Robert Loo, an eighteen-year-old who is, in Crabbe's eyes, a musical genius. He arranges and pays for Robert's trip to Singapore to record his music and has plans to obtain for him a scholarship to England (*Malayan Trilogy* 401). But Crabbe is taken aback when Robert shows no interest in getting his music performed there. Again, Crabbe is here assuming the "white man's burden", replicating the imperialist ideology that Malayan culture (in the form of music) has to be nurtured in Europe. When it is suggested to him the average Malayan would not care whether Malaya has a national music of its own, Crabbe retorts

> that's not the point. It's culture, and you've got to have culture in a civilised country, whether the people want it or not. That's one of the stock clichés—"our national culture". Well, here's the first bit of national culture you've ever had: not Indian, not Chinese, not Malay—Malayan, just that. (*Malayan Trilogy* 423)

Crabbe's argument is that a Malayan self-identity based on cultural production is achievable. However, that the text ends with Crabbe's death confirms the superfluity of his role and vision—and of the form of nationalism that Europeans envisaged for Malaya. As Geoffrey Aggeler points out, "[Crabbe's] belief that he is truly needed by Malaya is shown to be illusory" (50). The text makes the point that whatever future lies ahead for Malaya, it is beyond the imaginary of its former coloniser.

The irony regarding Robert's music is that when two American anthropologists finally hear it, it is, to their disappointment, not indigenous enough. They wanted to find "the real native artists":

> We've heard it all before. We can do it far better ourselves. In fact, we didn't come out these thousands of miles to see a distorted image of ourselves in a mirror. (Burgess *Malayan Trilogy* 572)

Perhaps the fate of Robert's music is also the postcolonial fate of newly independent nations. On the one hand, national culture has to be distilled from modular forms that first occurred in Europe, thus entering into a period of history through which Europe has already passed. On the other hand, when placed under the Euro-American gaze, the national culture of the ex-colony is dismissed as insufficiently indigenous and hence, inauthentic. However, if the final moment of *Beds in the East* is anything to go by, Robert's Loo's music does represent Malaya in an ironic way. For just as his music has unwittingly absorbed what he has heard from his father's jukebox, which plays the latest American popular songs, the end of the trilogy signifies a new era of American cultural imperialism, as represented by the fact that the United States Information Service has taken over the former British Residency (Burgess *Malayan Trilogy* 570). There are signs that Malaya is now oriented towards and by another form of imperialism. Syed Hassan, a Malay youth,

> began to feel resentment towards those English masters of his who had taught him English. It was colonial English they had taught him, that was it. But he would soon learn this new, free, democratic [American] English. (*Malayan Trilogy* 568–569)

The newspaper now "delivered to humble kampong folks who else would know nothing of the events in the great world outside" is printed in Arabic script and bears the name "*Suara Amerika* (The Voice of America)" (*Malayan Trilogy* 570).

The trilogy's ending is prescient in its anticipation of America's rise in cultural and economic influence. We will consider the phenomenon of American cultural imperialism in a later chapter. For now, we must recognise that while colonialism may be a thing of the past as far as contemporary Singapore and Malaysia are concerned, the same cannot be said of Malaysian and Singaporean nationalism, as well as the cultural imperialism of the West—topics also to be explored later.

In the works of Maugham and Burgess, we see moments when the English book is re-read and rewritten. If the above discussion focuses exclusively on Conradian moments in Maugham's writings, and Conradian and Joycean moments in Burgess' writings, it is because these moments enable us to explore the trope of domesticity in the works of Maugham and that of the jungle in the works of Burgess: Just as domestic tranquillity is shattered in so many of Maugham's stories, the Malayan jungle, the space beyond the domestic homestead, is no longer a site of conquest. As such, Malaya is no longer a homely and familiar site amenable to the construction of Englishness.

Unlike Swettenham, Bird, Caddy, and Innes, who wrote of Malaya as an extension of empire, Maugham and Burgess were more circumspect. In narrative after narrative, we are witness to members of the colonial administration who are flawed, disabled, and powerless. Warburton struggles to maintain a Victorian (and aristocratic) homestead in the tropics even as his powers are waning. Characters such as Leslie, who murdered her lover and who is found innocent in court, exemplifies the breakdown of not only Victorian familial values, but also of European law. Victor Crabbe is in many ways a tragic character who realises that he is superfluous in Malaya, while the likes of Nabby Adams and Robin Hood are portrayed primarily as comical and ineffectual. All of them are equally aware of the declining power of the British in Malaya. Especially with the rise of nationalism, Malaya is no longer tenable as a home to its colonisers. Yet traces of Englishness are not completely erased after colonialism's official end, for, as we shall see in the next chapter, the figure of the Englishman becomes an unhomely presence that haunts the landscape.

II
Nations
Malaya, Singapore, and Malaysia

4
'There is no way out but through':
Lee Kok Liang and the Malayan Nation

As we have seen in the previous chapter, in the work of W. Somerset Maugham and Anthony Burgess, Malaya has become a site that is politically and culturally uninhabitable to its colonial masters. Now we shall explore the other side of the colonial picture—that is, from the perspective of a colonised subject who had spent time in London, the imperial centre. In Lee Kok Liang's novel entitled *London Does Not Belong to Me*, London is a place of temporary abode: He has gone there from Malaya and is to return. There is an explicit recognition in Lee's writing that London is untenable as a centre for colonised subjects. In the novel and in Lee's short story "Return to Malaya", London is remapped in relation to Malaya. There is a need to re-site one's self and reclaim one's sense of home outside of the imperial centre.

Lee had acquired a reputation in Malaysia as a novelist and a writer of short stories. His novel *Flowers in the Sky* (1981) and his collections of short stories, *The Mutes in the Sun and Other Stories* (1963) and *Death is a Ceremony and Other Short Stories* (1992), explore the social and cultural landscape of Malaysia. He was known for his bleak portrayals of Malaysian life in work that nevertheless affirmed and celebrated the unrecorded minutiae of everyday existence. In the early 1950s, he spent two years in London completing a law degree, and it was during this period that he began writing a journal entitled *Sketches, Vignettes and Brush Strokes*, later renamed *Ramblings and Remembrances*, in which he recorded his observations, thoughts, and encounters. As Bernard Wilson points out in *"Sketches, Vignettes & Brush Strokes:* Portraits of the (Malaysian) Writer as a Young Man", the material in this journal formed the basis of his first novel, *London Does Not Belong to Me* (1).

Published posthumously in 2003, the novel depicts the experience of an unnamed protagonist of Chinese ethnicity in London. The novel may be described as a symphonic pastiche of discordant, half-fulfilled, and half-understood encounters that are rehearsals in anticipation of social and romantic consummation, perpetually deferring and frustrating the protagonist's attempt at penetrating the private spheres of London. The narrative revolves around the protagonist's increasing frustration as he tries to discover the reasons behind his Australian lover's betrayal and her sudden disappearance. Even as he searches for Cordelia, he finds himself entangled in webs of relationships among expatriates from different corners of the empire who seek solace in one another's company in what is depicted as the suffocating environment of London.

As K. S. Maniam observes, it was in this novel that Lee developed the themes of marginalisation and dissolution that were to inform his later work; for a Malaysian writer whose world was first mapped by colonialist texts catering to a metropolitan readership, when it came to engaging the metropolitan discourse, "There [was] no way out but through" ("Introduction" 7). Postcolonial writers are said to be involved in the project of writing back to and resisting an imperial centre. However, the act of resistance needs to be qualified not as rejection but as an expression of dis-identification with metropolitan discourse. It is not the case that the centrality of the imperial metropole is denied, denounced, or dismissed. Rather, its centrality is negotiated with so as to come to an understanding of the cultural significance of the periphery. In the final analysis, the centre informs the periphery as much as the periphery informs the centre. In *England through Colonial Eyes in Twentieth-Century Fiction*, Ann Blake, Leela Gandhi, and Sue Thomas draw from Mary Louise Pratt's notion of "contact zone" to argue that "'England' is a site of multivalent 'contact' for writers whose perspectives have been shaped by historically localized varieties of British colonialism and continuing processes of anti-colonialism and decolonization" (2). John McLeod makes the point in *Postcolonial London* that this contact zone "has long been an important site of creativity and conflict for those from countries with a history of colonialism" (6). From our point of view, *London Does Not Belong to Me* uncovers the marginal at the heart of the metropolitan centre, thus exposing the harsh realities of life for many residents of the metropole as these are veiled by the euphemism of "mother country". In doing so, the novel re-sites the metropolitan centre as a space of cultural trauma for people of colonised countries.

However, this reading begs another question: What options are left for postcolonial writers who do not identify with the metropole as a site of cultural discourse and who return to their native countries? Can such writers speak from another cultural site without positing that alternative site as peripheral to metropolitan space? This question of postcolonial travel, in which the colonised subject returns to his or her native country after having resided for a period of time at the imperial centre, will be addressed by way of "Return to Malaya". *London Does Not Belong to Me* and the short story present different aspects of the same discursive strategy. While the novel exposes the marginal within the metropolitan centre, the story brings the margins of empire to the centre of the narrative, with the implication that the centre is wherever postcolonial subjects find themselves to be.

Rewriting London: City of ghouls and vampires

Drawing from the work of Michel Pêcheux, the authors of *The Empire Writes Back* argue that the three modes of responses to ideology—identification, counter-identification, and dis-identification—may well serve as a framework with which one may understand literary production in the postcolonial context (Ashcroft et al. 167–169). To be sure, such a framework (and indeed the term "postcolonialism") have been subjected to trenchant critiques: Arun P. Mukherjee has made the point that Ashcroft et al. have "collaps[ed] ... separate histories in the name of a 'shared' ... post-colonial experience" ("Whose Post-colonialism" 5). Anne McClintock argues that the term "signals a reluctance to surrender the privilege of seeing the world in terms of a singular and ahistorical abstraction" ("Pifalls" 86), while Ella Shohat has drawn attention to its "depoliticizing implications" (99). Nonetheless, this tripartite framework is especially relevant to the point I wish to make while approaching literary production in Malaya and post-independent Malaysia.

Literary texts that identify with colonialist ideology affirm and perpetuate unequal power relations between the coloniser and the colonised, thus justifying economic exploitation under the guise of a civilising mission. In *Resisting Colonialist Discourse*, Zawiah Yahya has shown that embedded in the fictional works of Joseph Conrad, Somerset Maugham, and Anthony Burgess are portrayals of Malaya that are complicit with colonialist ideology. These works portray the society of Malaya as backward, thus justifying and identifying with colonialist intervention in the name of progress. It is not surprising to discover that the works of Maugham and Burgess were preceded by those of Frank Swettenham. Swettenham's short stories are often based on actual persons and events. He was widely considered authoritative. As a colonial administrator with expert knowledge of the Malay language and culture, and having worked on a Malay-English dictionary, his portrayals of the Malays as indolent and given to running amok at the slightest provocation were often taken at face value by British readers.

An instance of counter-identification with colonialism may be located in the rejection of the English language as a radical attempt at decolonisation. As Saran Kaur Gill notes, after having attained national independence, Malay was chosen to be the official and national language of Malaysia, and English was "relegated to being taught in schools as a second language", to the extent that "in the rural areas where there was almost no environmental exposure to the language, English was virtually a foreign language" (244). Hence, for writers active from the 1950s to the 1970s, the adoption of Malay as the national and official language repeats the Manichean dynamic of the colonialist ideology, privileging one language group over others. (We will later take up language policy in Malaysia as it has been changed in acknowledgement of the place English occupies as the *lingua franca* of business, science, and technology.) As a cultural policy, counter-identification is as oppressive as the ideology that is opposed. In the case of Malaysia, British colonialism is replaced with an internal colonialism as managed by the nationalist state.

In contrast, *London Does Not Belong to Me* exemplifies dis-identification as a more fruitful method of engaging colonialism, acknowledging its historical condition and working within its framework to seek release from its debilitating consequences. Dis-identifying with colonialism does not involve the setting up of a binary opposition between the coloniser and the colonised. Rather, through dis-identification the dominant ideology of the coloniser is undermined on its own terms. In literary productions, dis-identification involves not only the appropriation of the language of the colonial masters, but their discourse as well.

In *London Does Not Belong to Me*, metropolitan culture is viewed through the modernist tropes of cultural fragmentation and alienation. The opening scene of the novel is intriguing in that it draws our attention to the theme of dis-identification that is to pervade the novel:

> Two milk bottles stood on the table—one full, the other three-quarters full—and spreading out beneath them *The Times* lay prostrate, its columns dirtied with the spilt contents of chilli sauces and mashed pickled prawns that dripped from the abandoned bottles and vials … This was my dining table, a littered no-man's land … What was it she had said, as she scooped out the lychee, balancing the fruit on the tip of her forefinger? "Flesh pink," with a laugh, as she rested her hand against her bare throat. (*London* 9)

The depiction of the protagonist's dining table is akin to that of a modern still life painting. Yet it is a painting with a topography that has been remapped and transformed into what Wilson calls an "Eliotesque wasteland" ("Submerging Pasts" 318). The British newspaper and the milk bottles, images of conventional daily life in London, are spoiled and written over by the spilt contents of "abandoned bottles". While these spilt contents signal a human presence, it is a presence registered in a "no-man's land". The protagonist's experience of London is anticipated in this scene: Just as the topography of the dining table is disrupted and the scene dissolved by the fragmentary memory of a loved one scooping out a tropical fruit, the idea of London as an imperial centre is envisioned by the protagonist as a place of disenchantment, a topography of disaffection and emotions half-recollected in something other than tranquillity.

London Does Not Belong to Me presents a vision of alienation: The protagonist is not at home in London. But the novel tells of the protagonist's London experiences even as it is a testimony to the difficulty of writing about London. Prompted by a need to articulate as well as to exorcise the memory of what he has to say, the language is tentative and couched in uncertainty:

> Solitary like a spider, weaving a web, I had written to her. Not of love, because we did not speak of love. But of what I had dreamt, awkwardly framing the words, with the concentration of a child filling in his first notebook, intent to please, and words became my courage and her tribute. Not about the past either; for in this city, men and women submerged their past. I swam along with them, flipping my fins. (*London* 10)

We are told this is neither straightforward reminiscence nor autobiography; it is not about the past but about what is dreamed. The text presents not mimesis but introspection, not faithful description but a self-reflexive retelling, the work of a solitary protagonist "weaving a web", reconstituting his experience through the act of writing. The novel depicts the protagonist's experience of London inasmuch as it depicts what is involved in the writing of this experience. Yet the act of reconstitution is synonymous with the act of entrapment, as signalled by the metaphor of the web. If the narrative offers itself as a web, then what follows is an account of entanglement, entrapment, and reconciliation.

London in the 1950s is depicted in the novel as a city in decay. It is judged by its inhabitants to be a "diseased society" (*London* 88). According to another character, "London's full of ghosts and ghouls. Vampires" (*London* 14). At a social gathering, England is variously described as "a long-teated bitch", a "washout", a "great unending diarrhoea" (Lee *London* 53–54). It is depicted as a city inhabited by phantom-like characters whose pasts are often unclear and whose introductions often appear to be superficial, with the impression that they are intended to conceal rather than reveal:

> "Who's Ken?" I asked during the pause.
> "Ken, well he's just Ken." (*London* 25)

> "My name's Alpaca. My father's a shirt manufacturer in Sydney and somehow he was at a loss for a name when I was born a girl. Alpaca material was in fashion then. I play the zither on TV." (*London* 55)

"It seems to me everyone of us has a mystery," says the protagonist at an early point in the novel (*London* 22). Just as the backgrounds of the characters remain vague and unarticulated, the motivations behind their unsettling and often disturbing behaviour remain unclear most of the time. Tristam's account of how he first met Steve at the opera is contradicted by Guy, who claims to have introduced them. Of the relationship between Steve and Ken, the protagonist notes, "Their conversation was like an ocean full of ice-floes, three-quarters of the meaning being submerged, while on the surface the peaks reflected glints of anger and bitterness" (*London* 67).

The pervading atmosphere of ambiguity and malignancy is not limited to the protagonist's social circle but extends to the general society as well. Trivial, random, and meaningless acts constitute the everyday experience of London. Often, these acts are racist taunts. When the protagonist and Cordelia are seen in public, there are often signs of disapproval. A glare from a stranger recalls for the protagonist an earlier episode when a woman looks at him with contempt (*London* 141–142). Gopal, an Indian from Kenya who later suffers a nervous breakdown, endures the racist taunts of eleven-year-old girls (*London* 150).

Yellow skin, white mask, and the trauma of colonial desire

If London is a malignant and unhomely site, a site of trauma, it is the site out of which the protagonist negotiates his sense of place and identity. He has no illusions about how his race and country of origin are perceived by his interlocutors: He becomes, in effect, a signifier of cultural and racial difference. As he puts it, "the easy casual manner in which strangers picked me up frightened me, as if I were a bargain find or a trinket" (*London* 16). That his ethnicity is not mentioned throughout the novel is a significant point, highlighting the trauma of cultural dislocation and alienation. His Chinese name remains unpronounceable and unpronounced throughout: "I mumbled my name … I had to repeat it" (*London* 51). If the protagonist does not refer explicitly to his ethnicity, it is because he is painfully aware of his difference. In social encounters, he is never allowed to forget this difference that need not be named: "The men lifted their haunches when I held their hands, but the women flung up their bright faces and then lost interest in me" (*London* 52).

That language becomes a barrier to communication is symptomatic of this crisis of self-image. Speech becomes struggle, and every social encounter becomes a cultural-linguistic ordeal:

> [W]hen I talked my words became inconsequential, losing their force, and as I spoke I became conscious of my pronunciation. Marbles in my mouth: I spewed them out. I hated myself as soon as I began to speak, feeling inadequate. (*London* 25)

> "I'm sorry I must go now. Got to catch the tube." I nearly said, "Got to tube a catch." Language was a loose string of beads to me. (*London* 26)

As Wilson observes, "The narrator experiences the practical difficulties and misapprehensions of a Straits-Chinese communicating in British English" ("Submerging Pasts" 321). His attempts to communicate meet with difficulties, and thus his desire for social recognition remains acute. As he walks away from the scene of his initial social encounter with Cordelia, Beatrice, and Arlette, he is concerned as to whether his presence at the gathering is registered:

> I stood for a moment on the pavement under their window ... So soon they seemed to have forgotten about me. I walked away carrying the warm voice of the girl tucked in my heart like the secret hoard of a squirrel. I knew I would be going back to them again, not because I was lonely in this cold city, but perhaps because, like a man who had been introduced to a drug, I wanted it again. I wanted to be an addict. (*London* 27)

In this respect, his desire for social recognition becomes codified as a desire for romantic consummation. "I began to wonder how I should talk to *this* girl," he thinks to himself during his first meeting with Cordelia, "I began to wonder what could happen if I knew her better" (*London* 16–18).

In intimate moments such as the following, Cordelia is codified as a feminine representation of colonial difference. Her Occidental physical features become the depository of the protagonist's fantasy of the Other:

> I held my legs open as she eased her shoulders between my thighs, bending her head forwards slightly and crossing her arms over her knees. Her hair had the softness of a child's fingers as it lay in my palm; I had never expected so many shades of gold. Warm brownish gold at her crown flowing thickly into streams of pure hard sparkle at her back and turning into pale massed clouds the colour of dry white sands. Swiftly brushing, I perceived its strength. As I swept the brush upwards from the base of her neck, I caught a glimpse of whiteness, marred by a tiny patch—a small black O with darkish hairs—and then the hair slipped between my fingers. (*London* 29)

The recitation of Occidental features ("shades of gold", "warm brownish gold", "the colour of dry white sands", "a glimpse of whiteness") is indicative of the projection of desire for the cultural Other. As Wilson suggests, though Cordelia is Australian, she "is interchangeable as a symbol of the narrator's conflicting responses to London ... as symbolic of the coloniser/colonised dynamic" ("Submerging Pasts" 329). If, at the end of the novel, the protagonist is able to come to terms with Cordelia's disappearance and then return to Malaya, it is because this coloniser/colonised dynamic is finally dissolved.

The protagonist's relationship with Cordelia is framed in the novel in such a way that the sexual act operates as psychic metaphor. The consciousness of the protagonist is shown to be disintegrating and reconstituting around Cordelia:

> I had discarded my physical shell and was flowing towards Cordelia, drawn by her absorbing gaze, spilling and sprinkling parts of me all over her. Inside me a bowl of warmth radiated. I spoke without knowing, wrapped up in my reconstruction, releasing my memories of those bitter dreams, and when I had finished, Cordelia closed her eyes, quietly. (*London* 38–39)

This psychic union between Cordelia and the protagonist is achieved at a price, as he soon discovers. At the beginning of the novel, we are privy to the protagonist's nostalgic dream-image of Malaya as a scenic paradise, with "mynah birds shooting like beads along branches of casuarinas, and … pale spidery crabs on warm sands and the dark button-sized shells buried just above the tides" (*London* 9–10). However, to achieve this psychic (and physical) union with Cordelia, he forgoes this dream-image in favour of an English landscape:

> When I was with her like this, I forgot about the warm sands and spidery crabs and the day when the sun would beckon again to me. I love the English winter and the coalescence it brings to lovers, its shadows which hide the mind and soul unlike the fierce gaze of the sun in the tropics. (*London* 112)

It soon becomes obvious to the protagonist that Cordelia cannot be reconciled to his image of Malaya. He fantasises about Cordelia being in Malaya, "a pale figure with milky transparent skin, moving about the hawkers in the bazaar", but he could not tell her of it, for "in her mind she saw only the heat and the jungle and the flies" (*London* 84).

Just as Malaya is reconstituted in Cordelia's mind as a forbidding landscape marked by the absence of civilisation, the protagonist's self can be reconstituted only in the gaze of his beloved as an exotic Other:

> "How wide apart your eyes are," she said with a half-smile, lifting up her face to mine. I knew by that she was wondering whether the rest of my kind had the same wide-apart eyes. (*London* 85)

Thus, the relationship between Cordelia and the protagonist is marked by the wound of mis-recognition. Each is drawn to the other through a gaze that accentuates the exotic/Occidentalist difference from the self, reconstituting each in the other's eyes. It is this accentuation of difference that obstructs mutual recognition.

Just as London becomes the site of psychic injury and mutual mis-recognition in the protagonist's relationship with Cordelia, it is also constitutive of the colonial experience, an experience that the protagonist learns to recognise and work through. If the protagonist's crisis of self-image in London is conflated with his relationship with Cordelia, his epiphany at the end of the novel signals reconciliation with his romantic experience. It is in his relationship with Beatrice, a repetition of his relationship with Cordelia but with a difference, that we detect this reconciliation.

At a Chinese restaurant, when Beatrice is intrigued by the protagonist's expertise with chopsticks, he is reconciled to the idea that in her mind he would forever be associated with a fetishised portrayal of Chineseness, with "a memory of gold and reds and dragons":

> Should I also tell her about the dirt and the flies and the diseases? But what's the point anyway? Everyone of us must preserve a certain romantie [*sic*] viewpoint about far distant places to which the mind could return in the midst of our grimy surroundings ... And I on my part would recapture the glitter in her eyes ... I was conscious that I was a craftsman, weaving on the loom of memory, sending out a rhythm that would enfold our lives like the caresses of the waves on a sandy beach. I would then be standing on the edge of a warm sea, gazing across the horizon, trying to centre my attention on some point where I thought London would be, and in particular where she would be... (*London* 247–248)

During a late-night conversation, it is Steve who suggests a way for the protagonist to come to terms with his experience:

> There's one thing, however, I'm glad for. Little nuts of experience. That can never be robbed away, at least if you know how to store them. One must learn to be a squirrel. Store nuts to consume at our low ebbs, during hibernation from the harsh realities. It's the game that keeps us going ... One day I'll take a bite and understand something ... I suppose you'll be doing the same thing. (*London* 284)

It is this recognition of preservation of memory as premonition, of recounting as re-creation, of imagining a romanticised past for posterity that reconciles the protagonist with his experience of London. The act of resituating is intertwined with the act of writing, with the act of storing little nuts of experience. It is the writing of fiction not as a glossing over, not as forgetting, but as building an enabling narrative. If the beginning of the novel employs the metaphor of weaving a web to describe the act of writing, by the end of the novel, the connotations of entanglement and entrapment are replaced by a poetics of liberation and epiphany. If, with Cordelia, he is unable to rehearse his private image of Malaya even to himself, with Beatrice he is able to reconstitute his sense of place within his homeland and at the same time recognise the constructed nature of this reclamation. At the end of the novel, just as the protagonist's romantic relationships are reconstituted, so is London. London, the site of alienation, is no longer the centre of his experience; rather, "standing on the edge of a warm sea", London would have to be re-sited from the cultural location of Malaya. "Glad you won't have to face the cold any more", says Tristam to the protagonist at the point of the latter's departure from London (*London* 286). Yet, as we shall see later, even in tropical Malaya, the protagonist of Lee's short story "Return to Malaya" still feels the London cold. Like it or not, and the novel's title notwithstanding, London does belong to him.

Reclamation and interpolation in 'Return to Malaya'

If *London Does Not Belong to Me* depicts the marginal spaces within the metropolitan centre, "Return to Malaya" relocates the margins of the empire to the centre of the narrative. Both texts have similar discursive aims: They exemplify an interpolation of colonialist discourse wherein the colonised subject undermines forces seeking to portray him or her as an inferior Other of European modernity. As Ashcroft points out in *Post-Colonial Transformation*, interpolation is not the "utter refusal to countenance any engagement" with the dominant culture; rather, it "make[s] use of aspects of the colonizing culture so as to generate transformative cultural production" (47). In "Return to Malaya", published in Kuala Lumpur in 1963, about a decade after Lee's sojourn in London, the act of interpolation is at the same time an act of cultural reclamation.

In the story we are privy to the observations of a protagonist surveying the scene of his hometown in Malaya:

> – *Chek, chek, chek (Gurgles of laughter)*
> *He lost his spectacles-lah, Ai-ya! do you know what he looked like*
> – *Like what*
> – *Like a tortoise with goat's dung eyes, chek, chek*
> – *Ai-ya! yes-lah, and he lost them, the spectacles-lah*
> – *One two som, la-la-li-tum-bong, I won!*
>
> They spoke in a sort of Hokkien Chinese (towns in Malaya are dominated by different Chinese dialects) with a few Malay and English expressions thrown in. [emphases in original] ("Return" 186–187)

In the above, as in many instances in the story, the act of observing becomes the act of reclaiming. As Wilson points out, the story "provides a cross-section of the plural landscape" of Malaya ("Sketches" 10). Malaya is no longer "a world where fathers were adulterous and mothers vicious" (*London* 18). In contrast to the protagonist's experience of social and linguistic alienation in the novel, where "words bounced against [him] softly like ping-pong balls", the dialects, words, and gestures of those under observation in "Return to Malaya" are accessible to the protagonist to the extent that he is able to provide a gloss on the language (*London* 55).

As Ashcroft et al. point out, code switching and vernacular transcription signify the postcolonial writer's ability to appropriate and abrogate English as a medium of writing, thus refuting "the privileged position of a standard code in the language" (*Empire Writes Back* 40). In "Return to Malaya", the use of non-standard English is a mark of abrogation. It is English, but not quite, just as it is Malaya that is being depicted, but as we shall see later, this is not quite so either. As John Clement Ball puts it:

> When writers from lands that were colonized by Britain's erstwhile empire put pen to paper, a set of ideas that coalesce around the signifier "London" often shadows their work—especially if they … use the colonizer's language. (3–4)

"Return to Malaya" transforms the centre-margin binary into a hybridised discursive space, a space where London emerges as a disinterred site, creating unexpected hybrid moments in the postcolonial narrative. One such moment occurs as the protagonist approaches a hawker's stall:

> Fine fluffy snowy drops of drizzle blew against my face; and in the tropics this was like having points of sunlight on one's face on a cold winter's morning, say in London. ("Return" 189)

We must note in this passage the incongruity of the haunted moment as a function of interpolation. Robert Young draws our attention to the dual nature of the concept of hybridity when he points out that it

> works simultaneously in two ways: "organically", hegemonizing, creating new spaces, structures, scenes, and "intentionally", diasporizing, intervening as a form of subversion, translation, transformation." (*Colonial Desire* 25)

As Young puts it, hybridity is "of a doubleness that both brings together, fuses, but also maintains separation", and it is this separation that legitimises the postcolonial writer's non-English context (*Colonial Desire* 22). Malaya, as a cultural site, is shadowed by London in that hybrid moment. Yet it is a hybrid moment that subverts. Soon after the protagonist is reminded of snow in London, he is confronted by the material presences of his immediate surroundings:

> Around me were the rough wooden tables, midget stools, four-wheeled stalls with zinc roofs, long and low like those of the quayside sheds, and tiers of meat-balls, fish, noodles, red chillies, neatly stacked in pyramids, and storm-lamps and oil-burners in cylindrical frames which flashed out like beacons—all these transformed the alley into a busy night-harbour as the lights glinted and slithered across the wet, glossy surface of the road. ("Return" 190)

In the above catalogue of material presences, all that is solid about Orientalist assumptions of the Malayan landscape, as depicted in *London Does Not Belong to Me*, melts into air. From wooden tables to midget stools to storm-lamps and oil-burners, these objects constitute a scene of habitation and of human activity, thus negating Cordelia's image of Malaya as an arid site of "heat and the jungle and the flies" (*London* 84). It also negates the protagonist's initially nostalgic (and illusory) dream-image of Malaya as a scenic paradise, with its mynah birds, warm sands, and so on.

Another moment of interpolation centres on the abrupt appearance of an Englishman:

> Suddenly, striding down the alley, a belated theatrical figure made his appearance: tall, fearsome, high in the nose, with stormy sunset complexion, wearing a bow-tie and flowing nylon shirt; and, without turning his head, bore himself like a dreadnought throught [*sic*] the crowds as though he had a mission to fulfil, or as if, a neighbour commented, he was hunting for the lavatory. In other words, an Englishman had walked by. ("Return" 192)

The Englishman in Malaya is depicted here as an incongruous and improbable figure. He appears suddenly out of nowhere onto the crowded night-harbour scene among the hawker stalls, where families are at tables having their meals and where men are ogling women whom one may suppose are prostitutes. While the crowd is depicted as belonging to and inhabiting the scene, the Englishman is not. He is inexplicable, and his appearance is unhomely and out of place, a "theatrical figure [making] his appearance", wearing a bow-tie in the tropical heat. In this way Lee's writings offer a reversal of the notion of "British Malaya"—the imperial gaze is overturned, such that we are offered a momentary vision of a "Malayan Britain". The figure of the Englishman is unhomely, conjured up in the story only to be expelled, as a reminder of that which does not belong to Malaya.

"Return to Malaya", a story of homecoming, may be read as a conclusion to *London Does Not Belong to Me*. Both narratives, taken together, map a journey to and from the imperial centre. Steve Clark points out that "travel writing is inevitably one-way traffic, because the Europeans mapped the world rather than the world mapping them", especially when the journey is carried out under the aegis of colonialism (3). Yet for the postcolonial writer who resided in the metropolitan centre before returning to his or her colonised lands, the situation is more complex. There is a need to reaffirm one's centre of reference—one's home, as it were. London in Lee's novel is a temporary abode. Lee returned to Malaya, and hence writing was for him necessarily a matter of two-way traffic. London and Malaya are mapped in relation to each other. At the end of *London Does Not Belong to Me* and in "Return to Malaya", London is subjected to a dialogical remapping in relation to Malaya. The protagonist recognises that Malaya is no longer at the periphery; correspondingly, in the short story, London is no longer the centre for the former colony.

Taken together, *London Does Not Belong to Me* and "Return to Malaya" bear testimony to Ashcroft's proposition that "one does not need to speak *out of* otherness, in the voice of the other, in order to speak *of* otherness" [emphases in original] (*Transformation* 46). For even though London as "a metonym for imperial power" is a ghost that haunts much postcolonial writing, the postcolonial text subjects this haunting into a productive transformation as an act of reclaiming one's sense of place outside of the space of the metropolitan centre (Ball 4). In his writings, Lee was able to return to a vision of Malaya as home and nation. However, as we shall see in the next two chapters, subsequent political events which led to the emergence of Malaysia's ethnic nationalism have come to problematise this vision.

5

Nationalism and Literature:
Two Poems Concerning the Merlion and Karim Raslan's "Heroes"

The literary history of Singapore and Malaysia is a history of the discursive formation of the nation. One sees its early incarnations in the Malaya of the 1950s and 1960s, in the form of poetic experiments with Engmalchin (a linguistic combination of English, Malay, and Chinese). Anne Brewster examined these in *Towards a Semiotic of Postcolonial Discourse*. Engmalchin was a literary project that came out of an emergent Malayan nationhood—the same nationhood that animates Lee Kok Liang's *London Does Not Belong to Me*. The failure of Engmalchin, as Harper argues, was due to its "obsession with a didactic promotion of the 'Malayan' identity"; as such, "the credibility of new literature had been undermined" (299). This articulation of Malayan nationhood was also curtailed by subsequent political developments in Singapore and Malaysia.

Writers have since responded variously to the modern political landscapes of both countries. The current generation of writers include, among others, the poet Alfian bin Sa'at from Singapore and the fiction writer and journalist Karim Raslan from Malaysia. In their work, the conceptual categories of nation and nationalism and their deployment in official discourses come under persistent critique. Malayan nationhood was something sought after by writers of the 1950s and 1960s. In contrast, while nationalism today presents the nation-state as a home for its inhabitants, the work of contemporary writers disturbingly narrates a condition wherein one is not at home.

State-sanctioned nationalism in contemporary Singapore and Malaysia, in its attempt to consolidate nationhood after colonialism, embodies the contradiction of both rejecting and accepting the intellectual framework of post-Enlightenment Europe. Reflecting this, literary work that engages the themes of nation and nationalism exemplifies the contradiction of a state-sponsored discourse that seeks to contain and normalise a perpetual state of crisis in identity formation. Here we will consider Edwin Thumboo's "Ulysses by the Merlion", Alfian Sa'at's

"The Merlion", and Karim Raslan's short story "Heroes" to illustrate the fraught endeavour of articulating nationhood in Singapore and Malaysia.

Thumboo's poem was first published in 1979, less than two decades after Singapore acquired national independence, a time when the nation's political elite faced the challenge of uniting a community composed of several ethnicities into a cohesive society. Alfian's poem, which appeared in 1998, is a contrapuntal response to Thumboo's. A juxtaposed reading of the two works enables us to foreground the power of national symbols in the creation of a myth of the nation's origins; at the same time, we find the creation of such a myth to be an act of contrivance. Karim, as both journalist and short-story writer, has in the 1990s initiated public discussions regarding Malaysia's ideology of nationhood and its related policies. "Heroes" is especially insightful, for a case can be made that the story invites an allegorical reading that imparts irony to Malaysia's authorised story of nationalism.

Singaporean nationalism

Singapore achieved nationhood only after a long interim of local ideological strife that culminated in the rise of the People's Action Party (PAP) under the leadership of Lee Kuan Yew and his peers. As Michael Hill and Lien Kwen Fee point out, the earliest articulation of nationhood in Singapore occurred not in 1965, when Singapore separated from Malaysia, but in the aftermath of the Japanese occupation (1942–45), when the idea of a Malayan nation arose in the Malayan Union proposal of 1946 (3).

The prevailing sentiment after the Second World War was that since the British had surrendered Singapore to the Japanese, they had forfeited their right to govern the colony:

> My colleagues and I are of that generation of young men who went through the Second World War and the Japanese Occupation and emerged determined that no one—neither the Japanese nor the British—had the right to push and kick us around. We determined that we could govern ourselves and bring up our children in a country where we can be proud to be a self-respecting people.
>
> When the war came to an end in 1945, there was never a chance of the old type of British colonial system ever being re-created. The scales had fallen from our eyes and we saw for ourselves that the local people could run the country.
>
> In fact the local people did run the country for the Japanese military administration. (Lee Kuan Yew *Battle for Merger* 10–11)

Popular sentiment, as this quotation makes plain, was co-opted by a discourse of nationalism shaped as a struggle for political independence. After 1965, Singapore embarked on a programme of industrialisation fostered by what may be called the PAP's ideology of economic pragmatism, legitimised by the fact that previously, Singapore was thought to be unviable as an independent nation in terms of defence, economics, and politics.

Singapore's nationalism places emphasis on a postcolonialism that narrates a rupturing of history so as to create a national future premised on the vision of the ruling political elite. Thus, to be a citizen is to re-create oneself to embody the national and economic goals established by the governing party. Despite its intellectual roots in the socialism of early twentieth-century Britain, one may go so far as to say that the PAP subscribes to the Darwinian ideology of survival and competition that underpins capitalism. Issues of race and ethnicity did not surface in the party's ideological framework until the 1980s and 1990s, when the state developed a sudden interest in exploring "Confucian" and "Asian" social values. One may suggest that this is an attempt, on the one hand, to project onto other nations an "Asian" modernity that explains Singapore's (and East Asia's) economic success at that point in time. On the other hand, the discourse of "Asian" and "Confucian" values, with their emphases on communitarian virtues, serves to instil in the domestic populace a givenness to obedience to state authority.

After 1965, state formation in Singapore was thus intertwined with material and economic issues in accordance with how the political elite defined the nation. There was a noticeable shift away from the political debates that characterised the previous decades. For instance, the issue of ethnic rights, especially as it pertained to the question of designated privileges that might be accorded to Malays, was supplanted by a politics of national survival that legitimised the move towards an emphasis on the economy. As Lee Kuan Yew puts it at the end of the second volume of his memoirs published in 2000, one major factor in Singapore's success was that its political leaders acted to "[keep] the workers on [their] side and at the same time tend to the needs of investors whose capital, knowledge, management skills and overseas markets would enable [the people of Singapore] to make a living" (*From Third World to First* 758). By aligning national survival with economic survival, hegemony was purchased, and the populace's allegiance to the ideas and vision of the political elite legitimised.

To borrow the phrase Francis Fukuyama made current at the Cold War's end, the PAP's politics of survival culminates in the end of history. Fukuyama deployed the term in his argument that "liberal democracy may constitute the 'end point of mankind's ideological evolution' and the 'final form of human government'" (xi). Just as Fukuyama's thesis is teleological in its assumption that the clash of alternative ideologies belongs to the past, the PAP's politics of survival likewise assumes the end of history in that there is a closure to ideological struggle, and all that remains for Singapore to do is to refine its economic and administrative machinery in the interest of nation-building. This pragmatism is accompanied by Lee's attitude towards what he calls "pet theories", a term he uses to dismiss what he perceives as fruitless discussions of socio-political ideology (*From Third World to First* 759). As he puts it, he has "always tried to be correct, not politically correct" (*From Third World to First* 759). Singaporean writers, we will now consider, have responded to such an approach to nation-building in various ways.

The Merlion

Anglophone poetry in Singapore, some readers have noted, has been put into the service of the state's discourse on nation-building. Robbie Goh points out that from 1965 to the late 1980s "Anglophone poetry has played a distinctive and privileged role ... a role reinforced by deliberate institutional measures and for clear strategic reasons of nation-building and cultural unification" ("Imagining the Nation" 22). Edwin Thumboo is one of only four Anglophone poets to have received the Cultural Medallion, Singapore's highest award for artistic excellence, so indicating the degree to which his poetry has attained institutional recognition.

As a poet, literary scholar, and university administrator, Thumboo, who is of Tamil and Teochew-Peranakan parentage, is one of the few writers in Singapore who can claim to have shaped the literary consciousness of his generation and those that have followed. In his academic essays, Thumboo makes overt his commitment to forging an indigenous voice. In his introduction to *The Second Tongue: An Anthology of Poetry from Singapore and Malaysia* (1976), he makes the point that a poet, "whatever his [or her] inclination and individual gifts, writes within a given historical context [and] is inescapably a child of his [or her] times" (xii). His public poetry is particularly exemplary for its articulation of how the formation of the nation occurs in its discursive aspect. Poems such as "9th of August–I" and "9th of August–II" offer different ways of commemorating Singapore's national independence and its relationship with Malaysia. "Catering for the People", another public poem, likewise clarifies the need for the agenda of nation-building after 1965: "There is little choice—/ We must make a people" (*Third Map* 53).

Thumboo's poetry has engendered mixed reactions, and this is no surprise, given its public nature. His poem, "Ulysses by the Merlion", is much discussed in part because it lays bare the mechanisms of how national identity is constructed. The poem, some critics argue, articulates a national consciousness crucial to the formation of Singapore's national collective. Ee Tiang Hong writes of the poem in a celebratory tone. "Where [Thumboo's] voice in the earlier public poems was tentative," he points out, "it now had the force of conviction. Politics was now enmeshed with poetry" (46). Others look at the poem with suspicion, arguing that

"Ulysses by the Merlion" is an example of state propaganda disguised as poetry, that it is a product of an ideological state apparatus that presents a coerced rhetoric of nationalism. For Leong Liew Geok, the "patent artificiality" of the Merlion testifies to "Singapore's artificiality as polity and sovereign nation" ("Lyric Enterprise" 45).

In "Ulysses by the Merlion", the journey of Ulysses, hero of Homer's epic poem, is interrupted by his encounter with the Merlion:

> But this lion of the sea
> Salt-maned, scaly, wondrous of tail,
> Touched with power, insistent
> On this brief promontory ...
> Puzzles.
>
> Nothing, nothing in my days
> Foreshadowed this
> Half-beast, half-fish,
> This powerful creature of land and sea.
>
> (Thumboo *Third Map* 80)

Ulysses, an experienced journeyman who "sailed many waters, / Skirted islands of fire," is depicted as perplexed and overwhelmed by the figure of the Merlion (Thumboo *Third Map* 80). Thumboo's poem, in placing Ulysses by the Merlion, locates them on the same plane of mythic existence so as to legitimise the latter as a national symbol. Unwittingly, however, the poem reveals the problems that attend to the articulation of nationhood: It is ironic that in a work that explicitly seeks to articulate a national present that is advancing beyond a colonial past, the voice of the national bard is supplanted by the voice of Ulysses, so drawing from one of the foundational texts in the Western canon. Clearly, the anxiety of influence is at work here. Furthermore, the figure of the Merlion is problematic as a national symbol, for it was created by a government tourism board. As Brenda Yeoh and T. C. Chang point out, the Merlion statue, with the head of a lion and body and tail of a fish, is a state-manufactured icon, created in 1972 by the Singapore Tourism Promotion Board (now renamed the Singapore Tourism Board) as part of a marketing strategy for the tourism industry (34).

The Merlion as a state-manufactured icon underscores the poem's contrived and artificial attempt to foster and affirm an organic national identity. Yet the Merlion fails as an instrument of rule as it is a national symbol that draws attention to its own synthetic origin. As such, both statue and poem may be regarded as representing the national ethos in a highly ironic fashion. Celebrating as a national symbol an object contrived for the consumption of tourists, the poem dramatises its own precarious project of articulating a national identity that is subject to the logic of economic pragmatism and which compels all cultural productions into the service of this logic. Certain lines, indeed, invite this reading: "They make, they serve, / They buy, they sell" (Thumboo *Third Map* 80). What is finally bought and sold is "This lion of the sea, / This image of themselves" (Thumboo *Third Map* 81). As such, the poem succeeds in rendering into myth the nation's subjection to capitalism.

"Ulysses by the Merlion" demonstrates some of the ambivalence and tensions that accompany the formation of a national identity. Thumboo's use of myth-making to legitimise the nationalist agenda, and the problematic alliance of poetic vision with economic imperatives, sit uneasily with the generation of poets who came after him. In a further demonstration of the anxiety of influence, Thumboo's poem has sparked off a series of Merlion poems in Singaporean literature. They include Daren Shiau's "Merlion Speaks", Felix Cheong's "The Obligatory Merlion Poem", Alvin Pang's "Merlign" and Alfian bin Sa'at's "The Merlion". While each of these poems engages Thumboo's in dialogue, it is Alfian bin Sa'at's that can be singled out as a polemically anti-nationalist poem that is not without its own irony.

With the publication of Alfian's two poetry collections, *One Fierce Hour* (1998) and *A History of Amnesia* (2001), his prize-winning short-story collection *Corridor* (1999), and the staging of plays that address a wide span of political issues, Alfian has acquired a reputation as an anti-establishment writer in a span of less than five years. Angelia Poon draws our attention to Alfian's ethnicity when she points out that within "the context of Singapore's literary scene, [he] stands out for being Malay and writing both in English and Malay" (122). In his poem "Neighbours", we find an expression of alienation among members of the Malay community, one from another: "During Hari Raya she knocks on my conscience, / I knock on her door and I give her cakes" yet "in our hands we hold with fists clenched tight / The keys to our homes, each night we slam the door shut" (*Fierce Hour* 8). In "Singapore You Are Not My Country", Alfian launches his polemic against the discursive formation of the nation:

> O Singapore your fair shores your garlands your GNP.
> You are not a country you are a construction from spare parts.
> You are not a campaign you are last year's posters.
> You are not culture you are poems on the MRT.
>
> (*Fierce Hour* 41)

Alfian's poetry is a challenge to the transparently manufactured aspect of Singapore. His poems react against the malleability of the nation in the face of the governing party's nationalist and economic enterprise.

Alfian's poem "The Merlion" may be regarded as a contrapuntal response to Thumboo's "Ulysses by the Merlion". In contrast to the mythic lyricism evident in Thumboo's poem, Alfian's riposte is delivered in everyday language via a dialogue between two friends. The tone is irreverent, describing the Merlion as a grotesque and limbless monstrosity. The Merlion is a mutant "writhing in the water, / like some post-Chernobyl nightmare" (*Fierce Hour* 21). It is a dislocated being, "marooned on this rough shore, / as if unsure of its rightful / harbour" (*Fierce Hour* 21). However, the poem undermines its own staging of the improbability of the Merlion as a national symbol when the reader's attention shifts from the first-person speaker to his interlocutor:

> "And why does it keep spewing that way?
> I mean, you know, I mean …"
>
> "I know exactly what you mean," I said,
> Eyeing the blond highlights in your black hair
> And your blue lenses the shadow of a foreign sky.
> "It spews continually if only to ruffle
> its own reflection in the water; such reminders
> will only scare a creature so eager to reinvent itself."
>
> Another pause.
>
> "Yes," you finally replied, in that acquired accent of yours,
> "Well, yes, but I still do wish it had paws."
>
> (*Fierce Hour* 22)

The irony of the poem is that the critique of the Merlion is articulated by someone who is equally eager to reinvent his or her identity in Western terms; he or she is someone with "blond highlights in … black hair", "blue [contact] lenses the shadow of a foreign sky" and who speaks with an "acquired accent". One may regard this as a critique of the superficiality of Singapore's Westernisation. The Merlion, limbless, a lion's head and a fish's body, is said to be afraid of its own reflection, afraid to be reminded of its incongruous appearance, much like the friend with the blue-tinted contact lenses and blond-highlighted hair, except that the Merlion is cast as being aware of its own incongruity while the friend is not.

The friend is a latter-day national subject, circumscribed by a state-sponsored ideology oriented towards capital accumulation. In his attempt to dissociate himself from nationalism as monumentalised by the Merlion, he unwittingly reveals the shallowness of his own Westernised modernity and his critique. He infuses the image of the Merlion with irony precisely because he is afraid to confront his own self-reflection. The Merlion in Alfian's poem is Othered in the process of disavowal. It is both a screen and a mirror. It is a screen the friend hides behind so as to veil his own malleable identity, projecting this malleability instead onto the figure of the Merlion. It is a mirror in that the Merlion, finally, reflects the friend's own fraught condition of subject-formation.

Like Thumboo's "Ulysses by the Merlion", Alfian's poem also draws attention to the ambivalence that attends to the formation of national identity. The two poems display two different kinds of awareness of the essential conundrum. The first recognises the power of national symbols in the creation of a myth of the nation's origins, while the second reveals the dubious effects of such power as they become manifest in those subjected to it. Both poems testify to the difficulty of articulating the conditions of nationhood. The moment one presses for a nationalist agenda by constructing a national icon is the moment one inadvertently reveals the act of that construction as being premised on artifice. Likewise, as my reading of Alfian's poem demonstrates, the moment one articulates scepticism towards the legitimacy of a national icon is the moment one would have to examine the condition of one's own identity-formation leading to that articulation.

Malaysian nationalism and the maimed hero

One reason for the separation of Singapore from Malaysia in 1965 was that during the period of merger between 1963 and 1965, Lee Kuan Yew pressed for an economic nationalism based on the principles of meritocracy and multiculturalism as encapsulated in the phrase "Malaysian Malaysia", while the Malaysian government in Kuala Lumpur favoured an ethnic nationalism, as encapsulated in the phrase "Malay Malaysia" (Yeo 146). Much has been said on this point. Another factor in the merger's failure was that UMNO, the United Malays National Organisation, then as now Malaysia's premier Malay political formation, was apprehensive about the possibility that the Singapore government was planning a "Chinese-takeover of Malaysia" (Turnbull 284).

Post-1965 political developments in Malaysia further underscored the issue of race in its nation-building project. Contemporary Malaysian nationalism arose from race riots that broke out in Kuala Lumpur in 1969 and the social and political consequences of those events. As Barbara Watson Andaya and Leonard Y. Andaya point out, since Malaysia's independence from Britain, "Chinese entrepreneurs had flourished under the government's *laissez-faire* policies, and ... the income disparity between Malays and Chinese had worsened. Rural areas, where most Malays still lived, remained poor" (292). Thus, the political elite undertook several measures to eradicate poverty, particularly in the rural Malay population, and to promote a sense of national belonging among Malays.

These measures primarily took the form of education, language, and land-resettlement policies intended to redistribute wealth among ethnic communities (Andaya 291–303). In 1961, the Education Act abolished government aid to Chinese-medium secondary schools. From 1965, entry examinations into the University of Malaya, previously given in English, were also given in Malay. The national Language Bill, passed two years later, recognised Malay as the national language.

The economic policies aimed primarily at rural Malays took form by way of new and large government agencies. Agricultural programmes such as the Federal Land Development Authority (FELDA) and the Rubber Industry Smallholders

Development Authority (RISDA) were created. FELDA involved the resettlement of the rural Malay population onto land that had been previously developed into various agricultural plots, while RISDA provided funding to rubber smallholders to develop better-quality rubber trees. However, rural Malay poverty persisted because, first, the northern Malay states, the areas of greatest poverty, were not included in these programmes and, second, these programmes created a group of local politicians whose support had to be courted. Finally, in the case of RISDA the main beneficiaries were the more well-off Malay landowners. At the same time, many of the areas where as many as 500,000 Chinese squatters had been resettled had expanded into towns, yet funds were not channelled into these areas to develop even the most basic of amenities. Thus, just as there was Malay resentment against the government for having created a system wherein the Chinese prospered while they continued to cope with severe poverty, there existed a sense of discontent in the Chinese community that special privileges were accorded to the Malays and that their interests were not being served.

During federal elections on 10 May 1969, these grievances were made manifest. At the polls a fundamental shift took place. A political formation called the Alliance party, which was responsible for initiating these language, education, and economic policies, had won 58.4 per cent of the popular vote in the previous elections, held five years earlier. It was made up of UMNO, the Malayan Chinese Association, or MCA, and the Malayan Indian Congress, or MIC. The alliance retained its majority in the Dewan Rakyat (House of Representatives), but its share of the vote fell to 48.5 per cent (Andaya 297). Political parties such as the Gerakan Rakyat Malaysia (the Malaysian People's Movement), the Democratic Action Party (DAP), and the People's Progressive Party (PPP), which had protested the privileges given to the Malay community, thus secured enough seats to deprive the Alliance government "of the two-thirds majority which had previously enabled it to obtain constitutional amendments with ease" (Andaya 298).

On 12 May, Gerakan and DAP supporters launched a celebration in the streets of Kuala Lumpur; the following day, UMNO supporters staged a counter-rally. This was when ethnic violence broke out, prompting the declaration of the state of emergency. The fighting lasted four days, and official figures showed 196 fatalities and 409 injured, the property of 6,000 residents of Kuala Lumpur destroyed; most victims were Chinese (Andaya 298). The government subsequently sought to normalise and contain this failure. The emergency government formulated a national ideology, the Rukunegara (Articles of Faith of the State), which was formally announced on 31 August 1970 (Andaya 298). The Rukunegara reasserted the status in Malaysia of

> the Rulers, the position of Islam as the official religion, the position of Malays and other Natives, the legitimate interests of the other communities, and the conferment of citizenship. (Means 13)

The Rukunegara was further legitimised by constitutional amendments that decreed that "the powers and status of the Malay Rulers; citizenship rights of non-Malays; Malay special rights and privileges; the status of Islam as the official religion; and the status of Malay as the sole National Language" were issues prohibited from public debate (Means 14).

In short, the declaration denied the right of non-Malays to question Malay hegemony. The general perception in Malaysia remains that civic and national participation hinge upon acceptance of these decrees. As Shirley Lim puts it in her 1996 memoirs, "the May 13 riots provided the bloody revolution that changed Malaysia from the ideal of a multicultural egalitarian future ... to the Malay-dominant race-preferential practice in place today" (*Moonfaces* 209). Many commentators have noted that there is in Malaysian political discourse a "trend toward authoritarian rule" (Francis Loh "Introduction" 4). This is especially evident in its post-1969 language policies. Malay has been gradually advanced as the only language of instruction in secondary schools and universities since 1971, although, on utilitarian grounds, English has been used in certain subjects in universities since the 1990s (Francis Loh "Developmentism" 29).

Another aspect of Malaysian nationalism may be found in Mahathir bin Mohamad's book, *The Malay Dilemma* (1970). A physician at the time he wrote the book, he became Malaysia's prime minister from 1981 to 2003. According to Khoo Boo Teik, Mahathir's biographer and one of Malaysia's noted political scientists, *The Malay Dilemma* "is the definitive document of ... Malay nationalism" (25). Published a year after the race riots but banned for eleven years for fear it would incite further ethnic violence, *The Malay Dilemma* is regarded as both a response to the social tensions that led to the riots and as the blueprint for Malaysia's future economic, social, and political progress under Mahathir's leadership. *The Malay Dilemma* was intended to "spotlight certain intrinsic factors which retard the development of the Malays" (Mahathir 1). These factors, we read, were environmental and hereditary. The geographical environment of Malaysia is such that "No great exertion or ingenuity was required to obtain food" because of its "lush tropical plains with their plentiful sources of food" (Mahathir 21). Thus, the descendants of these Malays who grew up in a climate of abundance are by nature indolent. In contrast, "The history of China is littered with disasters, both natural and man-made [such that for] the Chinese people life was one continuous struggle for survival" (Mahathir 24). As a result,

> The Malays whose own hereditary and environmental influence had been so debilitating, could do nothing but retreat before the onslaught of the Chinese immigrants. Whatever the Malays could do, the Chinese could do better and more cheaply. (Mahathir 25)

The Malay Dilemma goes on to explain in detail the Malay character, which, one surmises, is meant to account for the race riots that occurred a year prior to its publication:

> Amok is a Malay word ... amok describes yet another facet of the Malay character. Amok represents the external physical expression of the conflict within the Malay which his perpetual observance of the rules and regulations of his life causes in him. It is a spilling over, an overflowing of his inner bitterness. It is a rupture of the bonds which bind him. It is a final and complete escape from reason and training ... Today the amok is only a legend. Civilization has subdued the Malay. He still harbours his resentment, but he is better able to control it. He is a better man for it. But it remains an essential part of his make-up, a basic part of his character. (Mahathir 117–118)

One may say, then, that Malaysian nationalism derives from a colonialist discourse (as examined previously) that reduces the image of the Malay to a caricature of indolence. The Malays' entry into the realm of modern nationhood is predicated on the disparaging of its own ethnic identity, for *The Malay Dilemma* depicts Malays as being inherently disadvantaged due to their indolence so as to legitimise and advance national policies that favour the ethnic group.

Many commentators have disputed the image of the indolent Malay. S. H. Alatas is of the opinion that Mahathir's "views on the Malays ... are dominated by colonial capitalism" (162). Nonetheless, *The Malay Dilemma* finds legitimacy since it is written by a man regarded by many as the prime minister who transformed the country into an economic powerhouse. Khoo points out that there are several paradoxes in Mahathir's thinking that suggest contradictions in the way the Malay identity is inserted into the discourse of nationalism. He argues that as a prime minister who is "(a)nxious to secure the survival of the Malays", Mahathir's "Social Darwinism accentuated his Malay nationalism [while his] Malay nationalism checked his Social Darwinism" (Khoo 9). Paradoxically, then, Mahathir sought to resolve the ethnic tensions between the Malay and Chinese communities by accentuating their supposed differences.

The New Economic Policy (NEP) implemented one year after the race riots was formulated on the assumption and image of the indolent Malay. It was meant to facilitate the rise of a Malay middle-class and thus balance economic capital among different ethnicities to secure the nation. As Harper argues, the notion of the "Malay *bumiputera*, or son of the soil, and of his entitlement to special rights and privileges in economic life, became the ideological cornerstone of the modern Malaysian state" (229). However, the NEP, which formally ended in 1990, may have failed in its intention of fostering a generation of disciplined middle-class capitalists, for as Mahathir himself has noted, it has created a class of Malays that is economically dependant on the state (Gomez 118). As such, under the shadow of the NEP, the modern Malay who is economically successful is haunted by the neo-colonialist caricature of indolence of the Malays as portrayed by *The Malay Dilemma*.

Even though the Malaysian state's negotiation with capitalism privileges an ethnic community, it has, since the 1980s, secured a certain measure of consent from prominent members of ethnic minority groups. As Edmund Terence Gomez and Jomo K. S. point out, from 1981 to 2003, Mahathir was supportive of "the development of Malay capitalism through political patronage" (117). This situation has given rise to the issue of "money politics", the collusion of political and business interests (Gomez 120). As Gomez and Jomo have further shown, non-bumiputeras well connected to the political elite benefit from the latter's patronage as well (152–165). Hence, there is a measure of disjuncture between official policy and actual practice.

In the 1990s, a new set of economic policies, advanced as "Vision 2020", have taken root. "Vision 2020" is so named because it was created with the aim of further developing Malaysia's economic, political, social, spiritual, and cultural spheres by the year noted. In this respect, there is a commitment expressed by the state to move beyond the ethnic-based policies developed under the NEP—although, as Gomez and Jomo point out, "the NEP emphasis on restructuring wealth along ethnic lines continues to shape implementation of the government's new policies" (177). One may suggest that a measure of political patronage and the system of "money politics" has persisted in the post-NEP era.

The Malay Dilemma, the NEP, and Vision 2020 may be seen as solutions that contain ethnic disparities within the Malaysian state. In this respect, one may argue that these are forms of multiculturalism. I employ the term "multiculturalism" in the sense that Ien Ang uses it. For her, "multiculturalism is based on the fantasy that the social challenge of togetherness-in-difference can be addressed by reducing it to an image of living-apart-together" as it "depends on the fixing of mutually exclusive identities" (Ang 14). Thus, Malaysia presents us with an instance of multiculturalism wherein, even as economic capital is ostensibly redistributed along ethnic lines, access to economic power is given to those who are well connected to the governing elite, regardless of ethnicity.

The writings of Karim Raslan are much influenced by the political, economic, and social upheavals that marked the early years of nation building in Malaysia. In addition to being a founding partner of a law firm, the author is a prominent journalist. *Ceritalah: Malaysia in Transition* (1996) is composed primarily of selections from his weekly column in *The Sun* newspaper. *Journeys through Southeast Asia: Ceritalah 2* (2002) consists mostly of his syndicated column "Writers Journal", published by *The Business Times* (Singapore), *The Star* (Malaysia), *Sin Chew Jit Poh* (Malaysia), and on an ad-hoc basis by newspapers in Hong Kong, Australia, and the Philippines. The two collections are candid portrayals and commentary on the Malaysian political economy. In addition, he has also written a collection of short stories entitled *Heroes and Other Stories* (1996).

Karim acknowledges that Malaysia's political climate has shaped his views and personality. Referring to Mahathir in a 1995 column, he wrote:

> the PM—a man who has been in power for well over 14 years—has, deliberately or not, shaped my life and my way of thinking. Malaysian political life for anyone in his or her early thirties is Datuk Seri Dr Mahathir. As such what he thinks and how he thinks has permeated the fabric of society, colouring it much like a dye, until the society resembles him. (Karim *Ceritalah* 122)

However, he also comments that there is a need to look beyond what Malaysia has become, to question the status quo and to interrogate the assumptions that have led to the creation of modern Malaysia:

> I recognise the nation's debt to him but end by asking whether the same pattern of policies can necessarily see us into the new millennia with quite the same success. (Karim *Ceritalah* 123)

Karim's writings enact a desire for a nationally defined selfhood, for finding a place within the discourse of Malaysian nationalism. His questions about his Malay identity come to the fore, and they are always questions about representation: "how could I say, 'We Malays' and get away with it? How could I ... possibly speak for a community of millions?" (Karim *Ceritalah* 15).

Karim's search for a self defined by nationality is a troubled one, and the sense of unease expressed in his newspaper columns is explored more fully in his fiction. While *The Sun* is regarded as an alternative paper that airs relatively critical views of the Malaysian political scene, it is nevertheless subject to state control through the Printing Presses and Publications Act (1984) and the Broadcasting Act (1988) (Hilley 141–147). As Karim puts it, when commenting on Malaysian politics, he is engaged in "the art ... of writing between the lines ... for the reader who is practised in the art of reading between the lines" (*Ceritalah* 28). His newspaper columns hint at what his fiction reveals.

In Karim's writings, there is a sense of dislocation whenever the personal pronoun is substituted for the collective. His unease with the collective "we" in his columns is magnified in his fiction. The pieces gathered in *Heroes and Other Stories* are narratives that testify to the contested image of the modern Malay. In "The Beloved", we witness a pair of lovers who choose pragmatism, economic security, and social conformity over the possibility of romance, thus betraying their love for each other and themselves; in "Go East!", we see a young man in denial of his gender identity as it goes against the central tenets of the state religion. It is with "Heroes", however, that we are alerted to how the image of the modern Malay is enmeshed with the political economy of Malaysia.

In "Heroes" the "we" is split: Part of the "we" knows the truth of the 1969 race riots, while another part is ignorant of it. "Heroes" is about a retired civil servant who is strangely reticent in revealing the role he played in the events immediately following the riots. His daughter, Fariza, who asks him repeatedly about his role in the events, represents another part of the national persona, one that queries the truth of the 1969 riots: "She wants me to write about my days in the administration and especially that troubled year" (Karim *Heroes* 32). However, for the protagonist, this is precisely the problem. Once the truth is out, there would be no peace and reconciliation:

> Truth and reconciliation? Truth brings chaos, destruction and death. There are times when whole nations are happier subscribing to the great 'lie' … They want results, they want homes, jobs, schools, electricity and water. That's the truth. (Karim *Heroes* 32)

"Part of the problem," the narrator tells us, "lies in the fact that [Fariza's] husband is not Malay. He is a Chinese and a journalist too" (Karim *Heroes* 32). Here, the collective "we" in Karim's newspaper column becomes an internally divisive pronoun. The events of 1969 are a reminder of the existing racial tensions in the country. On that day, "we" became "us" and "them". That moment has a different meaning for those who lived through it and for those born after it. For the narrator, the question of the Malay dilemma is a question of the survival of one's own race against the perceived onslaught of another. For the younger generation, it is normalised as Malaysia's entry into a conception of modern nationhood premised on wealth accumulation: "For them, the *Malay Dilemma* is little more than a question of whether or not to take the money" (Karim *Heroes* 33).

Just as *The Malay Dilemma* represents self-inflicted violence to the image of the Malay in order for Malaysian nationalism to proceed, "Heroes" is a story wherein the image of the modern Malay has first to be mutilated in order for the author's race and nation to thrive in the aftermath of the 1969 race riots. If the narrator is reticent about discussing the actions he took in the days immediately following 13 May, it is because he does not want to talk about his aide, Nazrin. Nazrin, we are told,

> was a young fellow in his early twenties and straight out of Universiti Malaya. He was just the sort of young, bright Malay boy that we wanted to see prosper in new Malaysia, just the sort of boy that we were afraid would slip through society's net if we didn't help him. (Karim *Heroes* 38)

The above passage would appear strange if read without the supplement of *The Malay Dilemma*: Nazrin is an intelligent university graduate, yet it is assumed that he and many like him would not be able to succeed in life without some form of assistance from the government. This passage would make sense only if it is understood by way of the social climate fostered by the NEP, with the assumption that Malay indolence by nature of heredity would lead to the expiration of the ethnic community unless policy is made to favour it: "In such an environment we had to be uncompromising and harsh. We had a burden, a mission which was all-important—the preservation of the Malay race" (Karim *Heroes* 33). Thus, the image of the Malay community would have to be mutilated if it was to survive.

"Heroes" turns out to be a story about sacrifice. In the immediate aftermath of the 1969 race riots, the protagonist of the story is entrusted with documents crucial to the rebuilding of the nation, and Nazrin is assigned to travel with him from Kuala Lumpur to Penang. On the way, their car collides with a Chinese woman on a bicycle and she is killed. Nazrin is left behind to be assaulted by an angry mob, while the cowardly narrator escapes to complete his mission, thus playing a significant role in helping to reconstruct the nation. "Heroes" is also a story about the contradictions of Malaysian nationalism. Nazrin's maimed condition, after he is assaulted, is a symbol of the maimed image of the Malay—that is, maimed if one is to believe in the hereditary disadvantages of being Malay. The rise of the Malay middle class is founded on this very image. It is Nazrin's sacrifice that enables the nation to move forward: He is the unsung hero of the story. Nazrin, as Fariza discovers, is paralysed from waist down and lives an impoverished existence. At the end of the story, the protagonist, regarded as a national hero, has this to say regarding his actions in 1969:

> I had witnessed my own "fall": lived through it. I had seen myself at my worst. Nothing I could ever do, would match this failure ... Words and phrases tumbled through my mind, in an uneven, ramshackle surge of fear: cowardice; betrayal; catastrophe; chaos ... self-destruction; loss of face ... death; promotion; disgust; contempt; endgame. I felt as if all of Syaitan's demons had enveloped me with their darkness. (Karim *Heroes* 47–48)

Malaysian nationalism is narrated here as a catastrophe and as an apocalyptic endgame for the formation of the modern Malay as a subject.

More than twenty years after *The Malay Dilemma* was written, the modern Malay is still ambivalent about his Malaysian identity. As Karim put it in a 1993 column:

> I am a child of the NEP, a product of the social and economic policy first conceived and executed in the late sixties and seventies. Without the existence of the NEP, it is highly unlikely that people such as me—educated, middle-class Malays—would be around at all. As a result, my debt to the NEP is total and I am forced to acknowledge it as such.
>
> Nonetheless, this does not mean that I am without criticisms of the policy. The NEP has cast such a long, and at times, not altogether happy shadow over Malaysian public life. For example, anything I achieve will always be clouded by the taint of tokenism and favouritism. (*Ceritalah* 93)

The Malaysian poet and journalist Salleh Ben Joned expressed the same sentiment in a 1992 newspaper column:

> To be or not to be part of a "protected species": that is the question. Whether it is nobler in the mind to "opt out" for the sake of necessary pride and independence and fidelity to ideas that transcend barriers of ethnicity—that, or to commit some kind of moral suicide by accepting unquestioningly those convenient pieties about ethnic survival and dominance. (70)

On the one hand, as a post-mortem of the 1969 race riots, *The Malay Dilemma* played no small role in providing solutions that led to the economic and political stability of Malaysia; on the other hand, it represents a self-denigration of the image of the Malay.

In both Singapore and Malaysia, state-sponsored discourses of nationalism, which mark entry into nationhood after colonialism in both cases, are built on ambivalence. In the case of Singapore, as we note in our reading of the two Merlion poems, even as the power of national symbols in the creation of a myth of the nation's origins is exerted in the name of inventing a tradition, it lends itself to critique, given the dubious effects of such invented traditions as they become manifest in those subjected to it. As our consideration of "Heroes" shows, the image of modern Malays has to be maimed by official policies in order for ethnic-based nationalism to proceed. This is a symptom at the heart of Malaysian nationalism, which seeks to contain ethnic differences within the boundaries of the nation-state.

If nationalism lays claim to a new nation's autonomy in determining its future and articulating its break with its colonial past, it nevertheless is haunted by these moments of ambivalence lying at the heart of its project. One cannot take for granted that a nation as engendered by contemporary nationalism is congenial to its people; one cannot forget that the nation as home is also a site of ideological contestation. Now we shall examine how two Singaporean novels engage the statist discourse of nationalism; then we will consider how the novels of K. S. Maniam do the same in the context of Malaysia's ethnic nationalism.

6

Irresponsibility and Commitment:
Philip Jeyaretnam's *Abraham's Promise* and Gopal Baratham's *A Candle or the Sun*

We can call the state-sponsored discourse evident in Singapore since 1965 one of responsibility. This discourse has been legitimised by the argument some made that Singapore was too small to defend itself, prosper, or govern itself as an independent nation. Even now, as the People's Action Party remains in power, we find the overriding concern to be as it was initially defined: to create a society capable of meeting the demands of capitalism. To take any responsibility for national survival is therefore to be responsible to the state—a responsibility reified by an orientation toward the dictates of economic pragmatism. Within such a discourse, how is one able to locate and identify the nation as home? This is the question we shall now address.

Given the discourse of reified responsibility by which the lives of citizens are governed, it is not surprising to find that we can identify Singaporean writers according to whether they write from a position of "responsibility"—or with a lack thereof. Edwin Thumboo, regarded by many as Singapore's unofficial poet laureate, is a responsible poet: His poetry demonstrates a commitment toward the state and its agenda of nation building. Thumboo's poetry testifies against Shirley Lim's statement that "[i]t is impossible to find in Singapore any writer who has explicitly accepted [all state policies] and made it his business to be a spokesman for them" ("The English-Language Writer" 523). It is telling that Ee Tiang Hong's book-length study of Thumboo's poems is entitled *Responsibility and Commitment*. The book's cover, indeed, is stamped with multiple figures of the Merlion—that peculiarly ersatz national icon. Yet the term "responsibility" encompasses a broad spectrum of meanings. It can denote a duty to obey, to abide by, to be accountable, to be autonomous, to respond, to intervene, or to challenge. In this respect, a responsible author may also be one who is "irresponsible"—one whose writings disrupt the state's discourse of responsibility.

From the 1990s onward, there emerged a body of literary work that disrupts and contests, in precisely this manner, state-sponsored assumptions as to one's commitment to the nation-building project in Singapore. Examples would include Alfian bin Sa'at's poetry, which we have looked at earlier, Lau Siew Mei's *Playing Madame Mao* (2000), which we will examine in a later chapter. Here, we will consider Philip Jeyaretnam's *Abraham's Promise* (1995) and Gopal Baratham's *A Candle or the Sun* (1991), examining in them the various permutations of responsibility and irresponsibility with regard to nationalism and nation formation. The protagonists of both *Abraham's Promise* and *A Candle or the Sun* are faced with a dilemma: To whom and to what end should one act responsibly or irresponsibly, and how may one exercise one's agency when it runs contrary to the state's discourse of responsibility? Ancillary questions follow these. Given that official nationalism in Singapore inscribes an idea of responsibility on the part of citizens that is oriented toward economic pragmatism and the maintenance of the state, how does a writer assume the responsibility of political critique if this critique amounts to opposition against the state? How are the terms "responsibility", "nation", and "nationalism" coordinated within literary texts?

Natio, nationalism, and responsibility

Benedict Anderson's notion of the nation as an "imagined community" (*Imagined Communities* 6) and Partha Chatterjee's objections to such a formulation (*The Nation and Its Fragments* 5) are by now well known. The same may be said of Timothy Brennan's distinction, expressed in his essay "The National Longing for Form", between the nation as nation-state imagined and organised by a political ruling class and the nation expressed as *natio* pertaining to the ordinary person or citizen (45). Several commentators have pointed out this distinction between the nation-state and *natio*, although the terms they used were different. In her 1975 paper entitled "Politics in an Administrative State: Where has the Politics Gone?", Chan Heng Chee argues that after 1965, there "has been the steady and systematic depoliticisation of a politically active and aggressive citizenry" (1–2). Given that the government is largely in the hands of one dominant party and that the voices of opposition party members are weak if not almost nonexistent, the citizenry is depoliticised because debates of ideological and political import no longer occur in the public sphere, but are embedded within the administrative and bureaucratic structures of the nation-state.

This state of affairs has led to a persistent estrangement between the government (in other words, the governing party) and the citizenry. In his memoirs, Lee Kuan Yew is unwavering in asserting, "The single decisive factor that made for Singapore's development was the ability of its ministers and the high quality of the civil servants who supported them" (*From Third World to First* 736). He has written about how he has "systematically scanned the top echelons of ... the professions, commerce, manufacturing and trade unions" in search of capable people to fill important posts (Lee *From Third World to First* 739). He has learned from corporate models of recruitment and promotion practice, especially that of the oil company, Shell, and adopted them for the public service (Lee *From Third World to First* 740–741). There have been criticisms of such a top-down and corporatist approach to governance. As Garry Rodan points out, even though there were economic reforms in the 1990s that rendered corporate and fiscal processes more open to public and international scrutiny in the interest of attracting foreign investment, "the meaning the Singapore government attaches to the concept of transparency is a limited one" (81). Chua Beng-Huat concurs with Rodan's observations when he notes that the style of governance of this core of trusted civil servants is "top-down and based almost exclusively on hyper-technical rationality, with little participation from the population who have to live with its decisions and policies" (*Communitarian Ideology* 204).

In 1994, an article by the novelist Catherine Lim entitled "The PAP and the People—A Great Affective Divide" appeared in the *Straits Times*. Lim employs the phrase "affective divide" to denote what she sees as an emotional estrangement between the PAP and the population:

> The Great Affective Divide has created a model of government-people relationship that must be unique in the world: solid, unbreakable unity of purpose and commitment on the economic plane, but a serious bifurcation at the emotive level. (*The Straits Times* 3 September 1994)

The method of governance of the PAP, as she puts it, is based on "logic, precision, meticulous analysis and hard-nosed calculation and quantification. Their style is impersonal, brisk, business-like, no-nonsense, pre-emptive." Here, Lim is describing what Rodan calls "bureaucratic authoritarianism" (48–49). Lim argues that people have always voted for the PAP because since the difficult years of 1965, the party has never failed them when it comes to economic matters. She writes that while the "disaffection [of Singaporeans] remains largely [on the level of] coffee-house and cocktail party rhetoric", the PAP has been criticised as being "dictatorial", "arrogant", "impatient", "unforgiving", and "vindictive". Lim suggests that

> while the PAP ideology remains the same, the people have not. Higher education, a more affluent lifestyle and exposure to the values of western societies, have created a new generation that is not satisfied with the quantitative paradigm but looks beyond it to a larger qualitative one that most certainly includes matters of the heart, soul and spirit. (*The Straits Times* 3 September 1994)

To be sure, there has never been a single and unchanging official nationalism or PAP ideology. C. J. W.-L. Wee has made the point that Lee Kuan Yew, Goh Keng Swee (at various times the minister of finance and defence) and Sinnathamby Rajaratnam (at various times the minister in charge of culture, foreign affairs, and labour) each articulated various versions of modernity that inform official nationalism (35–48). Nonetheless, all three of them have in common the notion that Singapore would survive only if it holds a "logical-positivist outlook on the world" (Wee 50). Lim's article exemplifies the paradoxical outcome of a programmatic nation. It is precisely the PAP's economic rationality that has enabled its populace to have access to an affluent lifestyle and to the ideals of liberal and participatory democracy.

The government's response to Lim's piece was severe and uncompromising. The prime minister's press secretary, Chan Heng Wing, wrote a stern reply that, ironically, reinforces Lim's statements: "[The Prime Minister] cannot allow journalists, novelists, short-story writers or theatre groups to set the political agenda from outside the political arena" (*The Straits Times* 4 December 1994). There is also the suggestion that if Lim wishes to engage with politics,

> then she should use her communication skills to articulate her philosophy of government, and take responsibility for her views. Let her follow the illustrious example of British novelist Jeffrey Archer, who became an MP and later Deputy Chairman of the Conservative Party to espouse his political beliefs. (*The Straits Times* 4 December 1994)

The government's reply is symptomatic of Singapore's political climate. (The reference to Jeffrey Archer is ironic only in hindsight: Archer was found guilty of perjury in 2001.) The only passport into the political sphere, thus, is for one to be a politician. Ernest Gellner, in *Nations and Nationalisms*, argues that industrialisation fosters a homogeneous community out of heterogeneous groups (40); the paradox is that industrial capitalism necessitates a division of labour that segments people into specialised fields, to the extent that journalists, novelists, short-story writers, and theatre groups should pursue their artistic endeavours without encroaching on the political sphere. Singapore's body politic is premised on the division between politics and the public realms of culture (in this case, literature). As political critique by non-politicians is not welcome, it is the government that sets an unchallengeable agenda for the populace. It comes as no surprise, therefore, that literary works that depict Singapore as an imagined community are necessarily ambivalent. This ambivalence may be a result of self-censorship, or, more likely, it might be an authentically felt ambivalence. Often slipping between critique and affirmation of the discursive formation of the nation, they display the vexed condition of the nation as designated by the state's discourse of nationalism and *natio* as a sense of national belonging and identification experienced by the ordinary person.

Abraham's Promise: **Fulfilment and denial**

Abraham's Promise is narrated by the character Abraham Isaac. Abraham is an idealist by nature, well-read in the classics, and is committed to being a responsible person: "Surely my life can withstand any scrutiny: it has always been an examined life, at every step I directed my energies towards becoming a good son, good brother, good husband, good teacher and good citizen" (Jeyaretnam 290). From the outset, the novel directs our attention to the actions of Abraham as he looks back on his life in a nation he recognises as home. It foregrounds the act of recollecting a time that has passed; concurrently, it acknowledges the difficulty of doing so: "Memories are elusive creatures, like butterflies. The more one tries to capture them, to put them on display, the more tangled one becomes in the net of one's remembrance" (Jeyaretnam 299). Both time past and time present are set up as the personal time of Abraham Isaac.

However, even though at times the narratives are nested one within another, as when Abraham is relating a moment in his past when he was telling a student of his childhood memories, the reader is never at a loss as to the historical background that informs these memories because of the novel's judicious deployment of historical markers. Through these markers, personal time is aligned with the time of the nation that readers can recognise. It is clear that the novel is addressing readers who are familiar with the history of Singapore. We are able to match the time-frames of the fragments of Abraham's memories and identify specific moments in Singapore's history because of lines such as the following:

> The *Prince of Wales* and *Repulse* are sunk. The Japanese have landed near Kota Bahru. (Jeyaretnam 288)

> Colonialism was fading, its shadow diminishing, and young saplings of independence were thrusting into the sunlight. (Jeyaretnam 276)

> The Party was swept into office. I was elated: now at last a vigorous hand could be set to the task of Singapore's development as an independent nation. (Jeyaretnam 343)

Abraham's personal time is aligned with the homogeneous empty time of the nation. Despite it being a first-person narrative, *Abraham's Promise* is able to evoke a world wherein events of historical magnitude happen simultaneously through the use of historical markers. In the above lines, among many others found in the novel, one detects a narrative of national history, from the British's surrender of Singapore to their return at end of the Japanese Occupation, from Malaya's experiments at self-rule to Singapore's eventual separation from Malaysia. Readers are addressed such that the world of the novel is recognised through (to use a term employed by Roland Barthes) the "reality effect" of the historical markers.

In first-person novels that engender the possibility of imagining a community as a nation, an appeal to the real-time content of the nation is inevitable, even necessary; for homogeneous empty time to be recognised as the time of a particular nation, one must appeal to the content of the novel. If *Abraham's Promise*, through the use of the first-person narrative, is nonetheless able to present to its readers the time of the nation, it is because the narrative is about a character who is attempting to reconcile his personal experience with the homogeneous empty time of a specific imagined community. While *Abraham's Promise* utilises the reality effect of historical markers so as to engender the possibility of an imagined community, this is a possibility the novel's content and plot ultimately deny. On the one hand, the novel presents a recognisable imagined community called Singapore; on the other hand, when one looks at the content and plot, one detects a fracture between the life of an individual and the nation. It is in this way that the novel becomes a critique of official nationalism in Singapore.

There is another "reality effect" in the novel that deserves mention. Philip Jeyaretnam's *Abraham's Promise* is dedicated to his father, the late Joshua Benjamin Jeyaretnam (1926–2008). Born in Jaffna, Sri Lanka, the senior Jeyaretnam had been a highly respected lawyer and one of Singapore's few opposition members of parliament. A series of highly publicised defamation suits lodged against him in the late 1990s had rendered him bankrupt in 2001. This had prevented him from participating in future parliamentary elections. The career of his son, however, has proceeded on an opposite trajectory. Currently a senior counsel and president of The Law Society of Singapore, he received the Young Artist of the Year award from the National Arts Council of Singapore in 1993 for his books of fiction, *First Loves* (1987) and *Raffles Place Ragtime* (1988). It is interesting that the narrator of *Abraham's Promise* is a political activist before independence and during the early years after it, and that he has a son whose law career is on the ascendant. This has invited speculation regarding the extent to which the novel is biographical.

To proceed to the plot, it outlines the first-person narrator's failed attempt to participate in the life of the modern nation. The novel's opening hints at the futility of asserting oneself against the narrative of official nationalism:

> History is written by its survivors, survival elevated into triumph ... He who captures the mind of the young is in truth the victor. And the young are so impressionable ... all that I have lived by will be forgotten. (Jeyaretnam 273)

The fate of Abraham Isaac in *Abraham's Promise* demonstrates the difficulty on the part of an individual of assuming the responsibility of imagining and participating in the life of an emerging nation. *Abraham's Promise* weaves between what is and what might have been, between past and present, memory and life, ideals and realities. Abraham is a teacher of Latin who knows that the time and place in which he finds himself have no use for him: "Did teaching always feel like this, as if one were a charlatan about to be unmasked: the old pontificating to the young when their own lives have fallen so short?" (Jeyaretnam 274). The novel is shot through with Abraham's sense of failure; the promise of his personal life as well as the life of a nation in which he is supposed to play a part have failed to come into being. As Dennis Haskell puts it, the protagonist "is Isaac to his nation's Abraham" playing the role of sacrificial lamb "in the name of disciplined nation building" (147). Hence, Abraham Isaac is more Isaac than Abraham, the biblical father of nations.

In the novel, Abraham articulates a postcolonial nation with democracy as a principle of self-rule. Reflecting on his father, who was one of the "cogs and wheels of the [colonial] system", he anticipates a future nation where the "arrogance of those who ruled ... must give way to the democratic participation of all" (Jeyaretnam 276). Abraham, as an idealist, is committed to the idea of participating in the life of the emerging nation, abiding by the ideals of the Enlightenment without being unaware of the problems of colonialism:

> I had been dreaming of a new nation, the possibility of rational men in power, disinterestedly taking those decisions that tended to the public good, seeing myself perhaps among them, Abraham Isaac, ushering in a new age of enlightenment, a new order. (Jeyaretnam 324)

When the head of the civil service union loses his job because he objected to the new terms of service proposed by a government that had recently come into power, the narrator comes to his defence in his capacity as a trade unionist. Following the appearance of an essay Abraham wrote for the teachers' union newsletter, Abraham is advised by the authorities to retract his statement and apologise. Because he refuses to do so, he is falsely accused of having been abusive to his school's principal and of abandoning his teaching duties. Following an inquiry, he loses his job and his licence to teach and is subsequently reduced to earning a living as a private tutor.

During a discussion with his student, Abraham speaks of the inevitability of Japanese surrender during the Second World War:

> "Ideas count, not just force. I knew that Britain would win in the end because they had better ideas, however imperfectly they practised them."
>
> "You mean Christianity must triumph ... democracy must win?"
>
> Was the boy mocking me? A moment earlier I had been so sure of my insight ... Yet stated like that, as a universal law, it sounded absurd. (Jeyaretnam 299)

Of course, the Japanese surrendered not because Britain had better ideas, but because of the show of a greater force. At a social gathering, Abraham has a heated exchange with Lau Teng Kee, an MP. The argument revolves around the notion of democracy. In Lau's speech, we hear the elaboration of "East Asian consensus" in language that recognisably derives from the 1980s and 1990s discourse of "Asian" and "Confucian" values:

> We East Asians do things by consensus. We all agree on a goal and then don't waste any more time talking about it. So we can concentrate on achieving the goal. But the Americans want us to argue with one another so that we lose sight of the goal. (Jeyaretnam 315)

In contrast, the narrator's words are interrogative, resting on the ideals of liberal and participative democracy: "How do you know that we all agree on your goals, if you do not ask us first?" (Jeyaretnam 315). He points out the contradiction in Lau's argument, arguing that during the occupation of Kuwait by Iraq, the Singapore government gave support to American bombers. Yet Lau wins his argument in the end, not through debate but through mockery:

> "They're not white knights in shining armour, you know, these American bom-*bers* as you call them."
>
> Suddenly everyone is laughing ... I have spoken other than in their manner of speaking, betraying my upbringing, my Tamil otherness, most of all my insignificance. What are the words of a Latin teacher to those of a man of influence, a man with business to turn your way? How could the others not laugh at me? (Jeyaretnam 316)

Given the mockery of Abraham's South Asian speech pattern at the core of this exchange, in effect, Lau wins the argument by way of a racist taunt.

The narrator's failure in public life finds a measure of resolution in the private domain. The final moment in the novel sees him embracing his son, from whom he is temporarily estranged upon finding out about the latter's homosexuality:

> I have done my best, and if I have lived too much like a butterfly, soaring upon the puffs of my youthful fancies, too easily beaten back by the world's winds, well here in my arms is a beetle, clinging stubbornly to every inch of ground he gains. He may never change the world, hardly wants to, but still, head down, he will hold his ground (Jeyaretnam 387)

Abraham is finally also able to accept the fact that his son has no interest in anything else apart from his career: "he abjures politics ... [he sees] no reason why anyone should risk his career ... for the sake of more freedom than he would know what to do with" (Jeyaretnam 301–302). However, this hardly comes close to what the novel promises. *Abraham's Promise* is the promise of a new nation free from the control of its former rulers. Yet the nation in which Abraham finds himself is not unlike Singapore under the colonial system. The irony of Singapore's nationhood is that the following quotation, which was relevant when Singapore was under colonial rule, is just as relevant since Singapore attained independence:

> The ordinary Singaporean was like Hamlet, his heritage despoiled by the interloping colonising Claudius. How then to act? (Jeyaretnam 332)

Against the nationalist discourse, one cannot act; instead, one is acted upon. *Abraham's Promise*, as a novel, assumes the responsibility of creating a possibility of imagining a community one may identify as a nation; however, through its plot and content, it also demonstrates the impossibility of fulfilling that responsibility. Abraham's promise is the promise of a nation that has been made to its people, but it is a promise left unfulfilled.

A Candle or the Sun: On acting responsibly and the death of an author

How then to act? Like Abraham Isaac, the protagonist of *A Candle or the Sun* finds himself asking this question. How does one assert his agency in a country shaped by a nationalist discourse that does not tolerate dissent? Hernando Perera, the protagonist of *A Candle or the Sun*, comes up with an answer, albeit one he eventually rejects: "I knew that I must find in words themselves a solution to my problem ... it came to me: compartmentalize. Yes, that was what I would have to do. Compartmentalize my life" (Baratham 86).

Gopal Baratham's novel is an interrogation of Singapore's political status quo. Hernando is a writer of short stories and the manager of a department store. When his job is threatened by a staff reorganisation, he accepts a job offer from his friend, Samson Alagaratnam, at the culture ministry. Apart from drafting articles and stories with a pro-government slant, he is also tasked with finding out the identities of those responsible for putting out a subversive street paper. He soon realises that his lover, Su-May, and her friends, belonging to a quasi-Christian group who call themselves the Children of the Book, are the ones responsible. At first, he surrenders their names to the authorities. It is during this period that Hernando writes three short stories that later serve as a guide to what he has to do. Eventually, Hernando helps Su-May and the leader of the group, Peter Yu, to escape. Hernando is later arrested by the police and subjected to torture. The last chapter of the novel, describing how he is beaten up by his interrogators, is reminiscent of the ending of Orwell's *1984*.

As Philip Holden speculates, while the manuscript of *A Candle or the Sun* was initially completed in 1985, there is a strong possibility that it underwent several revisions before it was published in 1991 ("Writing Conspiracy" 60). As such, it may be read as referring to the events now known as the "Marxist" conspiracy of 1987. In May and June 1987, twenty-two people, among them lawyers and social workers associated with organisations affiliated with the Catholic Church, were arrested and detained without trial under the Internal Security Act on the basis that they were involved in a plot to undermine the Singapore government (Lee Lai To 204–205). Public confessions were extracted, and upon their release, the alleged perpetrators retracted these confessions, claiming that they were coerced. Given that the alleged perpetrators were associated with the Catholic Church and that they claimed duress in explaining their confessions, it is probably hard to ignore the possibility that the plot of *A Candle or the Sun* is based, however loosely, on this incident. That Baratham could not get Singapore publishers to publish his manuscript in the aftermath of the arrests indicates that this is a point not lost on them. At the suggestion of a prominent book editor, Baratham sent his manuscript to the former culture minister, who responded by saying that "[he doesn't] see any harm in this ... this is not going to bring down the government of Singapore" (Klein 95). Despite this, publishing firms in Singapore refused to publish his book because of its "political content" (Klein 94–95).

At the beginning of this chapter, we have seen how there is a division between the realms of literature and real-life politics. This division preserves the state's sole control over the discourse of nationalism, a division further reinforced by the climate of fear on the part of publishers (and the rest of the populace) that they might be perceived as engaging in politics. What is valuable about *A Candle or the Sun* is that it foregrounds the collision between politics and literature that has been suspended in reality. The novel proposes that works of the imagination, by virtue of the fact that they engender a universe through narrative, are able to create a world that has yet to be permeated by the machinations of the nation-state. It also proposes that the responsibility for bringing that world into reality lies in the realm of personal action, even if these actions are curtailed by the state.

At first, Hernando regards his writings "as little indulgences ... to fill an existence in which not too much happened" (Baratham 6). He finds himself contemplating the idea of writing a story stripped of the contents of everyday life: "I was trying to fashion a man so totally liberated that he had nothing to do with events outside his imagination" (Baratham 7). That this story never comes to fruition is indicative of the events that are to overtake his life, and the creative futility of compartmentalising everyday life from imagination. Eventually, the stories Hernando writes turn out to be narratives that shape and inform his actions. The novel is interpenetrated by three short stories entitled "Kissful of Tears", "Double Exposure", and "Dutch Courage". While these stories were published previously in a collection by Baratham, in the novel they are presented as having been written by Hernando—suggesting that perhaps Baratham is the true protagonist of the novel. These stories form three crucial junctures within the novel that serve to illuminate the protagonist's predicament.

"Kissful of Tears", told from the point of view of Ju, is a modern rendition of the biblical narrative of Judas' betrayal of Jesus. The story ends with Ju embracing his leader; it is a heartfelt embrace that is at the same time a betrayal: "A great love welled up inside me. I walked over and took his face in my hands and kissed him. There was no way of knowing whether the tears I tasted were mine or his" (Baratham 31). This story resonates with Hernando's previous and future decisions and actions. Hernando is Ju, caught between multiple loyalties. By virtue of his relationship with Su-May, he is betraying his wife, Sylvie. By virtue of his work at the culture ministry, he has to betray Su-May. By virtue of having helped Su-May and Peter Yu escape, he betrays the trust of Samson, his friend and senior colleague at the ministry. Caught in this impasse, Hernando at first opts to "compartmentalize" his life, separating his political work from his personal relationships. But he realises that this separation comes at a cost: His writings no longer reflect his convictions. He now writes to obtain financial security. He must, in his own terms, "prostitute" his writings for the sake of his livelihood:

> The analogy with prostitutes was a good one. There must be prostitutes who were wives and mothers, who ran families, loved their husbands. Their salvation must lie in an ability to separate in their minds acts which were physically identical. (Baratham 86)

The second story, "Double Exposure", is about a relationship based on anonymity. Alagrajah has for the past six months been observing a woman going through her yoga exercises on her balcony across from his flat. He later receives phone calls from a Chinese woman named Lu Shan, who prefers to be called Shanti. Eventually, he realises that Lu Shan and the woman he has been observing are one and the same. The theme of anonymous intimacy presents the possibility of an imagined community of members housed in isolation from each other, an imagined community that exceeds the physical circumscription of flats or blocks of flats, which are here the visible symbols of state sponsorship and regulatory power over place and space.

In the novel that encompasses these stories, Samson's vulgar response (vulgar in both senses of the word) to "Double Exposure" demonstrates how the story is received by the authorities:

> "Too confusing, baby. Mixed-up like. Could be sugar, could be spice. Could be things that ain't too nice." He fiddled with a dial on his chair and his head began to bounce and wobble the way an Indian dancer's does. "You and I, Hern, we geddit. But we're word turds, man. For us it's slam, bam, I understan'. Peeping Tom sees girl one from back-room window. Zap. Single exposure." His head jerked once sharply. "Then Peeping Tom sees girl two from bedroom window, zap – ahrap, double exposure." His head jerked twice. "But

> will Mr Loh Ai Kew and," he rolled his eyes heavenwards, "the powers that be, figure it out? No way, Hern. No fist-fornicating way." (Baratham 100)

Samson is of the opinion that Hernando's readers, symbolised by the figure of Loh Ai Kew ("low IQ", as we can transliterate it), will miss the point of his story. He suggests to Hernando that the story be rewritten to serve the disciplinary ends of the state: "'Peeping Doesn't Pay'. Geddit, baby? Alliteration and all. And it will slip smoothly into our crime-prevention programme" (Baratham 101). Samson's response to "Double Exposure" exemplifies the notion that the politicisation of the literary sphere enables the authorities to shape narratives for their own ends. What Samson displays is the collaboration of writers and cultural practitioners with the state, a collaboration that he re-presents as market-savvy and streetwise, a sign of his own cleverness. "Double Exposure" celebrates a relationship that is not easily identifiable: Are Alagrajah and Lu Shan lovers, or are they strangers? Samson suggests that the relationship between Algarajah and Lu Shan be portrayed so as to render it criminal. This is a situation Hernando finds untenable:

> Words were ... the instruments with which [he] explored the world; [his] organs for tasting and testing it, smelling and sounding it, palpating and plumbing it. With them, [he] sensed the world and grasped it. They were [his] antennae and [his] tentacles. And by joining Sam [he] was betraying them. (Baratham 85–86)

If words are instruments through which Hernando explores the world, then allowing them to be shaped by the state would imply an outright betrayal of his vocation as writer. It is at this point that Hernando realises he can no longer compartmentalise his imagination from the world outside himself.

Eventually, fiction for Hernando becomes a guide to one's conduct in everyday life to the extent that characters in his writings begin to seep into reality. The protagonist of his third story, "Dutch Courage", becomes as real to him as the people he interacts with: "Cornelius kept close to me all the while, smiling, sitting on the edge of my desk as I typed ... I would stop typing and he would indicate the sentence or juxtaposition of words that did not meet with his approval" (Baratham 157–158).

"Dutch Courage" tells the story of Cornelius Vandermeer, who fights alongside communist guerrillas against the Japanese during the Second World War. After the war, when the communists are fighting against the British during the Malayan Emergency, he switches sides and is recognised as the indomitable leader of an anti-communist resistance group. At the end of the story, he sacrifices his life to save his wife and son from an ambush orchestrated by Peng, his former protégé, who is a communist guerrilla leader. One may hazard a guess that the character Peng is meant to allude to the leader of the Malayan Communist Party, Chin Peng, who opted for armed conflict against the British in 1948 so as to establish Malaya as a communist state. The plot of this narrative informs Hernando's later actions. It revisits the pre-independence history of Singapore, a historical juncture of nascent nationalisms, wherein different visions of Malaya are contested on the battlefield. After writing the story, the transference of responsibility for action from his character to himself is complete:

> Near the end [Cornelius] had realized that concern for the well-being of others is the only defence we have against terror and death. The Captain had learnt this from the circumstances of his life; I, by fabricating them. The pages of "Dutch Courage" lay before me, a blueprint for what I had to do. (Baratham 158)

Again, there is a parallel to be sought between Hernando's later actions and those of his character. The novel presents us with the triumph of a writer: Hernando comes to terms with his story and characters and attains a private epiphany. However, even as his actions are motivated by his commitment to his writerly (a)vocation, there is an acknowledgement that, ultimately, the words and actions of writers are ineffective in a world of *realpolitik*. As mentioned earlier, at the end of the novel, because of his convictions and subsequent actions, Hernando is detained by the police and beaten up by his interrogators.

A Candle or the Sun makes the relationship between fiction and politics its central theme; it explores how the realm of fiction may inform and critique the nationalist discourse of the state as it governs the everyday life of its citizens. Singapore's political landscape is premised on material accumulation and economic achievement. Yet as the novel demonstrates, this is not only inadequate to sustain meaningful lives but can actually destroy them. The novel has a double-barrelled message for its reader. As a work of imagination, it is able to bear the responsibility of political critique. Ironically, as the ending of the novel shows, it is futile to act on the basis of that critique.

Nationalism in Singapore is powerful not just because the city-state's size facilitates surveillance, command, and control. It attains its power based on the fallacy that nation formation comes under the sole charge of the state. We recall the distinction Brennan makes between the nation as circumscribed by nationalist ideology and *nation–natio* as affective community, is perpetually in the making yet never finalised. In Singapore, the responsibility of a citizen and of the citizen-writer is narrated as a responsibility to the state. Therefore, it is not surprising that a measure of ambivalence attends to literary works that engage with debates on nationalism and the nation. *Abraham's Promise*, as a novel naturally intended for public consumption, raises the possibility of a nation as an imagined community. Yet the novel's plot and thematic concern revolve around the failure of a nation born out of a liberal democratic ethos. Like *Abraham's Promise*, *A Candle or the Sun* bears the marks of a liberal democratic critique. Yet its ending, culminating in the death of the author-narrator, serves as a warning to those who wish to bring into reality that which is promised through fiction.

In "Dissenting Voices: Political Engagements in the Singaporean Novel in English", Leong Liew Geok states that since Singaporean authors are now more forthright in engaging with politics, "a more open political culture founded on trust in the citizen, and an acceptance of criticism in the spirit in which it is given" is a "future that must now be foreseen" (291). I find this statement too optimistic. Literary works such as *Abraham's Promise* and *A Candle or the Sun* that venture into the realm of politics are forthright only about their inability to bring about political change. The novels narrate a condition wherein one is not at home and is at odds with the political landscape of Singapore. If one is to draw a conclusion regarding what literature in Singapore can be responsible for, it will be an ambivalent conclusion, bearing the syntax of "yes, ... but". Yes, literature makes a promise to bear the responsibility of articulating a nation as *natio*, but this articulation is curtailed by the socio-political realities under which the promise is made. As both novels suggest, if one is attuned to the political circumscription of the state on its people, then one can never be at home.

III
Globalisation
Home is Elsewhere

The Post-Diasporic Imagination:
The Novels of K. S. Maniam

While the more politically engaged novels of Singapore narrate "not-at-home" as a condition within the Singaporean state, Malaysian Anglophone writers are not at home by virtue of their choice of language: It has been policy since the late 1950s that non-Malay writers who do not write in Bahasa Malaysia, the official national language, are excluded from the body of texts known as "National Literature" and are grouped under the term "Sectional Literatures" (Fernando 138). From the outset, the earlier generation of Malaysian Anglophone writers, to which K. S. Maniam belongs, has been conscious of its marginal status, given a statist discourse through which a literary canon that privileges Malay-language works is formed. Writers such as Ee Tiang Hong and Shirley Lim have opted to emigrate partly because of this. For those who chose to stay, their marginalisation is akin to the condition of internal exile, whereby "writers or … intellectuals … without being physically away from home remain outsiders in their own country due to certain circumstances in their history, language or education" (Meenakshi Mukherjee "The Exile of the Mind" 8). This is very much the condition experienced by Maniam, a third-generation descendent of South Asian migrants who worked as indentured labourers in the plantation estates of British Malaya.

There are signs, however, that things are changing today. Since 2003, language policy has changed significantly in acknowledgement of English as the *lingua franca* of the international community, particularly in areas of business, science, and technology (Gill 257). Public universities in Malaysia are gradually adopting English as the medium of instruction in these disciplines. Nonetheless, while this may mitigate to some extent the marginal status of Anglophone literary works, that English is adopted out of economic pragmatism indicates that there is still a bifurcation in terms of language use. English is gradually being adopted in instrumental spheres of learning, but it remains to be seen whether it will become an accepted language for literary production in Malaysia.

Maniam's novels are interesting because they draw from the vocabulary of diaspora to explore the condition of internal exile. And it is in this sense that I use the phrase "post-diasporic imagination". This denotes not only "time after diaspora" but also the sense that cultural memory has to be reworked even as one stays in place. When James Clifford argues that diaspora signifies "not simply ... transnationality and movement but ... political struggles to define the local", he may be said to be making a claim about the post-diasporic condition (252). "Diaspora" denotes transnational movement, but "post-diasporic imagination" denotes the sense of coming to terms with the transnational movement of the past rather than that of the present.

Maniam's novels foreground not a diasporic condition per se, but, rather, a struggle to recover the diasporic condition so as to interrogate the socio-political space of the nation. There is a tension between diaspora and national belonging: To invoke the condition of diaspora is to testify that one is not at home within the socio-political space of the nation and hence to reconsider issues of identity and representation. These issues are pertinent to Maniam's novels. Diaspora is an unhomely condition, and the post-diasporic subjects in Maniam's novels are neither here nor there: They are unable to identify fully with the ancestral homeland of India, and neither are they at home within the nationalist configuration of Malaysia.

Here we examine Maniam's three novels, *The Return* (1981), *In a Far Country* (1993), and *Between Lives* (2003) as they chart progressively the recuperation of a diasporic past to interrogate the post-diasporic national present. "It may be argued", writes Salman Rushdie, "that the past is a country from which we have all emigrated, that its loss is part of our common humanity" (12). For Rushdie, as in the case of *Midnight's Children*, India is a forsaken and idealised site of the past that he recreates textually for the global diasporic present as an imaginary homeland. His novel delivers a challenge to exclusionary nationalist, nativist, or ethnic definitions of "home" in relation to India. For Maniam, the diasporic past is recreated textually so as to enable the post-diasporic work of challenging the national present as it is inscribed by Malay nationalism.

Maniam's writings challenge some of the conceptual underpinnings of diaspora. Rey Chow makes the point that in the process of "writing diaspora", one has to "*unlearn* that submission to one's ethnicity ... as the ultimate signified" [emphasis in original] (25). Yet such a statement overlooks the situation in Malaysia. There may be nothing to unlearn and everything to relearn, since ethnicity has already to some extent been written over by the Malaysian nationalist discourse. While Paul Gilroy in *The Black Atlantic* is able to characterise the African diaspora in terms of flows, exchanges, and circulation, what emerges in Maniam's novels is a diaspora that remains in stasis: In his novels, it is not so much physical displacement as a sense of alienation that propels the diasporic consciousness.

As we shall see, Maniam's novels centre on the trope of memory. His characters return, obsessively, to the past in order to recover aspects of the diasporic cultural memory so as to make sense of their present. In succeeding novels, the act of returning to the past is elaborated to form an understanding of the characters' post-diasporic present in Malaysia.

First return

Maniam's characters are often portrayed as alienated from their immediate surroundings. The paths out of this prevailing condition of unease are presented in the three novels to different degrees. At the end of *The Return*, Ravi begins to move, however tentatively, toward an understanding of the reasons behind his father's erratic behaviour. The narrator commemorates his father's funeral with a poem that acknowledges the difficulty of articulating this disquieting condition:

> Have you been lost for words
> when they imprisoned
> your flesh, your thoughts,
> feelings that rose with the wind?
>
> (Maniam *Return* 173)

At the end of *The Return*, Ravi begins to understand his father's obsession with laying claim to the land of his adopted country. The poem presents the diasporic condition as a repression of affect, and it is a condition that remains to be articulated in the novel, for, as the poem tells us, "Words will not serve" (Maniam *Return* 173). If anything, *The Return* presents a partial return to the present, for the process of the recuperation of the diasporic past in *The Return* has yet to take place.

This condition of alienation finds further expression and resolution in the two later novels. Significantly, unlike *In a Far Country* and *Between Lives*, which employ the mode of magic realism to depict, interrogate, and move out of the debilitating present as governed by the discourses of nationalism and modernity, *The Return* acknowledges the failure of its own narrative. The novel, written in the mode of realism, does not and cannot inhabit the mental space of the protagonist's father. One may say that *The Return*, even as it constitutes a partial return, also constitutes a failed return, for the financial decline of Ravi's father and his consequent behaviour is narrated from a distance and attended to from the outside. Kannan begins to build a house by the side of a river, an action that in Ravi's eyes remains inexplicable. Just before his father's self-immolation, Ravi continues to be embarrassed by him: "He had lost touch with reality completely" (Maniam *Return* 168). The reality inhabited by Ravi's father that forms the lacuna in *The Return* finds articulation in the magic realism of Maniam's two later novels, and this articulation forms the base from which modernity and the national present are critiqued.

Second return

One may suggest that the magic realist moments in Maniam's writings decentre the hegemonic thrust of capitalist and nationalist discourses that foreclose alternative options of identity-formation. Magic realism is a subversive and counter-discursive force. In their introduction to *Magical Realism: Theory, History, Community*, Lois Parkinson Zamora and Wendy B. Faris make the point that magic realism disrupts the political and cultural status quo (6). Stephen Slemon, in his essay "Magic Realism as Postcolonial Discourse", argues that it is a counter-discourse to imperialism (422). In the context of reading Maniam's works, magic realism challenges the nationalist and ethnic agenda that dominates the social and political landscape of Malaysia. Maniam's novels are subversive because the very act of articulating an alternative to the socio-political imaginary of the nation-state is the first step to socio-historical transformation.

The plot of *In a Far Country* revolves around a successful businessman who has become increasingly reclusive. Rajan embarks on a metaphysical journey even as he recalls his childhood in a plantation estate. He remembers his father, a first-generation immigrant from India, as someone who feels trapped in a Malaysia he does not identify with. As Wilson puts it, the negotiation in Maniam's writing between the "individual ethnic identity" and "plural national identity" is an "exploration in metaphysical terms" ("Memory, Myth, Exile" 392). The narrative employs the mythic to articulate the characters' sense of unease and estrangement so as to foster a sense of belonging to the land, a sense that is not only free from the dictates of state discourse, but also from the essentialist paradigm of ethnicity. One may suggest, therefore, that the appeal to mythic time in *In a Far Country* interrupts the linear history of progress that attends the nationalist paradigm and at the same time avoids the pitfalls of ethnic essentialism. Rajan revisits his past encounters with Zulkifli and Sivasurian, each of whom offers different ideas regarding the constitution of self and identity. Rajan recalls that in his younger days, Zulkifli has tried to guide him into a ritualised journey of introspection, taking Rajan into the jungle in order for him to "become the tiger" (Maniam *Far Country* 100). Yet the tree stump they come across in the jungle, which is the boundary marker between the everyday world and the land of the tiger, is a "faulty compass" (Maniam *Far Country* 95). As David Lim points out, Zulkifli's tiger is "an integral symbol on Malaysia's national coat-of-arms" (176). Significantly, Rajan rejects this integration of self with this symbol of Malay hegemony: "All the time the chant poured from

Zulkifli's throat like an ageless invitation to disown whatever I was and to merge with the tiger. I didn't wait for that to happen" (Maniam *Far Country* 101).

It is Sivasurian's message to Rajan concerning transcendence of the self into a larger community that prompts the latter to revisit this trip into the jungle. "You've to go back the way you came so you can know where you are": This is the final injunction from Sivasurian to Rajan, which prompts the latter to embark again on that spiritual journey (Maniam *Far Country* 118). As Rajan ventures into jungle of the self, this time without Zulkifli as a guide, he achieves an epiphany, one that involves the abandonment of the self and at the same time avoids complicity with the tiger of Malay hegemony. The tiger Rajan finds himself in the presence of is not the same as Zulkifli's tiger. In this journey, Rajan confronts the tiger of the self: "I discover that the qualities of the tiger are not out there but lie dormant within me" (Maniam *Far Country* 143). Rajan confronts himself to move beyond: "What does that vision mean? I recognize that it is some kind of a purgation" (Maniam *Far Country* 143). After this purgation of the tiger within himself, Rajan comes to an understanding of the forces governing his life. This realisation allows him to recognise the hegemonic forces of nationalism and the "watch-dog institutions" that "work through existing customs and rituals practised by the various communities" that shape everyday life in Malaysia (Maniam *Far Country* 146).

The narrative following Rajan's return from his journey recalls an earlier moment in his youth when he witnesses the sacrifice of a goat called Mani. One may regard this penultimate section of the novel as a revisionist moment. We recall that at the beginning of the novel, Mani is sacrificed as part of a Deepavali festival. Yet in the penultimate section of the novel, this sacrifice is no longer presented as a religious rite, but as a political one. The Hindu festival, as an articulation of ethnic identity, is interrupted by representatives of the state. If Malay hegemony is symbolised in the form of the tiger, then Mani the goat represents that which has to be purged to maintain the hegemonic status quo of Malaysia. Mani is a troublesome creature. He is "almost human in the way he protects his freedom. He doesn't allow anyone to put [a] rope round his neck" (Maniam *Far Country* 147). He disrupts political rallies:

> The speaker continues with his praise of the administration's far-sightedness when we hear a bray, followed by the sound of someone urinating ... the air suddenly fills with the stink of a goat's pellet-dung. (Maniam *Far Country* 150)

A directive arrives from an unnamed state agency for the Tamil Indian community to witness the capture and slaughter of Mani. Just before Mani is killed, there is a moment when man and goat look into each others' eyes, and it is at this moment that Rajan identifies with Mani: "There is a rapport between the two of us" (Maniam *Far Country* 153). Immediately after the dismemberment and subsequent killing of Mani, Rajan finds himself the object of surveillance, his allegiance to the state questioned. In the end, unlike Mani, Rajan does not publicly express his discontent with the discursive enclosures of Malay hegemony. Instead, the consequences of Rajan's confrontation with the tiger are worked out in the private sphere of his marriage.

It is after having embarked on the second metaphysical journey that Rajan begins to understand the cause of his estrangement from his wife, Vasanthi. Just as Rajan's agency has been determined for him, Vasanthi's selfhood has been seized from her:

> Her life had not been her own. First, her parents had had designs and ambitions for her. They had sent her to school for some purpose only they knew; they stopped her from going to school for their own convenience. They had woven the garland of marriage around her neck even before she could work out for herself what she wanted to do. And when she met and married me, she became part of my purpose and ambition. The frightening thing about all this was that she had submitted so easily. (Maniam *Far Country* 179–180)

Here, Rajan admits his own complicity in determining his wife's selfhood and depriving her of agency. It is only after husband and wife acknowledge to each other the absence of any sense of individual agency in both their backgrounds that they begin the work of self-determination. One detects in the following passage not only a marital reconciliation, but also the need to reclaim the autonomy of selfhood:

> Something helped me to begin the unworking. Unworking the sari folds tucked so tightly, neatly, into her flesh. Undoing the cross-stitches of her and my sari-bordered life. It comes to me now, even as I write, this strange, unlooked for energy that dares to undo the network of inhibitions, prohibitions, history and predilections that we have cast about us. (Maniam *Far Country* 196)

In a Far Country ends with reconciliation and healing between husband and wife. Yet it is an ending that is less than what is promised. Is this renewal to be located only within the personal, within the domestic spaces of the familial? Can one pursue the emanations of this renewal in the public spaces of Malaysia?

In this respect, David Lim writes of Rajan's return from his metaphysical journey as a "non-arrival", pointing out that this is symptomatic of Maniam's recognition "that Malaysians have generally come to accept and even appreciate authoritarian rule, norms and institutions" (194). However, one may suggest that just as *In a Far Country* articulates the unease suggested at the end of *The Return*, *Between Lives* carries on the work of renewal hinted at the end of *In a Far Country*.

Third return

In *Between Lives*, the process of healing again occurs on the level of the familial. Sumitra is a social worker employed by a state agency known as the Social Reconstruction Department. Her family lives in relative comfort in a two-storey bungalow, surrounded by the usual accoutrements of an upper-middle-class existence. However, certain minor observations on the part of Sumitra hint at a larger, prevailing sense of discontentment. Sumitra's father is frequently away from home, so that Sumitra asks herself at one point: "if he enjoys a spacious house, why is he always rushing off to the flood-lit golf course?" (Maniam *Between Lives* 166). Her mother is obsessed with watching video tapes. Her grandmother has an inexplicable appetite for jewellery. Yet what her grandmother really craves is attention, which jewellery shop attendants are more than willing to supply. Sumitra and her mother occasionally play cruel pranks on the grandmother, such as pretending to forget where the car is parked so that the ageing woman, whose ego having recently been boosted by extravagant purchases of jewellery, is forced to climb up and down the staircases of parking lots with them. When relatives come for a visit, Sumitra is disturbed by the "fake affection" they bear towards her mother (Maniam *Between Lives* 172).

A parallel disquieting familial dynamic culminates in tragedy in another family. Hisham is the son of a prominent banker. Upon his return from his (uncompleted) studies in the United States, Hisham unaccountably falls into a chronic state of depression. His impeccable appearance is symbolic of the conditions of the two families, bearing all the signs of affluence and giving no hint of the underlying disorder: "He wore the most stylish clothes … shirts that were so soft they seemed to melt into his broad shoulders and slim waist! Trousers that never got crushed or creased!" (Maniam *Between Lives* 48–49). It is his mother, Puan Jamal, who requests Sumitra's assistance. Yet, inexplicably, during every visit she cuts short Sumitra's interview with her son the moment the latter is about to bring up family matters. Hisham, in the end, runs amok and stabs his father to death.

If the institution of the family is a function of "money politics" and the resultant materialism brought about by Malay(sian) nationalism, then it is these discourses that are critiqued in the novel through the mode of magic realism. Sellamma is another of Sumitra's charges, and she plays a pivotal role. Her life story is conveyed through an immersion into an alternative reality on the part of her listeners. As Sumitra puts it, "[Sellamma] doesn't only talk about her memories, she creates them in front of my eyes" (Maniam *Between Lives* 83). In this alternative reality, Sumitra becomes Sellamma's sister, Anjalai. When Sumitra's family members, who are concerned that she is spending too much time with Sellamma, arrive for a visit, they are likewise transformed into different corresponding members of Sellamma's family. During one of the periods when Sumitra is immersed in the dream-time of Sellamma's memories, she finally grasps the anomic condition of her existence:

> Yes, there is the silence that I've been living with all my life ... the silence behind the tapes my mother plays, and the silence when she withdraws into herself or into her reading; the silence behind the silence when my father looks proudly at his house in the warmth of all that admiration. (Maniam *Between Lives* 201–202)

Reliving the past through Sellamma's memories has the effect of recovering the frustrations of life in a rubber estate to chart a way out of the impasse in their present lives. As Sellamma says at several points in the novel, "You must bring back into life what was not living properly" (Maniam *Between Lives* 289). What is not living properly is the attempt at forging meaning, identity, and affect—in other words, creating a homeland out of the physical terrain of one's abode. Sellamma's memories are focused on her father, who, like Ravi's father in *The Return* and Rajan's father in *In a Far Country*, is concerned with making his adopted country his homeland throughout the period of colonial occupation, the Japanese occupation, and the period of emergent Malayan nationalism. Eventually, through the recovery of diasporic memories, Sumitra begins to question and oppose the political status quo that disciplines the national subject.

At the end of the novel, Sellamma hands over to Sumitra the title deeds to her house and the surrounding land. Sumitra, instead of handing them over to the state, which is her initial task, takes steps to prevent the house from being demolished. With the help of family and friends, Sumitra establishes boundaries and fences to mark off their land from the encroaching construction crew hired by a property developer. The conflict between Sumitra and the authorities is staged through the media. The state-sponsored newspaper carries two advertisement pictures. One of them is a scene of carnage reminiscent of the race riots of 1969 entitled "This?":

> Military and police trucks are ranged around the block, the soldiers and policemen holding their weapons in front as if ready for any surprise attack ... Here and there you see the flash of the curved parang or sickle, daggers, machetes, kitchen knives, as the men locked themselves into body-to-body struggles. Streaks of blood run down their bodies, and fall in splotches on the ground. Turbans and songkoks are knocked off. (Maniam *Between Lives* 376)

This picture recalls a traumatic moment in Malaysia's history, a moment when ethnic violence had torn apart the social fabric and martial law had to be declared. It is a warning to Sumitra because it suggests that her actions will lead to a repeat of the past and also the return of the repressed ethnic tensions that, at present, are contained by national agencies such as the Social Reconstruction Department. The violence depicted in the picture is certainly racialised: "Turbans and songkoks are knocked off", a woman's "sari [is] loosened and streaming through the billowing smoke" and "a dragon writhes in the last throes of death, spent fire spluttering from its jaws" (Maniam *Between Lives* 376). In contrast, the soldiers, the police, and the medics, as the embodiment of governmental intervention, are depicted as ethnically neutral. They are depicted here to be attending to the aftermath of ethnic violence.

The second picture, entitled "Or This?", is that of a luxury condominium block:

> Huge, ornate pots fill the balconies, the plants sending their lush foliage and colourful flowers over the balustrades. Children gambol in the sparkling waters of a small pool, and further on, adults swim in an Olympic-sized pool. Just beyond the pools, the other residents, dressed in traditional clothes, the seluar and baju, sarung-kebaya, vesti and jippa, salwar-kameez, sari and choli, and stylish suits are gathered at tables, heaped with food. (Maniam *Between Lives* 377)

In the juxtaposition of the pictures there is a suggestion that modernity and wealth accumulation, symbolised by the luxury condominium apartments, an Olympic-sized swimming pool, and expensive cars, are the solutions that contain ethnic differences within the nation-state. The state's imagined community is idealised here, as signified by the gathering of residents of various ethnicities wearing their traditional costumes. There is a conflation of social class and ethnic harmony in the picture, and one may suggest that the novel is offering here a critique of the "money politics" as we have previously described it. Sumitra is standing in the way of modernity and wealth accumulation that lies at the heart of Malaysia's nation-building project.

At the same time, the mission of the Social Reconstruction Department is revealed. Sumitra's colleagues arrive to show her a printout issued by the department:

> Study the newspaper story and the advertisements carefully. The older generations don't need reminders, but the young must learn to remember. There was only that one deviation in the history and development in our society. The SRD was set up to discover the reasons, and to prevent it from happening again. (Maniam *Between Lives* 378–379)

This evocation of the scene of 13 May 1969, when the race riots that broke out at the outcome of national elections indicated the erosion of Malay dominance in the government ("that one deviation in the history and development in our society"), is a warning that any deviation from the state's version of modernity would bring about the return of racial conflict. The newspaper pictures present a choice between devastation and a multicultural modernity. Yet this multiculturalism is an illusion.

At one point in the novel, Sumitra recalls her days as a student in secondary school. The school that Sumitra and her colleagues, Christina and Aishah, used to attend is revealed to be an ideological state apparatus under the aegis of the New Economic Policy. The racialised environment is enacted through dress and naming in the everyday praxis of the school:

> There is Chikgu Hamid in front of the classroom. He's wearing his songkok and declaiming on the events just after the Japanese occupation of the country. He takes slow, dramatic steps before the class. The Hassans, Ah Chongs and Ramasamys ... and the Hasnahs, Siew Meis and Sumitras, not to mention the odd, withdrawn Aishah, are responding to his lesson in their own ways.
> The Hasnahs watch and listen with bated breath ... The Siew Meis and the Sumitras keep their heads down, either in embarrassment or mild disgust. The odd Aishah looks at him with a sort of disdain. (Maniam *Between Lives* 233–234)

While the novel is oblique as to the nature of Chikgu Hamid's history lesson, one may guess at its contents from the different responses of the "Hasnahs" (the metonym for "Malay"), "Siew Meis" (the metonym for "Chinese"), and the "odd Aishah" (the metonym for the non-traditional Malay or perhaps "Eurasian"). (The novel is silent as to why other Malays regard Aishah as odd.) The nation has always been segregated along ethno-racial lines, and Sumitra is resisting the forgetting of this historical fact: "our past selves [are] now not to be veiled over by some comforting, superficial light" (Maniam *Between Lives* 385).

The final moment of the novel takes a meta-fictional turn. All that has been narrated thus far has been put on the Internet:

> This is the only way we can reach you—through our web site. If you've been with us this far, you'll understand. You'll understand why we, Aishah, Mei (Christina insisted she be called by that name now), and I, like you all, are gathered around the PC or laptop. This is our story. (Maniam *Between Lives* 384)

Even though the use of the Internet seems to imply that Sumitra is appealing to an international forum, it is clear, as articulated in the novel, that taking a stance against the state's version of modernity implies a commitment to the creation of a homeland out of contemporary Malaysia. As Aishah's father puts it, "We can't be like the people [who put] money in foreign banks. For stand-by properties, stand-by countries. To run away when trouble starts" (Maniam *Between Lives* 385–386). The final paragraph of the novel affirms exile as an accusation against the hegemonic forces of Malay(sian) nationalism:

> We've to listen to the slightest thoughts, to the faintest, disappointed sigh of our conscience. We must follow every twist and turn of our memories, fearlessly, so we won't be easily put off our tracks. We've been had once, we must not let it happen again. Then, maybe, we'll return from our exile ... yes, return from our exile. (Maniam *Between Lives* 388)

The post-diasporic condition is akin to the condition of exile. But here, the exile is in the form of cultural exile, wherein one's ethnicity finds no expression within the ambit of Malaysia's ethnic nationalism. Rushdie writes, "It may be that writers in my position, exiles or emigrants or expatriates, are haunted by some sense of loss, some urge to reclaim, to look back, even at the risk of being mutated into pillars of salt" (10). In the case of Maniam, it is not the land that has to be reclaimed but the memory of being at home in the land.

Between Lives represents the culmination of Maniam's work thus far. The use of magic realist moments initiates an exploration as well as articulation of the post-diasporic condition. The novel expresses a longing for national recognition; it carves out a cultural space within Malaysian social landscape even though this space has yet to find expression within the political discourse of nationalism. Unlike Rushdie's work, which has been criticised as privileging a form of imagination that is ahistorical and celebrates a free-floating form of subjectivity lacking in commitment to a particular locality (Ahmad 128), Maniam's writings commit themselves to a national home that is Malaysia.

Taken together, Maniam's three novels progressively dramatise a recuperation of a forgotten diasporic past, mapping it onto the national present in such a way as to submit it to critique. Ravi in *The Return* begins to understand his father's need to lay claim to the land of his adopted country. Yet the novel narrates this understanding at second hand, from the point of view of Ravi as he observes his father. The reality as experienced by Ravi's father is not made directly accessible to the reader, and hence the message regarding the post-diasporic condition is muted. In contrast, the next two novels we have examined, because of the use of magic realism, come closer to presenting the sense of alienation from the point of view of one who is experiencing it. Rajan in *In a Far Country* revisits his younger days to understand the nature of the "watch-dog institutions" that govern his life. It is the magic realist moments in Maniam's writings that lay bare the hegemonic thrust of capitalist and nationalist discourses, thus opening up alternative possibilities of identity formation. It is with Rajan's identification with a ritually slaughtered goat that the novel begins to interrogate the ideological enclosures that circumscribe his life. In *Between Lives*, Sumitra is immersed in Sellamma's memories, to return to the present to re-establish familial ties as well as to renounce her work at the Social Reconstruction Department. As the novel shows, the roots of Malaysia's ethnic nationalism can be traced back to the race riots of 1969, and it is this founding event that led to the post-diasporic condition as articulated in Maniam's writings. In all of Maniam's novels, this post-diasporic condition is claimed as a function of contestation against the hegemonic enclosures established by the nationalist discourse of the state. Taken together, they testify to the condition of being not-at-home and to an attempt to establish a home in the national present.

8

Two Singaporeans in America:
Hwee Hwee Tan's *Mammon Inc.* and Simon Tay's *Alien Asian*

The post-diasporic condition as exemplified in K. S. Maniam's novels is a function of the cultural dislocation brought about by Malaysia's ethnic nationalism. Now we shall examine another form of dislocation, that which is brought about by globalisation. Given that globalisation is ushering in a passage in history characterised by rapid flows of capital, commodities, and labour, how is the sense of home and belonging to be understood? Can one truly be at home anywhere in the world? We shall engage these questions by exploring how the Singaporean subject grapples with the changes brought about by globalisation; it focuses on how one is to narrate one's attempt at negotiating and finding one's self amidst the increasingly intertwined social landscapes of American and Singaporean modernity.

We shall "read" America via two very different Singaporean texts that nevertheless possess one common theme: Is it possible to claim an identity rooted in "place" in the face of increased mobility and interconnections between different localities? The two texts to be considered present transnational space as a function of transaction and negotiation between the social and cultural spaces of Singapore and America. In Simon Tay's *Alien Asian*, a travelogue consisting of observations, anecdotes, and commentaries, and Hwee Hwee Tan's *Mammon Inc.*, a novel that reactivates the trope of medieval romance within a contemporary landscape, we will explore how individual subjects grapple with issues of identity formation within a globalised paradigm.

This reading of *Alien Asian* and *Mammon Inc.* is situated within recent debates pertaining to globalisation and transnationalism. Much of the scholarship exploring the paradigm of globalisation and transnationalism, we must note at the outset, is devoted to the cultures and political economies of nations, and there is little work that looks at how the literary imagination is formed and informed by these worldwide processes. For example, in *Nations Unbound*, Linda Basch, Nina Glick Schiller, and Cristina Szanton Blanc locate transnationalism "as the processes by which immigrants forge and sustain multi-stranded social relations that link together their societies of origin and settlement" (7). Such a formulation of transnationalism overlooks short-term travel and temporary expatriation, and its empirical bases do not enable one to explore what Arjun Appadurai calls *"imagined worlds*, that is, the multiple worlds that are constituted by the historically situated imaginations of persons and groups spread around the globe" [emphasis in original] (33). But in reading Tay's travelogue and Tan's novel, we find that any pronouncements as to the forging of hybrid identities and an imagined multiplicity of worlds may be unduly celebratory.

Certainly, both Tay's and Tan's life experiences bear testimony to the kind of subjectivities made possible by globalisation. Both are accomplished Singaporean writers, and both have lived abroad and have spent a significant part of their lives in America before returning to Singapore. Tay is a law lecturer at the National University of Singapore and chairman of the Singapore Institute of International Affairs, a non-governmental think tank. Having served for a period as a nominated member of parliament under a scheme which allows citizens to engage in parliamentary debates, he is recognised as an alternative voice with respect to issues pertaining to the development of civil society in Singapore. However, it has to be said that there is a general public perception in Singapore that his voice has since, to some extent, been co-opted by the government. (Though to be fair, it can be said that everyone living in Singapore is in some measure complicit.) Tay's appointment as the chairman of the National Environmental Agency from 2002 to 2008 is indicative of his complex negotiations with state agencies. In 1995, Tay was named Singapore Young Artist of the Year in recognition of his literary works. Apart from a novel, *City of Small Blessings* (2009), a short story collection, *Stand Alone* (1991), and *Alien Asian* (1997), he has also written two collections of poems, entitled *5* (1985) and *Prism* (1980). *Alien Asian* collects a series of newspaper columns entitled "Fax from America" that Tay wrote for the *Straits Times*, Singapore's national newspaper, while he was studying for his master's degree in law on a Fulbright scholarship at Harvard University.

Hwee Hwee Tan is a journalist and a writer with an international reputation. Tan has received numerous awards, including those from the New York Times Foundation and the British Broadcasting Corporation. In 2003, she followed Tay as a recipient of the National Arts Council's Young Artist of the Year award. Born in Singapore, she lived for a period in the Netherlands and received her first degree from the University of East Anglia. She obtained a master's degree in English studies from the University of Oxford and a master's degree of fine arts, in creative writing, from New York University. Set in Singapore, the plot of Tan's first novel, *Foreign Bodies*, revolves around a Singaporean lawyer who comes to the help of a British friend arrested for masterminding an international gambling syndicate.

While the book explores the theme of Singaporean culture and expatriation, her second novel, *Mammon Inc.*, which is set in Singapore, Oxford, and New York, explores the exigencies of transnational identity formation in a world shaped by globalisation.

I emphasise the background of the authors at length because their work may be read as reflections of their personal experiences outside of Singapore. In many ways, Tay's travelogue is a work of auto-ethnography. I use this term in the same way Heewon Chang does, to refer to writing that "combines cultural analysis and interpretation with narrative details" (46). Certainly, much of what occurs in *Alien Asian* amounts to an exploration of Tay's personal experience of America as the author thinks through larger issues pertaining to cross-cultural engagement. While Tan's novel is, of course, a work of fiction, one may nevertheless note that much of what is narrated in it draws from her personal experience, given that the novel is about the experiences of a Singaporean Oxford graduate in America.

Globalisation and its discontents

> I was born American. Not in the country itself, but in its shadow. Coca-cola and jeans were always in, no matter how the governments of Singapore and of Asia railed against "yellow" culture in the 1960s and 1970s, or "decadent" Western values. By my late teens, McDonald's and other fast-food joints were the hangouts; others younger than I were born into that urban landscape and cannot imagine life without them. In our mindscapes, TV and movies made us visualise new places and situations. They taught us new words, ways of speaking and dressing, new lifestyles. Sex, drugs and rock-n-roll were part of it; the most censurable part. Harder to keep out (if anyone wanted to) were money, big business and cities with skyscrapers, cars and shopping malls, TV, movies and stars, consumer culture. The whole American cult.
>
> It did not matter that Singapore was almost exactly halfway across the world. (Tay *Alien Asian* 15)

The above passage, taken from Tay's travelogue, describes the interpenetration of Singapore's social landscape with that of America, as facilitated by the transnational flows of images, products, and attitudes.

The passage can be better appreciated when we consider the changes Singapore has undergone in terms of how it engages with what it perceives as the West. In the late 1960s and 1970s, the rhetoric against Western (read American) decadence was prevalent in the form of notices in post offices informing everyone that males with long hair would be attended to last, while at the Singapore customs, male foreigners with long hair were not allowed into the country until they had their hair trimmed. This was the era belonging to the Woodstock generation of America, the time when the guitar riffs of Jimi Hendrix and songs of rock bands such as the Grateful Dead were regarded with disdain by the political authorities. The newly assembled Singaporean government, with its memory of ejection from the Federation of Malaysia still fresh, had by then embarked upon a national campaign of modernisation and frenetic industrialisation. Images of rebellion from abroad were policed. Discipline and thrift were the order of the day, while decadence in the form of drug culture and "free love" as espoused by the Woodstock generation of America were viewed with suspicion and proscribed.

Fast-forward to the 1990s, and things had undergone a sea-change. Instead of sending government scholars to traditional British centres of learning such as Cambridge and Oxford universities, the government of Singapore was sending its best and brightest—those being groomed for important government posts—to American universities on the assumption that these scholars, when they returned, would be familiar with the conditions of a globalised economy as a result of having lived in the United States for a period of time. This attitude towards America had been sustained for well over a decade. Davinder Singh, a lawyer and an MP, contributed an article to the *Straits Times* in 2004 wherein he argued that to survive what he called the "New World Order" shaped by the forces of globalisation, Singapore has to emulate America by maintaining an open-door policy when it came to the influx of foreign labour (*Straits Times* 17 August 2004). The urgency with which Singh regarded the theme of globalisation is not singular. Rather, it is exemplary in the way the flow of labour and capital is linked with urgency to the trope of national survival and inserted into Singapore's public discourse.

If I have emphasised at length the local conditions of Singapore, it is because Tay's travelogue is addressed primarily to local readers, given that it was published by a Singapore publisher that, by and large, distributes locally. Singaporeans who encounter the above passage would read it as a commentary on their everyday lived experiences and on the changes to which they bore witness within less than two decades. The general tenor of Singaporean society with regard to its openness to American influence as registered in Singh's article, read alongside Tay's travelogue, gives us a sense of Singapore's contemporary moment of transition. This gradual transition, from suspicion to embrace in the matter of different aspects of American culture, is congruent with Singapore's entry into a late modernity as characterised by the vicissitudes of globalisation.

If mobility engenders cross-cultural engagements, then what is valuable about Tay's travelogue is its sensitivity to the nuances that attend to the act of representing the self as well as another culture. The travelogue narrates Tay's experiences as a law student at Harvard and on a farm in Vermont, where he and his wife stayed for a period while she was completing her master's dissertation. In it, Tay calls attention to the fictive nature of the image of America:

> Between and beyond New York and Los Angeles, the usual depictions of the mass media, there is something different. The Mid-West and the South, the mountains and the coasts, the small towns and rural communities: regions differ—not only in geography, but also in culture, people, industry, lifestyle, past and future, needs and aims ... The picture of America that is broadcast across the world, across the Pacific, is too simple. (26–27)

Similarly, as Tay recognises, to Americans the term "Asian" is a monolithic term that glosses over significant differences among Asian ethnicities and nationalities, within which Singaporean identity is erased. An incident narrated in *Alien Asian* serves to demonstrate the extent of these cultural misapprehensions. When Tay tries to rent an apartment from a landlord concerned about good housing maintenance, he and his wife have to take pains to present an act of "strategic essentialism", to borrow a term from Gayatri Chakravorty Spivak ("Criticism" 11). Strategically, they adopt the stereotype of "the new Asian" to distinguish themselves from "Asians [who] had a reputation from the smell and mess of Chinatown":

> We complained about the slummy houses we had seen and the mess that students—mainly American—had left behind. We expressed disdain for loud and messy parties. Jin Hua played the role of dutiful Asian wife and home-maker ... We were ... the more monied and house-proud new Asian. One stereotype was exchanged for another. This time, however, to our benefit. (Tay 43–44)

In this respect, cultural misrepresentation becomes a deliberate act, one performed so as to secure an economic transaction. What matters is not so much the authenticity of identity formation but a strategic and essentialised performance of it for the purpose of economic exchange.

There is in Tay's travelogue a sense of disenchantment with the futility of representation. His is not so much a disenchantment with America but with the failure of equal exchange on the field of representation: "All of us, and all the wider world we represented, were just an island in America's vast continent" (Tay 205). *Alien Asian* lays bare the gap that has to be breached in mutual representations among nations, and this asymmetrical relation between two nations is enacted through the American media. In 1994, when America's attention was drawn to Singapore during the Michael Fay incident, what resulted was a deliberate will-to-misrepresentation. Michael Fay was an American teenager arrested in Singapore for defacing several cars in late 1993. He pleaded guilty to vandalism and was sentenced to jail and six strokes of caning. The sentence was subsequently reduced to imprisonment and four strokes of the cane. This incident served only to widen the gap between both nations. Tay was asked if he would want to appear on the "Larry King Show" to give a Singaporean perspective on the incident: "They wanted a person with an opinion that was wholly in favour of the punishment and about Asia's right to stand up to America. Or they would have a Singaporean ... who was clearly against what his government was doing" (Tay 111–112). As Tay observes, whenever the issue was discussed, "It was not a conversation about Singapore, but one about America. It was also a conversation in which both sides seemed to speak, without listening to each other" (115). America was interested in Singapore in so far as it was Asia. The Michael Fay incident became a debate about Asia standing up to America rather than about the two nations' different attitudes to crime.

There is no real dialogue; or rather, dialogue between Singapore and America occurs not as a mutual exchange of ideas and opinions but on the plane of commodity circulation. Thus, the identity formation of the Singaporean in America has to be negotiated, structured, and mapped onto the plane of commodity exchange to find recognition. As Tay observes, the American supermarket

> had everything: chilli and other sauces and *bok choy*, fresh *kway chap* and *char siew pau* made for the microwave, the *tau hwei chui* ... even frozen durian ... There were familiar brands like Yeo's and Amoy Canning. There were mysterious packages and tins that I had never seen and knew nothing about, from Vietnam, China and other parts of Asia. (Tay 40)

While commodities from Asia are present in the American supermarket, what is absent in America is an awareness of the cultural specificities of different groups of Asians. When an American couple expresses surprise that Tay's Singaporean friend, Karen, could speak grammatically correct English but could not understand the Thai or Vietnamese label on a package, the narrator realises that "to White eyes, Singaporeans, Malaysians, Chinese, Koreans, Japanese, Thais, Vietnamese, Burmese, all ... Asians, were the same" (Tay 41).

When, in his critique of capitalism, Marx elaborates on the concept of commodity fetishism, whereby people's social relations are transformed by capitalism because they "do not come into social contact with each other until they exchange their products", he does not foresee that identity markers are likewise susceptible to commodification and objectification (77). As the various moments noted in *Alien Asian* demonstrate, under the aegis of globalisation, the production of identity is based not on nation formation but on the momentary, day-to-day transactions between human agents. Identity formation is formation with a purpose; one's self-identification as of a given ethnicity is not an end in itself, but a means to a pragmatic end. This is the situation encountered by the protagonist in Tan's *Mammon Inc.*, as well.

Playing with mistaken identities

> There seemed to be nothing that [the company] didn't own or couldn't buy. Whether you were in London, Singapore or New York, you would find people in mcJeans drinking mcLite beer while talking about the latest mcMovie. I looked at the headlines of the *mcTimes*, which announced that Mammon Inc. was taking over Apple Computers to form a new company—mcMac. (Tan 4)

The plot of *Mammon Inc.* revolves around the dilemma faced by Chiah Deng Gan, a recent Oxford graduate offered the post of a research assistant to Professor Ad-oy. At the same time, she is the only candidate on the shortlist of Mammon CorpS, a subsidiary of Mammon Inc., the largest corporate entity in the world. The transnational corporation is depicted as one that has achieved global domination through the control of global commodities, from mcJeans to the mcMac. While such a caricature of an American corporation with global reach may find resonance among those who argue that globalisation is synonymous with American imperialism, the novel is interesting because it draws attention to the agency of the individual subject.

Chiah Deng is invited to undergo a series of tests for the position of an "Adaptor", someone who helps international professionals such as diplomats, bankers, and lawyers adapt to different cultures to gain an edge in their professional expertise. The tests require that she transform herself into a member of the Gen Vex, a group of ultra-chic New Yorkers, advise her sister on how to be accepted into Oxford society, and train Steve, her British friend, to pass himself off as a Singaporean. While Chiah Deng agrees to undergo these three tests to try out for the position, she is of two minds about accepting the job.

Like *Alien Asian*, *Mammon Inc.* makes the statement that global capitalism necessitates a renegotiation of one's identity as a result of the shifting relations between global capital and labour. Global corporations, because of their transnational networks, require that their employees have a certain transnational capability to negotiate for themselves a social space situated in multiple localities. As this negotiation occurs on the individual level, it requires an agency invested with a critical consciousness that recognises the drawbacks of identifying oneself solely with communities situated in one specific locality. There is an implication here that a subjectivity created via an appeal to national identification may no longer be a viable option within a paradigm of globalisation.

By employing multiple settings in Oxford, New York, and Singapore, *Mammon Inc.* focuses our critical attention on the transnational paradigm. Oxford, we are told, is home to the English intellectual tradition; it is a place that offers respite to dons such as Professor Ad-oy, who muses upon the Christian mystics. The home of intellectual and spiritual contemplation, however, is prone to exclusivity and racism, as when Chiah Deng and her British friend, Steve, are ostracised by the student population as the former belongs to a different ethnic group while the latter is of a different socio-economic class. New York is the domain of the Gen Vexers, a high-flying, wealthy, and glamorous elite. "The Gen Vexers," we are told, "were cosmopolitan citizens of the world ... equally well versed in the work of George Lucas and Joseph Campbell to be able to analyse the mythological archetypes in *Star Wars*" (Tan 143). (There is another allusion to *Star Wars*: Professor Ad-oy is the novel's version of Yoda.) Glamour and intellectual flair go hand in hand in New York; despite their intellectual wit, however, the Gen Vexers are shallow, "created purely by external details: their jobs, quips, zip codes, CD collections, choice of gyms, Palmpilots and other consumer products" (Tan 149). The novel is offering at this point a critique, alerting one to the possibility that these Gen Vexers are free-floating subjects uncommitted to local and specific national ties. They identify themselves instead with consumer products and services such as CDs, gyms, and hand-held electronics.

At the same time, Tan's book draws attention to the possibility that Singapore, in its quest to be a global city like the New York of the Gen Vexers, has become another version of corporate and consumerist-oriented America. Singapore is depicted as "an American strip mall running through the middle of a tropical botanical garden" (Tan 244). This is the point at which claims to a unique Singaporean identity are placed under scrutiny. At various moments in the novel, the enactment of a Singaporean identity is just that—a performance lacking in cultural depth. In her attempt to communicate with students from Oxford, Chiah Chen, the sister of Chiah Deng, tries to engage their interest in Singaporean culture by explaining the significance of the miniature plastic Merlion statues and the rice dumplings she is giving out, and what follows is a presentation of historical kitsch. (We have to bear in mind that Chiah Chen is portrayed throughout the novel as a character motivated by the material aspects of life and uninterested in matters of cultural import.) Chiah Chen tells them of the thirteenth-century prince Sang Nila Utama, who travelled by sea to the island where he encountered a lion. "So Sang Nila Utama decided to call the island a new name, 'Singa-pura', which means 'Lion City'. That's how my country got its name" (Tan 194). As for the rice dumplings:

> You eat it during the dragon boat festival. There was a poet called Qu Yuan. He did many good things for the people, but the bad people in the King's court didn't like him, so they kicked him out. After that, he went round China, writing about all the bad things he saw. But one day, he was so sad about all the bad things he saw that he jumped into the Mi Luo River and killed himself. When the fishermen found out, they got in their boats to look for him. That's how the dragon boat festival started. But they couldn't find his body. So the people threw the rice dumplings into the river to protect Qu Yuan, so that the fish would eat the dumplings and not bite his body. (Tan 196)

The above exemplifies the creation and sustenance of identity by appeals to originary myths. Yet it is interesting to note that these myths emerge as part of the myths of other cultures. Despite the fact that they do not emerge organically but are state-manufactured, these myths take a place in Singapore's national culture. The Merlion, as we noted earlier, is a creation of the tourism authorities, while the dragon boat festival may be seen as the way Chinese Singaporeans affirm a form of cultural-historical genealogy reaching back into China's mythic history. Given the way Chiah Chen is characterised in the novel, *Mammon Inc.* presents historical kitsch as exemplary of mistaken self- and national identity in an ironic and self-conscious manner.

As Ien Ang puts it in her book *On Not Speaking Chinese* (2001), "any identity is always mistaken" (viii). Ang's statement is interesting in proposing that there is no such thing as a correct or authentic identity. Any attempts to present identity as "correct" is to arrest its fluid and negotiated nature. As Chiah Deng explains to Steve when the latter asks for Singaporean food:

> There's no such thing as Singaporean food, really. Which is why I find it really weird in England when I see restaurants offering Singaporean noodles, or see a Singapore stir-fry sauce in the supermarket. I mean, you can get Chinese or Malay or Indian food, but there's no dish that you can say is specifically Singaporean. (Tan 224–225)

The above passage demonstrates why it is so difficult to speak about national identity. How may one do so without resorting to stereotype and essentialism? This applies to ethnicity as well. Chiah Deng's British friend, Steve, understands Chinese identity only through stereotypes:

> "Well, you're not very Chinese. You never do any Chinese things."
> "What Chinese things *don't* I do?"
> "Plant rice." [emphasis in original] (Tan 153)

Steve goes on to list out why Chiah Deng is not very Chinese.

> "I mean, you don't have any Chinese friends. You dress like any other student. You don't have any Chinese art in your room. You don't even use chopsticks. You don't do *anything* that's Chinese. All you've done for the last three years is study English books and loiter in the pub with me."
>
> "I do Chinese things," I said, "only you don't know they're Chinese."
>
> "Like what?"
>
> I paused to think. I couldn't think of anything Chinese. What *was* Chinese anyway? "That's not the point. Being Chinese isn't just about eating sweet-and-sour pork, and hanging calligraphic scrolls in my room." [emphasis in original] (Tan 153)

The above examples of misidentification illustrate the habit of thinking via stereotypes; the construction of an ethnic identity leads to a predisposition to thinking about self and others in terms of stereotypical representation. Perhaps one may say that any attempt at representation is necessarily a misrepresentation.

What then, is Singapore? Or, to put it in another way, what is Singapore for America? What emerges in the novel is that Singapore is subsumed under the category of "Asia", which is constituted as a commodified signifier of sophistication. As depicted in the novel, America's understanding of Asia is not really of Asia per se but of a certain kind of Asia, an Asia that has been commodified. A photo-spread entitled "Go Orient Yourself" in the lifestyle magazine *Generation Vexed* offers the following advice on how to be culturally sophisticated:

> A smiling Buddha and a lacquered screen might make your local sushi den look Asian, but here at *Gen Vex* that just doesn't cut the wasabi. Forget the futon and ditch the bamboo prints. Mod-Asia is all about the energy and eroticism of the urban east. Venetian blinds play with the shadows across the room and increase the rectilinear divisions of the space. Hazy fluorescent lighting drifts up to the tenth floor—perfect for the complexion of the millennium Madame Butterfly, who kicks off her Jimmy Choo heels and sparks up a Mi-Ne cigarette. Out on the terrace, the violet panorama of the city seems ethereal. She stares out at the horizon, wondering if she's lost her Orientation. (Tan 109–110)

One must be a certain kind of Asian to be accepted in America—an Asian framed by the Orientalist requirements of mystique and eroticism coupled with urban sophistication. Asia finds recognition in America only when it is reconstituted, fetishised, and transformed into "Mod-Asia" on the plane of commodity exchange. Otherwise, as Tan cleverly puts it, it does not cut the wasabi. In such terrain, what option is left for individuals who wish to embed their subjectivity meaningfully within a foreign landscape? If no one knows Singapore, then an identity rooted in "place" would find no purchase in America. It is only after Chiah Deng undergoes a twenty-day exercise routine with Iron Belle, an exercise instructor she consults after seeing her on a Nike television advertisement, after an appointment with Monsieur Lucien, whose hair salon "looked like a high-tech alchemist's lair, like Merlin meets *Battlestar Galactica*", and after a trip to a fashion boutique that Chiah Deng finally feels confident enough to enter into the society of the Gen Vexers (Tan 128).

Mammon Inc. makes the proposition that one's identity within a transnational paradigm would have to be reconstituted by selecting different components from what may be called a "cultural supermarket". Gordon Mathews in *Global Culture/Individual Identity* proposes the notion of the cultural supermarket as the "multiplicity of information and potential identities" on offer and made available by the media and communications technology (20). As in the case of Chiah Deng, individuals may re-create their identities by aligning themselves with cultural icons or through the purchase of commodities that best articulate their sense of self. While Mathews makes the point that one is not absolutely free to re-create one's self, as the ability to do so depends on one's predisposition, level of education, affluence, and access to magazines, books, films, and the Internet, one may argue that within an affluent society the cultural supermarket is ever-present in the form of popular entertainment (21). In modern societies, one may easily find lifestyle magazines the equivalent of *Generation Vexed* on shelves of bookstores. In this respect, identity is simply how one labels oneself by presenting in an ostentatious manner the choices one makes from this cultural supermarket.

Thus, a transcendental, free-floating subjectivity may be fashioned by selectively appropriating images and meanings from the cultural supermarket. Yet such subjectivity is not posited uncritically in *Mammon Inc*. As evident from its title, the novel's Faustian drama is staged right from the beginning:

> No man can serve two masters; for either he will hate the one and love the other, or he will be devoted to the one and despise the other. You cannot serve God and mammon. (*The Holy Bible*, Matt 6:24)

Caught in the no-(wo)man's-land between East and West, between her interests in theological literature and the seductive excesses of consumerist culture, Chiah Deng is Eve to the serpent of global capitalism. At the end of the novel, Chiah Deng opts for the abyss of the empty signifier. She succumbs to the seduction of late capitalism and embraces, as it were, a transnational subjectivity that is, at the same time, transcendental, "like a plug-and-play peripheral ... like one of those PCMCIA cards that you can just take out of the box and slot into any computer, anywhere" (Tan 64). So is the embrace of global capitalism depicted as a Faustian pact: It is difficult to see how one can be a citizen of the world and at the same time remain loyal to local and specific national ties.

As a global nomad, Chiah Deng expresses her sense of belonging as an agent of global capitalism by articulating her non-attachment to other localities. As a member of an elite group of CorpS, she belongs by not belonging. As an Adaptor working for Mammon CorpS, her job is to help professionals adapt to different cultures. She is by nature of her professional skill able to belong everywhere—yet, at the same time, nowhere. However, it is clear that the novel does not posit rootless existence as an ideal solution; it is rather critical of its own ending, as Chiah Deng's embrace of the transcendental subjectivity requires nothing less than collusion with the devil, demanding the abandonment of a prelapsarian existence:

> I would rather die in the company of demons than live in heaven and be alone on earth. Christ's crucifixion brought him the kingdom of heaven but I didn't have the strength to go through that, couldn't imagine being without the love of my loved ones for the rest of my earthly life.

> I saw in Christ's eyes the pearl of a great price, but realized that in order to follow him, I would have to weep those tears as well. I wasn't Christ, but was merely Eve. I didn't have the stamina to bear the cross. (Tan 276)

Mammon Inc. is satiric in its presentation of identity under the aegis of global capitalism. While national identity relies on historical kitsch, participation in global flows involves the loss of prelapsarian innocence. The novel suggests that an identity constructed under the aegis of global capitalism is not a perfect substitute for that which is shaped by appeals to nationality: If the latter is a function of misrecognition, the former appears to be diabolical, predicated on the erasure and denial of the national.

In so far as globalisation fosters a dense network of interdependencies and connections among people from different localities, it necessitates the renegotiation of their subjectivities. As identities forged via appeals to the nation as an imagined community may no longer be viable within a transnational paradigm, mobile subjects are obliged to renegotiate their identities, playing with stereotypes, personae, and images so as to find recognition. In *Mammon Inc.* and *Alien Asian*, we see human social exchanges operating in an analogous manner with commodity exchange. Tay and his wife have to perform a strategic essentialism to secure a lease on a house, while Chiah Deng has to recreate herself to be accepted into the society of *Gen Vex*. Globalisation may thus be said to bring about another level of commodity fetishism, whereby Asian subjects find social acceptability by renegotiating their identities through the conduit of the cultural supermarket, selecting from a number of available manufactured images, narratives, and stereotypes appropriate to the occasion. In so far as globalisation brings into intimate contact people from different localities, it brings about asymmetrical social relations between subjects of different nationalities. While Arjun Appadurai may argue that "the United States is no longer the puppeteer of a world system of images but is only one node of a complex transnational construction of imaginary landscapes", one may nevertheless point out that America is still perceived as the world's dominant economic, political, and cultural Goliath (31).

One must pay heed to the alarm sounded in Tan's novel and Tay's travelogue, both of which are cultural texts narrating the experiences of Singaporeans in America. Any claims to a subjectivity that is based on the notion that one can be at home anywhere in the world would have to take into consideration how identities are commodified. For if we were to extrapolate from these narratives the operations of cultural transactions between Singapore and America, then there is more that can be done in terms of determining how people from different nations may seek to address one another on equal terms.

9
Writing Back Home:
Tash Aw's *The Harmony Silk Factory*, Vyvyane Loh's *Breaking the Tongue*, and Lau Siew Mei's *Playing Madame Mao*

In the past decade, an emerging body of Anglophone literary work about Malaya and modern Singapore and Malaysia has appeared under the conditions of expatriation, emigration, and diaspora. These novels include Hwee Hwee Tan's, one of which we have examined in the previous chapter, Shirley Lim's *Joss and Gold* (2001) and *Sister Swing* (2006), and Hsu-ming Teo's *Love and Vertigo* (2000) and *Behind the Moon* (2005). All of these books are by writers based outside of Singapore and Malaysia and were published elsewhere, as well. They reflect the experience of living abroad and their creators' attempts to recover personal histories as well as the social histories of their countries of origin.

At the outset I argued that there is transactional and transnational representation at work in Anglophone work by Singapore and Malaysian-born authors who are based in the two countries. The recent emergence of literary texts written by authors outside of Singapore and Malaysia extends this transnational politics of representation. This tells us there is a need to consider how these transnational categories shape themes in literary texts. The national, it would seem, is already transnational. The term "transnational" and its corollaries, "diaspora", "emigration", and "expatriation", are useful as a way of bypassing an exclusivist and essentialist insistence on identity markers. A judicious use of these terms would allow one to demonstrate the fallacy of the claim that only a "local" author is able to represent authentically the conditions of his or her own culture. At the same time, these are also categories under which an author may be identified as interrogating the exclusivist nature of a nationalist canon formation. This is the critical strategy we employed in Chapter 7, where we examined, under the category of diaspora, the work of K. S. Maniam. He resides in Malaysia and writes about it, but he enjoys no recognition within the national literary canon because of his ethnicity and choice of language.

The life trajectories of the three authors whose works we are examining here, along with the international acclaim they have earned, are testimony enough to the transnational arena of literary production and reception. Tash Aw was born in Taiwan to Malaysian parents, brought up in Malaysia, and is currently based in London. Vyvyane Loh was born in Malaysia, educated in Singapore and America, and is currently based in Boston. Lau Siew Mei was born in Singapore and has emigrated to Australia. Unlike *Mammon Inc.* and *Alien Asia*, which construct a discursively stable and recognisable site of departure from which one enters into the globalised and alienating space of America, Aw's *The Harmony Silk Factory* (2005), Loh's *Breaking the Tongue* (2004), and Lau's *Playing Madame Mao* (2000) constitute an interrogation of normative histories that renders unfamiliar the discursive sites of Malaya and modern Singapore. In the novels, home is unmade. *The Harmony Silk Factory*, set in the period of the impending Japanese invasion of British Malaya, presents three incommensurable narratives surrounding the life of Johnny Lim. The cumulative effect of this incommensurability draws attention to the epistemological instability of what we know as Malaya. *Breaking the Tongue*, set in Singapore in the same time period, moves not only between time past and narrative present, but also between different narrators in the retelling of history, such that we are presented with a history composed of multiple narratives. In *Playing Madame Mao*, the events surrounding the "Marxist Conspiracy" of 1987, noted earlier in relation to Gopal Baratham's *A Candle or the Sun*, are juxtaposed with the Chinese Cultural Revolution, such that one is no longer sure whether the novel is set in Lee Kuan Yew's Singapore or Mao's China.

Given their experiences of expatriation and emigration, these three authors do not fall into the category "Singapore and Malaysian authors" in a normative sense. In one way or another, they are all writing about homes they have left behind. These novels have much in common with what Linda Hutcheon identifies as "historiographic metafiction": They offer "a sense of the presence of the past, but a past that can be known only from its texts [and] its traces" (125). However, as texts that reread the past and draw attention to the constructed nature of the past, they have achieved different results in terms of opening up alternative possibilities that interrogate the present configuration of power. It is my argument that Aw's *The Harmony Silk Factory* and Loh's *Breaking the Tongue* lack the critical force one finds in Lau's *Playing Madame Mao*.

The Harmony Silk Factory: The absence of narrative harmony

Set in Malaya from the 1930s to the 1950s, *The Harmony Silk Factory* is divided into three narratives that revolve around the life of Johnny Lim. Each narrative, taken on its own, is not unlike the Harmony Silk Factory that Johnny builds, filled with secrets and hidden mechanisms that are not immediately obvious. It is only when the narratives are juxtaposed that attention is drawn to their incommensurability. Each narrative is partial, and the true story of Johnny Lim resides not within a single one but is dispersed among the three of them.

Part One of the novel is narrated by Jasper, who presents us with "The True Story of the Infamous Chinaman Called Johnny (Early Years)". Here, the life of Johnny Lim is reconstructed partly from Jasper's memory and partly from his research into the archives of libraries and government offices. Jasper claims to "have read every single article in every book, newspaper and magazine that mentions [his] father" and claims to be "particularly well placed to relate the truth of [his] father's life" (Aw 6). He believes that he has "constructed a clear and complete picture of the events surrounding [his] father's terrible past" (6). According to Jasper, Johnny has maimed his father-in-law for life and is most likely to have murdered his business mentor for personal gain. He is also a communist who betrayed his comrades to the Japanese to gain their favour.

In Jasper's reconstruction of Johnny's life, the narrative present becomes an extension of the legacy of Malaya's colonial past. Jasper inserts the story of Johnny into a script that is confluent with the colonial discourse; he makes no secret of his reliance on colonial archives. Hence, the colonial text becomes a text of authority that shapes Jasper's narrative. In Jasper's account, the story of Johnny's early life is juxtaposed with observations of Malaya obtained from a colonial textbook:

> In order to give you an idea of what [Johnny's] life might have been like ... I am able to provide you with a few of the salient points from the main textbook [on peasant life in Malaya], R. St J. Unwin's masterly study of 1954, *Rural Villages of Lowland Malaya.* (Aw 10)

Given a life of hardship and the lack of basic amenities in rural Malaya, "[c]hildren therefore did not 'play'" and were "expected to help in the manual labour" (Aw 11). As such, "rural children became hardened early on. They had no proper toilets, indoor or outdoor" (Aw 12). Jasper then urges his readers to "imagine a child like Johnny, growing up on the edge of a village on the fringes of a rubber plantation", making the point that Johnny, brought up in a backward, impoverished, and underprivileged background, "would have no idea of the world around him" (Aw 13). We considered earlier the colonial stereotype of the Chinese in Florence Caddy's travel book and found them portrayed as a mass of undifferentiated bodies at work, carrying loads, bearing bamboo poles, and pulling rickshaws. Jasper's narrative, like Caddy's text, interpellates the Chinese as the source of raw physical power amenable to the colonial economy. Jasper's account of Johnny's life is filtered through colonial taxonomies of racial categories. Thus, when a Chinese individual of rural peasant background becomes a singularly prosperous and worldly merchant, there is a suggestion that his wealth and status were most likely to have been obtained through unscrupulous means. Thus, it is not surprising, that Jasper's depiction of Johnny as "a liar, a cheat [and] a traitor" is drawn from the stock colonialist portrayal of the Chinese male as a corrupt and untrustworthy businessman (Aw 4). Also, according to Jasper, Johnny's involvement with the Malayan Communist Party is the result of his thirst for violence for its own sake rather than his ideological commitment. It is at the moment when Johnny is fascinated by a communist's display of fighting skill with a *parang*, a type of machete common in Malaya, that "he knew he was truly and irreversibly a communist" (Aw 49). In Jasper's narrative, the colonial subject is stripped of ideological agency.

As we proceed to the second section of the novel, we begin to realise that Jasper's narrative may not be as reliable as he claims. Part Two consists of entries in the journal of Snow Soong, Johnny's wife, from September to November 1941. While some of the events in the entries overlap with those found in Jasper's account, there are points of contradiction, especially in the retelling of how Johnny and Snow first met. Much of this material revolves around Johnny and Snow's honeymoon trip to the Seven Maiden Islands to escape the impending Japanese invasion. In contrast to Jasper's account, Johnny is portrayed as a naïve and trusting husband. To Snow, Johnny "seemed a mere child ... [she] knew that [she] would soon bring [his] fleeting happiness to an end, and all traces of the child in him would die" (Aw 151). Snow is about to leave her husband for Mamoru Kunichika, a Japanese professor of linguistics and anthropology who (unknown to her) turns out to be the much-feared leader of the *Kempeitai*, the Japanese secret military police, in Malaya.

Part Two has all the elements of a Gothic text. Snow's journal entries, consisting of fragmented thoughts and observations, is characterised by events the significance of which eludes their narrator. During their journey to the Seven Maiden Islands, while in the middle of nowhere, the group repeatedly meets a fruit-seller who possesses no apparent means of transport. There is a suggestion that the group is under surveillance, with figures hidden among trees and appearing at the edge of their vision. At the Seven Maiden Islands, Snow is convinced that someone is secretly reading her journal. Inexplicable wails are heard at night, and the death of Frederick Honey, one of the members of their group, is left unexplained. That her narrative hints at its own unreliability underscores the sense of the readers' disorientation in their encounter with it:

> I do not know which came first, or which is stronger: the failure of my memory to record events accurately or the failure of my belief in what is true. All I know is that we are here and we are alive. I know, too, that we have no idea where *here* is. (Aw 191)

Snow's journal constitutes moments when characters confess their inability to grasp the reality that surrounds them. Events are inconclusive, and the motivations of characters are inexplicable.

Part Three of the novel is narrated by Johnny's British friend, Peter Wormwood. The friendship begins with a chance meeting: Peter is fascinated by his encounter with a Chinese man reading Shelley in a coffee shop in a Chinatown alley. For Peter, Johnny is a person of enigma and contradiction: He is a communist who possesses an "instinctive trust, communicated by an intimacy that ... the cold West lost many years ago" (Aw 271). Peter's portrayal of Johnny is a function of his Orientalist perspective. Malaya is "where [he] would find [his] paradise, [his] tropical Arcadia, [his] vision of perfection"; it is Peter's notion of a prelapsarian idyll (Aw 242). Peter's narrative is likened to the cultivation of a garden: "In creating a garden, we acquire, by force, a patch of land from the jungle; we mould it so that it becomes an oasis amid the wilderness" (Aw 257). Given this, Peter's last name, Wormwood, is suitably ironic. We are told that wormwood, a plant that produces a bitter extract used in the making of absinthe, thrives "(e)ven after the garden began its descent into dilapidation" (Aw 289). As written, the novel reminds us that according to the Bible, during the coming of the apocalypse, a star falls from the sky and turns a third of the sea into wormwood (Aw 290).

Peter's narrative, entitled "Eden", turns out to be a narrative of revelations. It is in Peter's narrative that the mystery surrounding Frederick's death is solved: He is the one who kills Frederick because he is angered by what Frederick says about the true purpose of their trip to the Seven Maiden Islands. According to Frederick, Johnny is to become good friends with Kunichika during the trip, eventually becoming his chief informer in Malaya, and Snow is the sexual bait for Kunichika. Peter is unable to reconcile his vision of Malaya as a tropical Eden with the possibility of such duplicity. According to Peter, Johnny is later threatened with the loss of his wife and wealth if he does not become Kunichika's informer. Despite Peter's best efforts to preserve his Malaya as a paradise, and to intervene in the emotional bond between Snow and Kunichika, he ultimately betrays Johnny, having seduced his wife. "Eden" is a narrative of confession: "I had not suffered enough; I had not atoned" (Aw 316).

The Harmony Silk Factory presents us with three narratives that are compromised by elisions, discourses of power, and the narrators' hate and guilt. Jasper's story of Johnny represents a narrative present that is shaped by the authority of colonial discourse and Jasper's own desire; just as its portrayal of Johnny is characterised by hate, the narrator's reliability is threatened by ignorance with regard to his own parentage. Snow's journal entries present an unmediated depiction of Johnny's life and the events that occurred during their trip to the Seven Maiden Islands, yet its immediacy is characterised by confusion, paranoia, and guilt pertaining to her intention to betray her husband. Peter's narrative fills in significant gaps in the other two, yet it is compromised by its nostalgia for Malaya as a tropical Eden. His narrative follows the tripartite biblical teleology of the prelapsarian state, the fall and regeneration, attempting to seek closure on the narrator's past and projecting hope onto the future, a future his biological son inherits: "Jasper. Clear as crystal, the foundation of a new Jerusalem" (Aw 362). Ironically, of course, Jasper's narrative is far from being as clear as crystal, and the same may be said of the narratives of Peter and Snow.

The Harmony Silk Factory draws attention to the problem that attends the writing of history. As one of the characters puts it:

> It's always the case that details are lost in the retelling of stories. Sometimes things are forgotten, sometimes things are added. The tale of History is most unreliable. It is, after all, reconstructed by human beings. (Aw 155)

Confronted with a novel that is an assemblage of fictionalised archives, readers are made to do the work of historians. History is mediated through narrative texts; however, a single document is always a partial narrative, while the perusal of multiple documents does not necessarily lead one to form an internally consistent historical narrative. Even as the novel ends on an ironic note of finality, "*Consummatum est*", the project of coming to terms with the past is far from finished (Aw 362).

Yet apart from its foregrounding of revisionism, *The Harmony Silk Factory* lacks a focused critical agency. The novel suggests that all historical narratives are equally valid, first, because they are reconstructions and, second, because details have been omitted. The novel achieves this in a rather paradoxical manner, for it places its readers in a position of omniscience in relation to acts of revisionism: We are not implicated in the historical reconstructions and amnesias. Rather, we are detached from this assemblage of fictionalised archives, self-satisfied in our knowing position as readers of the assemblage. By the end of the novel, we realise that, unknown to Jasper, he may not be Johnny's son. Johnny the villain may actually be a victim. Peter Wormwood, the flamboyant homosexual aesthete, may have cuckolded his best friend, and the professor of linguistics and anthropology may turn out to be the much-feared leader of *Kempeitai*. Malaya may have been rendered unhomely, unfamiliar and unknowable, but precisely because readers are able to read its unreadability, it becomes the "inscrutable East" that is familiar in the discourse of Orientalism.

Breaking the Tongue: History and the body in pain

The revisionist theme of *Breaking the Tongue* may be found in the following passage:

> You too can make history, write it down. The thought is so clarifying, so renewing that you hardly feel the slap. Too busy with possibilities, too delighted by options ... You too have a creative task; you too have an opportunity to perform. (Loh 33)

Loh's novel, like *The Harmony Silk Factory*, foregrounds the act of historical revisionism. It is excessive in its revisionism because it refuses to take a critical stance regarding what is to be narrated. In Loh's novel, history is perpetually deferred, with one construct replacing another. In this regard, the project of writing about home, instead of drawing from the force of historical specificity to critique dominant and reified nationalist narratives of the present, falls prey easily to a reading that converges with Frederic Jameson's "Third World" allegories: One may say, for instance, that the period of the novel's setting is an instance of a "Third World" zone struggling to find a national voice.

Breaking the Tongue depicts the fall of Singapore to the Japanese in the Second World War and is set in approximately the same time period as *The Harmony Silk Factory*. Through flashbacks and multiple narrators, the novel depicts the lives of individuals in wartime Singapore. Claude Lim is arrested and tortured by his Japanese interrogators. He is made to tell the story of his friendship with Han Ling-li, a spy working for the British, and Jack Winchester, an Englishman who falls ill and is cared for by Claude and Ling-li during the war. An unnamed fifth columnist trails Ling-li and concocts stories about her spying activities. Humphrey, Claude's father, is an Anglophile whose faith in the British is shattered when Singapore is surrendered to the Japanese. Cynthia, Claude's mother, has a series of affairs with white men. The New Zealand-born Patrick Heenan of the Indian Army is a spy for the Japanese, providing them with information about British military bases in Malaya. After Claude is released by his captors, he revisits moments of his interrogation in his dreams, during which he communicates with Ling-li, who describes to him the details of her torture at the hands of the Japanese. What is interesting about these conversations—and this is a point to which we will return later—is that they are written in Chinese.

In the novel, the characters' bodies serve as a metaphor and as sites where cultural and historical narratives are played out. When it becomes clear that the British have surrendered and the Japanese have control of Singapore, Humphrey, the anglicised, Straits-born Chinese whose faith in the British is shattered, suffers a stroke and receives a beating from Japanese soldiers for refusing to bow to them. His body is no longer capable of functioning in the Japanese-occupied regime. His wife, Cynthia, has the habit of burning her wrists with lighted cigarette ends out of self-loathing for having affairs with white men. The body of Ling-li's uncle, Hong-Seng, is the body of the Chinese-speaking working class, physically strong and, in this case, skilled at carpentry. Jack Winchester inexplicably falls ill during the Japanese invasion of Malaya, his body unable to withstand the coming of the Japanese.

Even as these stories are told, we are brought back time and again to the narrative present, which is the scene of Claude's torture. In *The Body in Pain: The Making and Unmaking of the World*, Elaine Scarry makes the point that physical pain is ultimately indescribable and is accompanied by a dissolution of language (4). And if language is one of the major ways through which the world is articulated and constituted for the self, then "[i]ntense pain is world-destroying" for the individual (Scarry 29). In this respect, torture "permits one person's body to be translated into another person's voice ... [it] allows real human pain to be converted into a regime's fiction of power" (Scarry 18). Claude is not Claude but "Claude the Body" in the hands of the Japanese (Loh 22). His body is made an object and made to represent the physical terrain of Malaya. His torturers carve with a knife the route of the Japanese invasion of Malaya on Claude's body, beginning with Thailand on his face and proceeding southward, ending with Singapore at his groin:

> – A brief history of the Japanese liberation of Malaya, he declares to the room. A little refresher course for you, my friend. Let us say this is Kota Bharu ... He places the knife in the narrow pass between the right temple and the earlobe. When the Body flinches, he uses the other hand to grasp its chin. A pair of hands clamps down on the sides of its head.
>
> – December eight, 1941, he drones on. There are two other landings that day, in Thailand, at Singora and Patani.
> The knife marks the crown of the head, where the soft spot grew in after birth, and then another point beside it, to the right. (Loh 188)

Claude the Body in the hands of the Japanese is the body of Japanese-occupied Malaya. The body is made to form part of a larger envisioned history, for the Japanese regarded their conquest of Singapore, which they renamed Syonan (Light of the South), as part of the Greater East Asia Co-Prosperity Sphere, which included Burma, Thailand, Indo-China, the Philippines, and Indonesia (Thio 95). Torture is part of a regime of violence that subjects and incorporates the body so that it might be released back into a Japanese-occupied Singapore that is part of a larger world of the regime's making.

What is interesting about the torture scene is that a narrative of resistance emerges, one that converts the story of Japanese-occupied Malaya into a story of the nation. If Claude the Body is mapped out as the site of "Japanese liberation", the spirit of Claude that hovers above it, watching with disinterest the torture that is taking place, challenges this narrative, in effect giving birth to the nation as an imagined community even as the body is under the threat of castration:

> Is it possible to see so much, to be an entire people all at once? Is it possible to bear such knowledge? Weightless like this, the possibilities are infinite. But most of all, you are drawn to the body below: Claude, clod, clot, cloth, clout, clown; you, light as floating cloud, possessor of a broken arm and cracked ribs, the English-educated boy from Bukit Timah, you the practical, level-headed Ling-li, you the peanut vendor dragging his cart behind him, you the Malay clerk in City Hall, you the Chinese women labourers laying down roads and fearlessly scaling flimsy wooden scaffolding to erect the growing skyline of Shenton Way, you the pommified soul of Humphrey Lim and associates, you the Bengali doormen of vaulted

banks and airy hotels, you the tormented psyche of Cynthia Lim, you the satay-seller, you the scrofulous gangsters and clan leaders in the querulous heart of Chinatown, you the sometime Voice of a confused and cantankerous city. More than that, you are witness to all that has brought about the fall of the city, the many and petty English foibles that have changed the course of history. Or obeyed it. (Loh 39–40)

In the above, various ethnic and occupational categories are collapsed into a national mosaic of "an entire people". From the anglicised Chinese (Claude) to the nationalist spy (Ling-li) recruited by the pro-communist Tan Kah Kee to work for the British, from Malay clerks to Chinese *samsui* women labourers, from Bengali doormen to gangsters in Chinatown, such a mosaic is fashioned into a collective voice, a voice that finds its place in history. The nation is historicised, its emergence grafted onto the history of the Second World War. Just as the passage resists the history of Japan's Greater East Asia Co-Prosperity Sphere, it is also the answer to a question posed by the chauffeur of Claude's family in the first chapter of the novel: "What is this place? It's not India, it's not China … It's nothing" (Loh 31). If Claude's body represents Malaya, his coming-of-age as depicted in the narrative flashbacks is also the coming-of-age of the nation. Claude's childhood in an anglicised family is such that he becomes a mimic man. However, there is "something inside him" that makes him uncomfortable with this subject formation: "he wants more than anything to be white, and English, and yet something inside him prevents him from admitting it, from wanting it even" (Loh 144). That "something", one may suggest, is the desire for nationhood. Out of British- (and Japanese-) controlled Malaya emerges the nationhood of Singapore; it is a nationhood naturalised in the boy's resistance to his own desire of wanting to be a white man and articulated at the moment of torture in the hands of the Japanese.

As Holden points out, the novel reiterates "a racial governmentality in which Chineseness is moulded", and this form of governmentality is associated with the modern state's discourse of nationalism ("Histories" 7). In a 1978 lecture, Foucault made the point that "the state can only be understood in its survival and its limits on the basis of the general tactics of governmentality" ("Governmentality" 103). Foucault's analysis alerts us to the notion that governance is by no means brought about only through political institutions. Rather, a wide array of institutions, from private corporations to the media, participate in shaping and moulding behaviour by inducing in the modern subject a state of constant vigilance over the self. As Mitchell Dean puts it, "government encompasses not only how we exercise authority over others, or how we govern abstract entities such as states and populations, but how we govern ourselves" (12). One may speculate that Dean is drawing from a moment in Foucault's analysis of the "microphysics of power" when he was elaborating on the operations of Bentham's Panopticon (*Discipline and Punish* 201). The disciplinary power of the Panopticon is such that it compels the inmates to govern their own behaviour. Likewise, the disciplinary power of the state and various other institutions is such that it compels subjects to govern their own behaviour, and this is made manifest in the novel.

In the novel, Chineseness is placed at one pole of a binary opposition, defined as freedom from the formal and restrictive codes of behaviour of the West. This is played out in the contrast between two schools in Singapore. Claude envies the Chinese-educated students from Hwa Ming over the plight of their English-educated counterparts from Littleton:

> Suddenly he knows what it is about them that he envies. It's their spontaneity, their way of yelling at each other and making a god-awful row and not caring. Littleton boys are always on their guard and at their best—there is always the feeling of being watched, of being afraid to be disgraced with a mispronounced word or gauche behaviour. (Loh 67)

Chineseness is also defined against decadence, indiscipline, and ineffectiveness. Just as the students from Hwa Ming are far more effective in fire-fighting than those from Littleton, the committed members of Dalforce, an anti-Japanese battalion composed largely of Chinese volunteers, is contrasted with the Australian and British deserters of their respective armies. At one point, Ling-li, who is tasked to help two Chinese informers wanted by the Japanese to leave Singapore, is disgusted by the fact that they are accompanied by four British Army escorts who are equally anxious to leave.

The novel depicts Claude's effort to learn Chinese as a demonstration of his recovery of Chineseness. After he is released from prison, he begins to speak and write Chinese under Hong-Seng's tutelage:

> Each word must be learnt, its design imprinted on the memory, but more than that, the strokes comprising each character are to be constructed in precise, predetermined ways. "Your hand must know where to go without your brain thinking" (Loh 466–467).

Chinese characters are depicted as extensions of the Chinese body. At the same time, they are sites where the nation is embodied. Earlier in the novel, Ling-li relates to Claude the story of Yue Fei, the Song Dynasty general, on whose back his mother tattooed the characters "精忠报国", translated in the novel as "The Ultimate Loyalty Is to Serve Your Country" (Loh 36). Claude recalls the Chinese character for "endurance" (忍), which he first learnt from Ling-li, a character comprised of the character for "knife" poised over the character for "heart": "For what is endurance but the strength of the heart under knife-blade?" (Loh 60). Just as it is this character that sustains Claude during his period of torture under the Japanese, it is this character that is written over the body of Malaya: The present is to be endured for the sake of the birth of the nation in history.

In the final section of the novel, Claude is visited by Ling-li in his dreams, where she describes for him in Chinese her torture and rape at the hands of her Japanese interrogators. As she is blindfolded, she requests that Claude provide her with descriptions of her tormentors, which he does in Chinese. Just as Claude's body in the hands of the Japanese is rendered into a historical and cultural site, so is Ling-li's. Claude is, in effect, witnessing and relating in part the rape of Singapore by the Japanese, and out of his testimony would emerge a history of the nation. As she says to Claude,

> If you won't witness this, who will? … If you won't remember and record this, who will? This is how our history starts and is transmitted, Claude. Witness and transmission of Story. 事实的见证和传述是历史. [History is the witnessing of the truth and its transmission] (Loh 480)

In this scene, Jack is also present. Yet he is emotionally detached from what he is made to witness. As Ling-li tells Claude, "Jack can afford to close his eyes, he can afford to turn away. In a few years, it will be over, and he will return to his country … He will be able to put his memories behind him, especially things he did not see" (Loh 480). Jack's presence is forgotten in the rest of the dream, as if to suggest that the witnessing and transmission of truth—in other words, the history of the nation—no longer require the intermediary presence of the British.

Given that the dialogue between Claude and Ling-li at this crucial point in the novel is written primarily in Chinese, one may suggest that Chineseness as a racial and cultural matrix is built into the history of the nation. Holden identifies this narrative move as affirming and reifying the racial governmentality at work in the state's construction of Singapore's nationalist discourse. As he points out,

> Loh's novel … reiterates, rather than challenges: rather than providing a genealogy of the present, it accepts hegemonic constructions of the present, and history's place within the present, at face value. ("Histories" 8)

However, Holden's analysis overlooks one of the points the novel is making—that the version of history provided by Claude and Ling-li is, after all, a version. At first reading, it may seem that the novel adopts a culturalist framework aligned with Singapore's nationalist project. After all, the novel's epigraph consists of a statement by Lee Kuan Yew made during the 1978 National Day Rally:

> I may speak the English language better than I speak the Chinese language … But I'll never be an Englishman in a thousand generations and I have not got the Western value system inside; it's an Eastern value system. (Lee "Excerpts of a Speech" 8)

Claude is in many ways like Lee; both were educated in English and are fluent in it, and both grew up within a particular historical time span in Singapore's history. However, at several self-reflexive moments in the novel, the omniscient narrator expresses surprise at Claude's ability to concoct stories: "Who suspected you would have such a perverse delight in fictions, versions, variations? History: the Detour. And you, its author" (Loh 43). The narrative of the nation—its truth and its transmission—that is historicised in the novel is presented as one out of many possible variations: "The truth has countless permutations. The lie, on the other hand, if correctly told, is specific, clearly defined, embedded with details and incidentals" (Loh 238). While the novel acknowledges the normative history of the nation as engendered by the state's discourse of nationalism, it reminds its readers that this is but one out of many possible narratives.

It is significant that in the final moments of the novel, Claude, the character who in many ways resembles Lee Kuan Yew, tears out his tongue. To destroy the tongue is to undo the authority of the single narrative—one that reifies the state's discourse of nation formation—the tongue has learned to speak. The tearing out of Claude's tongue, the mutilation of the part of the body responsible for speech and storytelling, creates a pain and a wound out of which new narratives may be articulated. The novel here is making the point that there is a need for the Singapore story to be rewritten. One is reminded here of the final moment in J. M. Coetzee's *Foe*, where Friday, who is unable to speak because he has no tongue, possesses a voice that overpowers all other narrative voices in the novel.

Breaking the Tongue offers a history; yet even as it gives this history a defining moment—that of the birth of Singapore's nationhood—it reminds us of the need to regard this history as a continuing project rather than as a fossilised legacy. The final words of the novel, which the narrator directs at Claude, draw attention to the malleability of narratives; they are a stricture against conferring authority onto a single narrative and a reminder that one has always to speak anew:

> Words, history, narrative can all be manipulated. And if you don't
> want [Ling-li] dead, then it's time to resurrect her, time to defy and
> outdo the construct once again. (Loh 489)

The ending of the novel reminds its readers that new stories, where categories such as nation, culture, race, and history are reconfigured anew, remain to be told. It speaks of a need to resurrect Ling-li, not as the story-teller who narrates the self-same story of the birth of the nation, but as one who is able to give another version of history.

Both *The Harmony Silk Factory* and *Breaking the Tongue* may be seen as postcolonial projects of writing about home. It has to be said that both novels are directed at a community of readers located primarily in Anglo-American locales. That Aw is based in London and that his novel was long-listed for the Man Booker

Prize in 2005 are noteworthy, especially if we recall Graham Huggan's critique regarding how literature of, from, and about the margins is marketed. Likewise, judging from the reviews in the *Washington Post*, the *Dallas Morning News*, the *Boston Sunday Herald*, and the San Jose *Mercury News*—parts of each grace the cover of *Breaking the Tongue*—it is clear that the book has been advanced as an "Asian-American" novel. The act of writing about home is not the same as writing *back* home, for it does not direct itself to the purpose of critically loosening the hold of dominant narratives of the present. Neither do the novels engage in dialogue the present dominant narratives of Singapore and Malaysia. Both texts are capitalising on the fact that they are not at home: Rather than interrogating the present, the novels are ideologically compromised.

Playing Madame Mao: Cultural revolution in Singapore

There is an instance in *Playing Madame Mao* when one of Kundera's novels, *Life is Elsewhere*, is mentioned, setting off common thematic resonances (Lau 218). Lau's novel is a political allegory. Hence, the comparison with Kundera's work is not far-fetched. Like Kundera's novel, *Playing Madame Mao* sets the personal against the political in contrapuntal balance, playing off a personal, intimate history of the self against the larger, impersonal, and often ruthless history of politics. Both novels suggest that, given the violence inflicted upon the fabric of everyday life by what has been deemed a political necessity, the personal has no choice but to be located elsewhere. As a result, life *is* elsewhere; it just is never where one happens to be. This novel, then, is motivated by a need to bring about alternative narratives. Given that the novel was published in Australia and that Lau emigrated there in 1994 because of a perceived lack of freedom from the "all-inclusive ideological boundaries of the state", there is certainly an autobiographical element in this work (Chin 14). In narrating another experience of the national, the novel suspends a constraining reality for a universe of multiple possibilities. As the protagonist puts it:

> At the end of dreaming, it is only a little room with cream walls that I wake up in. The curtains flap in the dust and smell of city living. It is a narrow area, and I am driven by desperation to look for a space beyond. (Lau 22)

Composed of fragmented scenes and half-revealed imagery, it has multiple narrators and different levels of realities, ranging from the mythic to the historical to the contemporary.

Tamara S. Wagner points out that *Playing Madame Mao* presents "[h]istory as an elusive, indeterminate [and] polymorphous process" (282). One may surmise that a novel that regards history as an on-going project would necessarily place any normative version of history—such as that fostered in Singapore's official discourse of nationalism—under critique. However, Holden in "Writing Conspiracy: Race and Rights in Two Singaporean Novels" warns against placing "too much celebratory faith in the power of ... texts [such as *Playing Madame Mao*] to question" (59). This is because while the novel "raise[s] questions regarding everyday politics in Singapore", it ultimately reaffirms rather than challenges "many of the discursive parameters of the Singaporean governmentality expressed through the management of ethnicity in the city-state" (Holden "Writing Conspiracy 67). For Holden, the novel diagnoses "the state's response to the Marxist conspiracy as a manifestation of an essential Chineseness, rather than proceeding from a specific mode of governmentality that reconstructs and utilises Chinese identity" ("Writing Conspiracy" 66). I argue that it is precisely this mode of governmentality that the novel submits to critique.

Playing Madame Mao is a postmodern novel insofar as one may define postmodernist aesthetics in its literary-textual manifestations: It incorporates "the textualized past into the text of the present" through the use of parody (Hutcheon 118). It is parody, a strategy absent in *The Harmony Silk Factory* and *Breaking the Tongue*, that gives the novel its critical force. The novel presents a dystopian and phantasmagoric vision of Singapore through the principle of mirroring, to the extent that the distinction between reflection and the reflected is blurred. It recalls the actual events of May 1987 in Singapore, when a Marxist conspiracy was supposedly uncovered, resulting in the arrest and detention of twenty-two people without trial under the Internal Security Act. In the novel, one historical moment is rendered into a parody of others. The conspiracy recalls the early history of Singapore's nation formation, when those regarded as communists in the People's Action Party left the government. This is juxtaposed with Mao's China, a China that came into being after the nationalists left the country.

The novel begins with the arrest of Tang Na Juan, a polytechnic lecturer who has written several articles attacking the government in a Catholic newsletter. His wife, Ching, trained as a Chinese opera actress, seeks a form of vicarious vengeance by playing Madame Mao:

> With my husband taken from me, all I have left now is revenge. Hui has asked me to help him redraft the play. I will play a dominant role, going over each word, taking the actors through the rehearsals, making sure each intonation, each gesture, each movement, betrays a hidden intent: to satirise Them. (Lau 22)

It is unclear, however, what Ching intends to achieve. The narrative at various moments subsumes character motivation and action under swift, often dizzying transitions among different levels of reality. The novel is a labyrinth of mirrors: We are presented with an actress, Ching, who plays on stage the historical Chiang

Ching, who was Mao's third wife and an actress who was eventually to play a key role as one of the "Gang of Four" during the Cultural Revolution. Ching's best friend, a journalist named Roxanne, is a mirror image of Roxane Witke, the American historian who went to China to study the plight of women under the Cultural Revolution. Witke eventually became the confidante and official biographer of the historical Chiang Ching. Ching's dissident husband, Tang Na Juan, has a historical counterpart in the person of Tang Na, a film critic and founding member of the communist-sponsored Art Society and rumoured to be Chiang Ching's former husband (Witke 133).

Playing Madame Mao is a carnivalesque disruption of history and the political status quo. It presents history and political reality not as finality but as a set of open-ended dynamics. As Mikhail Bakhtin argues in *Rabelais and His World* (1984), the medieval carnival

> offered a completely different, nonofficial, extraecclesiastical and extrapolitical aspect of the world, of man, and of human relations; [it builds] a second world and a second life outside officialdom, a world in which all medieval people participated more or less, in which they lived during a given time of the year. (5–6)

One may argue that *Playing Madame Mao* is an example of Bakhtin's thesis that carnival has migrated from the social sphere into the novel. The novelistic carnivalesque represents a suspension of authority, order, and hierarchy much in the same way as the medieval carnival did. *Playing Madame Mao* creates numerous parallels between Mao and Lee Kuan Yew, then the prime minister of Singapore. As in the carnival, where rulers and fools exchange places, the novel makes a parody out of Singapore's foremost figure of authority:

> I think of making the Chairman appear like a figure in a Theatre of the Absurd. I write down his common nickname: Hairy. I pretend he is not the demigod he is in reality, presiding over our lives; he … keeps the masses in slavish adoration. A good explanation for his prolonged popularity among the populace, who return him to power every election with the highest percentage of votes. How else can I explain this phenomenon? (Lau 23)

Even though his name is never mentioned in the novel, we know that the Chairman is the textual version of Lee Kuan Yew, who was known as Harry Lee when he was a student at Cambridge.

The themes of acting and staging are in the foreground of the novel. Apart from the protagonists's profession, there is Chiang Ching in history. At the height of her power, the historical Chiang was a cultural commissar who supported, wrote, and staged works sympathetic to communist politics. Theatre thus plays a disruptive role in the contexts of Singaporean politics (in the novel) and in the Chinese Revolution (in history). *Playing Madame Mao* interrupts Singapore's political status quo through textual deployment. The text inserts feminist presences derived from a pastiche of strong women drawn from the recesses of Chinese history. Ching would "learn to be a warrior woman. Like Hua Mu Lan" (Lau 140). She would also recall the deeds of "empresses and mother dowagers, and of the one empress in the long Chinese history who actually ascended the male-dominated throne, the Empress Wu Tse-tien" (Lau 140). This is where the novel's dialogic nature comes to the fore. On the one hand, the novel utilises descriptions of the excesses of the Chinese Cultural Revolution as a commentary on Singaporean politics; on the other, it comments on how blame for the excesses of the Cultural Revolution has been deflected from Mao and placed largely on the supposedly ruthless ambition of the historical Chiang Ching.

In this way, the novel launches a powerful satire against Singaporean nationalism. Through the mirroring and counter-mirroring of political narratives, *Playing Madame Mao* presents a dystopian portrayal of Singaporean politics seen through the lens of Mao's China—as Mao's China was seen, in turn, through the eyes of Madame Mao (which is, again in turn, seen through the eyes of an opera actress). Multiple realities and personalities collide to form a disorientation—a fruitful disorientation that serves to highlight the similarity within differences. The Chairman is

> a man born under the sign of the Virgo: intellectual, meticulous, a tough opponent. But not one to look too deeply into matters of the heart. His hirsute attributes are rather diminished near the temples. He reveals a grand sweep of the forehead, a pock-marked nose, and thin lips ... [He has] a fiery temper, a cutting tongue and an intolerance for fools. Fools, he believes, compose 99 per cent of the population he rules. (Lau 22)

It is tempting to think of the Cultural Revolution as a one-off affair in the history of politics, yet history, as the saying goes, repeats itself: "Chairman Mao's ambitions are reminiscent of the overwhelming desire of the First Emperor of China to control time and in so doing, also history" (Lau 17). The novel stops short of suggesting that Lee does the same, though it is disturbing to find that descriptions of Mao apply just as well to Lee.

Rather than accepting the parameters of Chineseness as constituted by the state's discourse of Singaporean nationalism, the novel parodies the process of its constitution so as to place it under critique. As Hutcheon puts it, "To parody is not to destroy the past; in fact to parody is both to enshrine the past and to question it" (126). If Lee Kuan Yew is likened to Mao, who is in turn likened to Chin Shih Huang Ti, the "despotic" first Emperor of China who "had wanted time and history to begin with him", it is to uncover the genealogy of racial governmentality essentialised and reconstructed in the politics of modern Singapore (Lau 17). The text mimics and parodies such a strategy when it utilises literary and historical figures such as Hua Mu Lan and Wu Tse-tien so as to establish a narrative that is contrapuntal to the history of racial governmentality as constituted by the patriarchal genealogy. In doing so, the novel utilises historically and politically essentialist constructs of Chineseness against themselves. Rather than reifying and privileging a particular mode of Chineseness, *Playing Madame Mao* employs the trope of theatricality to draw attention to Chineseness—not as a given, but as a script to be performed.

The novel, by juxtaposing Lee Kuan Yew's Singapore with Mao's China, bears the revelation that Singapore's economic success and its passage from third-world status to first-world nation within a few decades is a consequence of nothing less than a cultural revolution of sorts. The following quotation demonstrates the social contract between the government and the citizens of the state, one constitutive of the narrative present that underscores the government's subtle strategy of social control:

> MIND YOUR OWN BUSINESS. It is written upon my forehead, everyone's forehead. The business of the state is not to concern me, only basic necessities like how to earn enough money to feed my belly and put a roof over my head. I am not to make comments on things I can have insufficient information on. (Lau 20)

Contemporary Singapore, then, is the utopia created by a cultural revolution brought about through social control. This revolution is made possible not by street demonstrations and open denunciations (though there are denunciations), but through careful social engineering and efficient administration utilising policies and bureaucratic procedures with the consent of the populace. In *Playing Madame Mao*, Singapore's political landscape is shown to be part of a Chinese genealogy. Lee's Singapore is likened to Mao's China which in turn is likened to the China of Chin Shih Huang Ti. The narrative present, then, is constituted out of historical moments, each of which is a parody of its others, such that the novel presents a satirical critique of the power of those in the government.

As works written under conditions of expatriation, emigration, and diaspora, the novels just considered are uneven in terms of enabling us to consider what constitutes a critique of "local" conditions. The authors are not at home, both in the literal sense and also in the sense that they are alienated from the political and social climate that is their background. Yet by itself, distance is not necessarily a condition that enables critique. *The Harmony Silk Factory*, as an assemblage of fictionalised historical documents, highlights the problem inherent in any claim to a history that is authoritative. Malaya is unknowable, but its unknowability ushers in the return of the Orientalist trope of the inscrutable East. *Breaking the Tongue*, while acknowledging a normative history of the nation, confesses to a need for a narrative space for a renewed envisioning of history. However, the novel's tinge of nostalgia for an essentialist national narrative is problematic. Both of these novels ultimately translate Malaya and Singapore into textual products for readers outside of Singapore and Malaysia. In contrast, in *Playing Madame Mao,* the juxtaposition of Lee's government with that of Mao's forces us to see a genealogy of governance that we may otherwise choose not to see. The novel interrogates not just the process of writing history but, more important, any form of governmentality legitimised by history. Its revisionist momentum subverts the reification of history and the current nationalist discourse in Singapore.

Conclusion

We have traced through a range of Anglophone literary texts of Malaya and those of post-independence Singapore and Malaysia a history of anxiety that attends the condition of being not-at-home. One finds in colonialist writings and in literatures written after colonialism a situation in which cultural signs are continuously formulated, investigated, and reformulated. In all of these works, identities are contested and reformulated because governing ideological discourses offer a subjectivity that is limiting.

The narratives of Bird, Innes, and Caddy, each in its own way, reaffirm the assumptions of colonial rule; these are writings based on domestic ideological discourses of the late nineteenth century. However, there are ways of reading against the grain of colonialist discourse. The trope of amok deployed in Swettenham's writings may be read as an unhomely signifier that exceeds its colonialist frame, indicative of the coloniser's anxiety over the extent of their control over the colonised. Similarly, one may read the Malayan fiction of Maugham and Burgess as exemplifying the anxiety that attends to the realisation that the East can no longer be circumscribed as the site of colonial adventure.

There are disjunctions and continuities to be found between colonialism and nationalism, even though nationalists would claim that they are presiding over a national present that constitutes a complete break from the colonial past. A vision of Malaya as home and nation was articulated in the works of Lee Kok Liang, only to be curtailed by history. As the novels of K. S. Maniam remind us, Malaysian nationalism and multiculturalism circumscribe a limit that excludes those who are of non-Malay ethnicity. Yet this is not to say that the Malay subject as constituted by the discourse of Malaysian nationalism is unproblematic. For, as Karim's short story "Heroes" demonstrates, it is based on a maimed image of the Malay subject. Identity, as generated by colonialism and nationalism, is based on exclusion.

In the Singaporean context, the nationalist discourse is associated with a Darwinian ideology of survival and competition that underpins modernity.

Hegemony has been purchased, and the populace's allegiance to the ideas and vision of the political elite legitimised, by aligning the theme of national survival with that of economic survival. This is exemplified by Edwin Thumboo's "Ulysses by the Merlion", which seeks to naturalise and elevate a tourist symbol into a national myth. Singaporean nationalism comes under critique with Baratham's *A Candle or the Sun* and Jeyaretnam's *Abraham's Promise*. Both novels depict the political landscape of Singapore as premised on command and control, whereby the responsibility of a citizen and the citizen-writer is narrated as a responsibility to the state. As both novels show, there are boundaries that, when transgressed, exact a price on the part of the transgressor.

Does this imply, therefore, that subjectivity may locate its freedom outside of the enclosures as enacted by colonialist and nationalist discourses? Is it possible for one to seek freedom by declaring that one is at home anywhere in the world? As Tan's *Mammon Inc.* and Tay's *Alien Asian* remind us, Asian identity has to be negotiated, structured, and mapped onto the plane of commodity exchange to find recognition. My answer is that work has to be done in terms of re-visioning the history that has led to the present. Even then, one has to make distinctions regarding the critical agency of works of historiographic metafiction such as *The Harmony Silk Factory*, *Breaking the Tongue* and *Playing Madame Mao*.

Colonialism may be a thing of the past, but the same cannot be said of nationalism and the cultural imperialism of the West. The everyday present brings us new critical challenges, one of which is to learn to heed the momentary and momentous call of the unhomely with its promise of freedom.

Works Cited

Abdullah bin Abdul Kadir. *The Hikayat Abdullah*. Trans. A. H. Hill. Kuala Lumpur: Oxford University Press, 1970.
Achebe, Chinua. "An Image of Africa: Racism in Conrad's Heart of Darkness". *Hopes and Impediments: Selected Essays*. Achebe, NY: Doubleday, 1989; Great Britain: Heinemann, 1988. 1–20.
Aggeler, Geoffrey. *Anthony Burgess: The Artist as Novelist*. Alabama: The University of Alabama Press, 1979.
Ahmad, Aijaz. *In Theory: Classes, Nations, Literatures*. London: Verso, 1992.
Alatas, Syed Hussein. *The Myth of the Lazy Native: A Study of the Image of the Malays, Filipinos and Javanese from the 16th to the 20th Century and Its Function in the Ideology of Colonial Capitalism*. London: Frank Cass, 1977.
Alfian bin Sa'at. *One Fierce Hour*. Singapore: Landmark, 1998.
———. *Corridor*. Singapore: Raffles, 1999.
———. *A History of Amnesia*. Singapore: Ethos, 2001.
Andaya, Barbara Watson and Leonard Y. Andaya. *A History of Malaysia*. 2nd ed. Basingstoke: Palgrave, 2001.
Anderson, Benedict. *Imagined Communities: Reflections on the Origin and Spread of Nationalism*. Rev. ed. London: Verso, 1991.
Ang, Ien. *On Not Speaking Chinese: Living Between Asia and West*. London: Routledge, 2001.
Appadurai, Arjun. *Modernity at Large: Cultural Dimensions of Globalization*. Minneapolis: University of Minnesota Press, 1996.
Ashcroft, Bill. *Post-colonial Transformation*. London: Routledge, 2001.
Ashcroft, Bill, Gareth Griffiths, and Helen Tiffin. *The Empire Writes Back: Theory and Practice in Post-colonial Literatures*. 2nd ed. London: Routledge, 2002.
Aw, Tash. *The Harmony Silk Factory*. London: Harper Perennial, 2005.
Bakhtin, Mikhail Mikhailovich. *Rabelais and His World*. Trans. Hélène Iswolsky. Bloomington: Indiana University Press, 1984.
Ball, John Clement. *Imagining London: Postcolonial Fiction and the Transnational Metropolis*. Toronto: University of Toronto Press, 2004.
Ban, Kah Choon. "Narrating Imagination". *Imagining Singapore*. Eds. Ban Kah Choon, Anne Pakir and Tong Chee Kiong. 2nd ed. Singapore: Eastern Universities Press, 2004. 1–15.

Baratham, Gopal. *A Candle or the Sun*. London: Serpent's Tail, 1991.
Barlow, H. S. *Swettenham*. Kuala Lumpur: Southdene, 1995.
Barthes, Roland. *The Rustle of Language*. Trans. Richard Howard. New York: Hill and Wang, 1986.
Basch, Linda, Nina Glick Schiller and Cristina Szanton Blanc. *Nations Unbound: Transnational Projects, Postcolonial Predicaments and Deterritorialized Nation-States*. Pennsylvania: Gordon and Breach, 1994.
Begbie, Peter James. *The Malayan Peninsula: Embracing Its History, Manners and Customs of the Inhabitants, Politics, Natural History, & c. from Its Earliest Records*. [Madras]: Vepery Mission Press, 1834.
Bhabha, Homi K., ed. *Nation and Narration*. London: Routledge, 1990.
———. *The Location of Culture*. London: Routledge, 1994.
Bird, Isabella. *The Golden Chersonese and the Way Thither*. [1883]. Kuala Lumpur: Oxford University Press, 1967.
———. *Letters to Henrietta*. Ed. Kay Chubbuck. London: John Murray, 2002.
Biswell, Andrew. *The Real Life of Anthony Burgess*. London: Picador, 2005.
Blake, Ann, Leela Gandhi, and Sue Thomas. *England through Colonial Eyes in Twentieth-Century Fiction*. Houndmills, Basingstoke, Hampshire; New York: Palgrave, 2001.
Bloom, Harold. *The Anxiety of Influence: A Theory of Poetry*. 2nd ed. Oxford: Oxford University Press, 1997.
Brennan, Timothy. "The National Longing for Form". *Nation and Narration*. Ed. Homi K. Bhabha. London: Routledge, 1990. 44–70.
Brewster, Anne. *Towards a Semiotic of Postcolonial Discourse: University Writing in Singapore and Malaysia*. Singapore: Heinemann, 1989.
Brewster, J. W. "The Amok of Imam Mamat". *The Perak Government Gazette* 4 (13 March 1891): 131–133.
Brontë, Charlotte. *Jane Eyre: An Authoritative Text, Backgrounds, Criticism*. Ed. Richard J. Dunn. New York: Norton, 1971.
Burgess, Anthony. "Introduction". *Maugham's Malaysian Stories*. Ed. Anthony Burgess. Kuala Lumpur: Heinemann, 1969. vi–xvii.
———. *The Malayan Trilogy: Time for a Tiger, The Enemy in the Blanket, Beds in the East*. London: Vintage, 2000.
Caddy, Florence Caddy. *To Siam and Malaya in the Duke of Sutherland's Yacht 'Sans Peur'*. [1889]. Singapore: Oxford University Press, 1992.
Chan, Heng Chee. "Politics in an Administrative State: Where has the Politics Gone?" Singapore: Institute of Southeast Asian Studies, 1975.
Chan, Heng Wing. "PM Goh Remains Committed to Consultation and Consensus Politics". *The Straits Times*. 4 December 1994: 3.
Chang, Heewon. *Autoethnography as Method*. Walnut Creek, CA: Left Coast Press, 2008.
Chatterjee, Partha. *The Partha Chatterjee Omnibus: Nationalist Thought and the Colonial World; The Nation and Its Fragments; A Possible India*. New Delhi: Oxford University Press, 1999.
Cheong, Felix. *I Watch the Stars Go Out*. Singapore: Ethos, 1999.
Chin, Grace V. S. "The Anxieties of Authorship in Malaysian and Singaporean Writings in English: Locating the English Language Writer and the Question of Freedom in the Postcolonial Era". *Postcolonial Text*. 2.4 (2006): 1–24.

Chow, Rey. *Writing Diaspora: Tactics of Intervention in Contemporary Cultural Studies*. Bloomington: Indiana University Press, 1993.
Chua, Beng-Huat. *Communitarian Ideology and Democracy in Singapore*. London: Routledge, 1995.
Clark, Steve. "Introduction". *Travel Writing and Empire: Postcolonial Theory in Transit*. Ed. Clark. London: Zed, 1999. 1–28.
Clifford, Hugh. *Saleh: A Prince of Malaya*. Singapore: Oxford University Press, 1989 [1926].
Clifford, Hugh and Frank Athelstane Swettenham. *A Dictionary of the Malay Language: Malay-English*. Taiping, Perak: Government Printing Office, 1894–1902.
Clifford, James. *Routes: Travel and Translation in the Late Twentieth Century*. Cambridge, MA: Harvard University Press, 1997.
Coetzee, J. M. *Foe*. London: Penguin, 1987.
Conrad, Joseph. *Almayer's Folly*. Cambridge, MA: R. Bentley, 1971 [1895].
———. *An Outcast of the Islands*. London: T. F. Unwin, 1896.
———. *The Rescue*. Harmondsworth: Penguin, 1920.
———. *A Personal Record*. London: Dent, 1946.
———. *Youth/Heart of Darkness/The End of the Tether*. Ed. John Lyon. London: Penguin, 1995.
Dean, Mitchell. *Governmentality: Power and Rule in Modern Society*. London: Sage, 1999.
Defoe, Daniel. *Robinson Crusoe*. Oxford: Oxford University Press, 1999.
Ee, Tiang Hong. *Responsibility and Commitment: The Poetry of Edwin Thumboo*. Ed. Leong Liew Geok. Singapore: Singapore University Press, 1997.
Fanon, Frantz. *Black Skin, White Masks*. Trans. Charles Lam Markmann. New York: Grove, 1967; *Peau Noire, Masques Blancs*. Paris: Editions du Seuil, 1952.
———. *A Dying Colonialism*. Trans. Haakon Chevalier. Harmondsworth: Penguin, 1970; *L'An Cinq de la Révolution Algérienne*. Paris: François Maspero, 1959.
Fauconnier, Henri. *The Soul of Malaya*. Trans. Eric Sutton. Singapore: Archipelago, 1980 [1930].
Fernando, Lloyd. *Cultures in Conflict: Essays on Literature and the English Language in South East Asia*. Singapore: Graham Brash, 1986.
Foucault, Michel. *Discipline and Punish: The Birth of the Prison*. Trans. Alan Sheridan. London: Penguin, 1977.
———. "Governmentality". *The Foucault Effect: Studies in Governmentality*. Eds. Graham Burchell, Colin Gordon and Peter Miller. London: Harvester Wheatsheaf, 1991. 87–104.
Frawley, Maria H. *A Wider Range: Travel Writing by Women in Victorian England*. London: Associated University Presses, 1994.
Fukuyama, Francis. *The End of History and the Last Man*. New York: The Free Press, 1992.
Gellner, Ernest. *Nations and Nationalism*. Oxford: Basil Blackwell, 1983.
Gikandi, Simon. *Maps of Englishness: Writing Identity in the Culture of Colonialism*. New York: Columbia University Press, 1996.
Gill, Saran Kaur. "Language Policy in Malaysia: Reversing Direction". *Language Policy*. 4 (2005): 241–260.
Gilroy, Paul. *The Black Atlantic: Modernity and Double Consciousness*. London and New York: Verso, 1993.
Goh, Robbie B. H. *Contours of Culture: Space and Social Difference in Singapore*. Hong Kong: Hong Kong University Press, 2005.
———. "Imagining the Nation: The Role of Singapore Poetry in English in 'Emergent Nationalism'". *Journal of Commonwealth Literature*. 41.2 (2006): 21–41.

Gomez, Edmund Terence and Jomo K. S. *Malaysia's Political Economy: Politics, Patronage and Profits.* Cambridge: Cambridge University Press, 1997.

Gullick, John. "Florence Caddy: A Biographical Note". Florence Caddy. *To Siam and Malaya in the Duke of Sutherland's Yacht 'Sans Peur'.* Singapore: Oxford University Press, 1992. v–xiv.

Harper, T. N. *The End of Empire and the Making of Malaya.* Cambridge, UK: Cambridge University Press, 1999.

Haskell, Dennis. "Memory and Romanticism in Philip Jeyaretnam's *Abraham's Promise*". *Interlogue: Studies in Singapore Literature, Volume 1: Fiction.* Ed. Kirpal Singh. Singapore: Ethos, 1998. 145–156.

Hill, Michael and Lian Kwen Fee. *The Politics of Nation Building and Citizenship in Singapore.* London: Routledge, 1995.

Hilley, John. *Malaysia: Mahathirism, Hegemony and the New Opposition.* London: Zed, 2001.

Holden, Philip. *Orienting Masculinity, Orienting Nation: W. Somerset Maugham's Exotic Fiction.* Westport, CT: Greenwood, 1996.

———. "Love, Death and Nation: Representing Amok in British Malaya". *Literature and History* 6.1 (1997): 43–62.

———. "Histories of the Present: Reading Contemporary Singapore Novels between the Local and the Global". *Postcolonial Text* 2.2 (2006): 14pp. <http://postcolonial.org/index.php/pct/article/view/431/190>. Date Accessed: 25 June 2006.

———. "Writing Conspiracy: Race and Rights in Two Singapore Novels". *Journal of Postcolonial Writing* 42.1 (2006): 58–70.

Holy Bible, The. Revised Standard Version. London: Thomas Nelson and Sons, 1952.

Hooker, Virginia Matheson and M. B. Hooker. "Introductory Essay". *John Leyden's Malay Annals.* Trans. Leyden. Malaysia: Malaysian Branch of the Royal Asiatic Society, 2001. 1–72.

Huggan, Graham. *The Postcolonial Exotic: Marketing the Margins.* London and New York: Routledge, 2001.

Hunter, G. K. *Paradise Lost.* London: George Allen and Unwin, 1980.

Hutcheon, Linda. *A Poetics of Postmodernism.* London: Routledge, 1988.

Innes, Emily. *The Chersonese with the Gilding Off.* Vols. I and II. [1885]. Kuala Lumpur: Oxford University Press, 1993.

Jameson, Fredric. "Third-World Literature in the Era of Multinational Capitalism". *Social Text* 15 (1986): 65–88.

Jeyaretnam, Philip. *Tigers in Paradise: The Collected Works of Philip Jeyaretnam.* Singapore: Times Editions, 2004.

Jonas, Klaus W. "Maugham and the East". *The World of Somerset Maugham.* Ed. Jonas. Westport, CT: Greenwood Press, 1972. 96–141.

Joyce, James. *A Portrait of the Artist as a Young Man: Complete, Authoritative Text with Biographical and Historical Contexts, Critical History, and Essays from Five Contemporary Critical Perspectives.* Ed. R. B. Kershner. New York: Bedford Books of St. Martin's Press, 1993.

Karim Raslan. *Ceritalah: Malaysia in Transition.* Singapore: Times Books International, 1996.

———. *Heroes and Other Stories.* Singapore: Times Books International, 1996.

———. *Journeys through Southeast Asia: Ceritalah 2.* Singapore: Times Books International, 2002.

Khoo, Boo Teik. *Paradoxes of Mahathirism: An Intellectual Biography of Mahathir Mohamad.* Kuala Lumpur: Oxford University Press, 1995.
Klein, Ronald D. "Gopal Baratham". *Interlogue: Studies in Singapore Literature, Vol. 4: Interviews.* Ed. Klein. Singapore: Ethos, 2001. 80–102.
Krenn, Heliéna. *Conrad's Lingard Trilogy: Empire, Race and Women in the Malay Novels.* London: Garland, 1990.
Kundera, Milan. *Life is Elsewhere.* Trans. Peter Kussi. New York: Knopf, 1974.
Kuo Pao Kun. "The Coffin is Too Big for the Hole". *Images at the Margins: A Collection of Kuo Pao Kun's Plays.* Singapore: Times Books International, 2000.
Kwa, Chong Guan. "From Temasek to Singapore: Locating a Global City-State in the Cycles of Melaka Straits History". Eds. John M. Miksic and Cheryl-Ann Low Mei Gek. *Early Singapore, 1300s–1819: Evidence in Maps, Text and Artefacts.* 124–146.
Lau, Albert. "The National Past and the Writing of the History of Singapore". *Imagining Singapore.* 2nd ed. Eds. Ban Kah Choon, Anne Pakir and Tong Chee Kiong. Singapore: Eastern University Press, 2004. 34–53.
Lau, Siew Mei. *Playing Madame Mao.* New South Wales, Australia: Brandl and Schlesinger, 2000.
Lee, Kok Liang. "Return to Malaya." *The Mutes in the Sun and Other Stories.* Lee. Kuala Lumpur: Rayirath (Raybooks), 1963. 182–204.
———. *Flowers in the Sky.* Kuala Lumpur: Heinemann, 1981.
———. *Death is a Ceremony and Other Short Stories.* Singapore: Federal, 1992.
———. *London Does Not Belong to Me.* Eds. Syd Harrex and Bernard Wilson. Petaling Jaya, Malaysia: Maya Press, 2003.
Lee, Kuan Yew. *The Battle for Merger.* Singapore: Government Printing Office [1961].
———. "Excerpts of a Speech made by the Prime Minister, Mr. Lee Kuan Yew, at the National Day Rally held at the National Theatre on 13 August, 1978". 17pp. Speech-Text Archival and Retrieval System. National Archives of Singapore. <http://stars.nhb.gov.sg/stars/public/> Date Accessed: 20 December 2005.
———. *From Third World to First, The Singapore Story: 1965–2000, Memoirs of Lee Kuan Yew.* Singapore: Times Media, 2000.
Lee, Lai To. "Singapore in 1987: Setting a New Agenda". *Asian Survey* 28.2 (1988): 202–212.
Lee, Tzu Pheng. "My Country and My People". Society of Singapore Writers. *Tides of Memories and Other Singapore Poems.* Rev. ed. Singapore: Asiapac Books, 2002.
Leong, Liew Geok. "'We must make a people': The Lyric Enterprise of Edwin Thumboo". *Interlogue: Studies in Singapore Literature, Volume 2: Poetry.* Ed. Kirpal Singh. Singapore: Ethos, 1999. 35–49.
———. "Dissenting Voices: Political Engagements in the Singaporean Novels in English." *World Literature Today* 74.2 (2000): 285–292.
Leyden, John, trans. *John Leyden's Malay Annals.* Malaysia: Malaysian Branch of the Royal Asiatic Society, 2001.
Lim, Arthur Joo-Jock. "Geographical Setting". *A History of Singapore.* Eds. Ernest C. T. Chew and Edwin Lee. Singapore: Oxford University Press, 1991. 3–14.
Lim, Catherine. "The PAP and the People: A Great Affective Divide". *The Straits Times.* 3 September 1994: 34.
Lim, David C. L. *The Infinite Longing for Home: Desire and the Nation in Selected Writings of Ben Okri and K. S. Maniam.* Amsterdam; New York: Rodopi, 2005.

Lim, Shirley Geok-lin. "Finding a Native Voice: Singapore Literature in English". *The Journal of Commonwealth Literature* 24.1(1989): 30–48.

———. "The English-Language Writer in Singapore". *Management of Success: The Moulding of Modern Singapore*. Eds. Kernial Singh Sandhu and Paul Wheatley. Singapore: Institute of Southeast Asian Studies, 1989.

———. *Writing S.E./Asia in English: Against the Grain, Focus on Asian English-Language Literature*. London: Skoob, 1994.

———. *Among the White Moonfaces: Memoirs of a Nonya Feminist*. Singapore: Times Books International, 1996.

Lim, Suchen Christine. *Fistful of Colours*. Singapore: EPB Publishers, 1993.

———. *A Bit of Earth*. Singapore: Times Books International, 2001.

Loh, Kok Wah Francis. "Developmentalism and the Limits of Democratic Discourse". *Democracy in Malaysia: Discourses and Practices*. Eds. Loh and Khoo. Richmond, Surrey: Curzon Press, 2002. 19–50.

Loh, Kok Wah Francis and Khoo Boo Teik. "Introduction". *Democracy in Malaysia: Discourses and Practices*. Eds. Loh and Khoo. Richmond, Surrey: Curzon Press, 2002. 1–18.

Loh, Vyvyane. *Breaking the Tongue*. New York: W. W. Norton, 2004.

Mahathir Mohamad. *The Malay Dilemma*. Singapore: Times Books International, 1970.

Maniam, K. S. *The Return*. London: Skoob, 1981; 1993.

———. *In a Far Country*. London: Skoob, 1993.

———. *Between Lives*. Selangor, Malaysia: Maya Press, 2003.

———. "Introduction." *London Does Not Belong to Me*. Lee Kok Liang. Eds. Syd Harrex and Bernard Wilson. Petaling Jaya, Malaysia: Maya Press, 2003. 1–8.

Marx, Karl. *Capital: A Critique of the Political Economy*. Vol. 1. Trans. Samuel Moore and Edward Aveling. Ed. Frederick Engels. Moscow: Progress Press, 1954.

Mathews, Gordon. *Global Culture/Individual Identity: Searching for Home in the Cultural Supermarket*. London: Routledge, 2000.

Maugham, W. Somerset. *Collected Short Stories: Volume Four*. London: Pan, 1976.

McClintock, Anne. "The Angel of Progress: Pitfalls of the Term 'Post-colonialism'". *Social Text* 31/32 (1992): 84–98.

McLeod, John. *Postcolonial London: Rewriting the Metropolis*. London; New York: Routledge, 2004.

Means, Gordon P. *Malaysian Politics: The Second Generation*. Singapore: Oxford University Press, 1991.

Meyers, Jeffrey. *Somerset Maugham: A Life*. New York: Alfred A. Knopf, 2004.

Miksic, John N. and Cheryl-Ann Low Mei Gek, eds. *Early Singapore, 1330s–1819: Evidence in Maps, Text and Artefacts*. Singapore: Singapore History Museum, 2004.

Mills, Sara. *Discourses of Difference: An Analysis of Women's Travel Writing and Colonialism*. London: Routledge, 1991.

Milton, John. *Paradise Lost*. Ed. Alastair Fowler. London: Longman, 1968.

Morgan, Susan. *Place Matters: Gendered Geography in Victorian Women's Books about Southeast Asia*. New Brunswick, NJ: Rutgers University Press, 1996.

Muhkerjee, Arun P. "Whose Post-colonialism and Whose Postmodernism?" *World Literature Written in English* 30.2 (1990): 1–9.

———. "Some Uneasy Conjectures". *Interrogating Post-colonialism: Theory, Text and Context*. Eds. Harish Trivedi and Meenakshi Mukherjee. Shimla: Indian Institute of Advanced Study, 1996. 13–20.

Mukherjee, Meenakshi. "The Exile of the Mind". *A Sense of Exile: Essays in the Literature of the Asia-Pacific Region*. Ed. Bruce Bennett. Western Australia: The Centre for Studies in Australian Literature, the University of Western Australia, 1988. 7–14.

———. "Interrogating Post-colonialism". *Interrogating Post-colonialism: Theory, Text and Context*. Eds. Harish Trivedi and Mukherjee. Shimla: Indian Institute of Advanced Study, 1996. 3–11.

Orwell, George. *1984*. New York: New American Library, 1949.

———. *Burmese Days*. London: Secker and Warburg [1949].

Pang, Alvin. *City of Rain*. Singapore: Ethos, 2003.

Poon, Angelia. "Performing National Service in Singapore: (Re)imagining Nation in the Poetry and Short Stories of Alfian Sa'at". *Journal of Commonwealth Literature* 40.3 (2005): 118–138.

Pratt, Mary Louise. *Imperial Eyes: Travel Writing and Transculturation*. London: Routledge, 1992.

Press, John, ed. *Commonwealth Literature: Unity and Diversity in a Common Culture*. London: Heinemann Educational Books Ltd., 1965.

Raffles, Thomas Stamford. *Statement of the Services of Sir Stamford Raffles*. Kuala Lumpur: Oxford University Press, 1978.

Reid, Anthony. *Charting the Shape of Early Modern Southeast Asia*. Singapore: Institute of Southeast Asian Studies, 2000.

Rhys, Jean. *Wide Sargasso Sea*. New York: Norton, 1982.

Rodan, Garry. *Transparency and Authoritarian Rule in Southeast Asia: Singapore and Malaysia*. London: RoutledgeCurzon, 2004.

Rushdie, Salman. *Imaginary Homelands: Essays and Criticism, 1981–1991*. London: Granta, 1991.

Said, Edward W. *Culture and Imperialism*. New York: Vintage, 1993.

———. *Orientalism*. New York: Vintage, 1978.

Salleh Ben Joned. *As I Please*. Singapore: Times Editions, 2003.

Scarry, Elaine. *The Body in Pain: The Making and Unmaking of the World*. New York: Oxford University Press, 1985.

Sheppard, M. C. *The Adventures of Hang Tuah*. Singapore: Donald Moore [195–].

Shiau, Daren V. L. *Peninsular*. Ethos, 2000.

Shohat, Ella. "Notes on the 'Post-Colonial'". *Social Text* 31/32 (1992): 99–113.

Singh, Davinder. "Are We Prepared for New World Order?" *The Straits Times*. 17 August 2004: 13.

Slemon, Stephen. "Magic Realism as Postcolonial Discourse". *Magical Realism: Theory, History, Community*. Eds. Lois Parkinson Zamora and Wendy B. Faris. Durham: Duke University Press, 1995. 407–426.

Smith, Roland, ed. *Postcolonizing the Commonwealth: Studies in Literature and Culture*. Waterloo, Ontario: Wilfrid Laurier University Press, 2000.

Spivak, Gayatri Chakravorty. "The Rani of Sirmur". Eds. Francis Barker et al. *Europe and Its Others, Volume One: Proceedings of the Essex Conference on the Sociology of Literature, July 1984*. Colchester: University of Essex, 1985. 128–151.

———. "Criticism, Feminism, and the Institution". *The Post-colonial Critic: Interviews, Strategies, Dialogues*. Ed. Sarah Harasym. New York: Routledge, 1990. 1–16.

Spores, John C. *Running Amok: An Historical Inquiry*. Athens, OH: Ohio University Center for International Studies, 1988.

Stape, J. H. "Conrad's 'Unreal City': Singapore in 'The End of the Tether'". Ed. Gene M. Moore. *Conrad's Cities*. Amsterdam: Rodopi, 1992. 85–96.

Swettenham, Frank Athelstane. *The Real Malay: Pen Pictures*. London: John Lane, 1900.
——. *Footprints in Malaya*. London: Hutchinson, 1942.
——. *British Malaya: An Account of the Origin and Progress of British Influence in Malaya*. 1906. Rev. ed. London: George Allen and Unwin, 1948.
——. *Malay Sketches*. [1895]. Singapore: Graham Brash, 1984.
Talib, Ismail S. "Malaysia and Singapore". *Journal of Commonwealth Literature* 39.4 (2004): 71–96.
Tan, Hwee Hwee. *Foreign Bodies*. London: Penguin, 1998.
——. *Mammon Inc*. London: Penguin, 2002.
Tay, Eddie. "Hegemony, National Allegory, Exile: The Poetry of Shirley Lim". *Textual Practice* 19.3 (2005): 289–308.
Tay, Simon. *5*. Singapore: Department of English Language and Literature, National University of Singapore, 1985.
——. *Prism*. [Singapore]: [S. Tay], 1980.
——. *Stand Alone*. Singapore: Landmark, 1991.
——. *Alien Asian: A Singaporean in America*. Singapore: Landmark, 1997.
——. *City of Small Blessings*. Singapore: Landmark, 2009.
Tennyson, Alfred Lord. "Ulysses". *The Poems of Tennyson in Three Volumes*. 2nd ed. Ed. Christopher Ricks. Essex: Longman, 1987. 613–619.
Thio, Eunice. *British Policy in the Malay Peninsula, 1880–1910*. Singapore: University of Malaya Press, 1969.
Thomas, Nicholas. *Colonialism's Culture: Anthropology, Travel and Government*. Cambridge: Polity Press, 1994.
Thumboo, Edwin. "Introduction". *The Second Tongue: An Anthology of Poetry from Singapore and Malaysia*. Ed. Thumboo. Singapore: Heinemann Educational Books (Asia) Ltd, 1976. vii–xxxv.
——. *A Third Map: New and Selected Poems*. Singapore: UniPress, 1993.
Trivedi, Harish and Meenakshi Mukherjee, eds. *Interrogating Post-colonialism: Theory, Text and Context*. Shimla: Indian Institute of Advanced Study, 1996.
Turnbull, C. M. *A History of Singapore, 1819–1988*. 2nd ed. Singapore: Oxford University Press, 1989.
Viswanathan, Gauri. *Masks of Conquest: Literary Study and British Rule in India*. London: Faber, 1990.
Wagner, Tamara S. *Occidentalism in Novels of Malaysia and Singapore, 1819–2004: Colonial and Postcolonial Financial Straits and Literary Style*. Lewiston, NY: Edwin Mellon Press, 2005.
Wee, C. J. W.-L. *The Asian Modern: Culture, Capitalist Development, Singapore*. Hong Kong: Hong Kong University Press, 2007.
Wilson, Bernard. "Memory, Myth, Exile: The Desire for Malaysian Belonging in K. S. Maniam's *The Return*, 'Haunting the Tiger' and *In a Far Country*". *Textual Practice* 17.2 (2003): 391–412.
——. "*Sketches, Vignettes & Brush Strokes:* Portraits of the (Malaysian) Writer as a Young Man". *Jouvert: A Journal of Postcolonial Studies* 7.2 (2003): 13pp. <http://social.chass.ncsu.edu/jouvert/v7i2/bwils.htm> Date Accessed: 25 November 2004.
——. "Submerging Pasts in *London Does Not Belong to Me*." *London Does Not Belong to Me*. Lee Kok Liang. Ed. Syd Harrex and Bernard Wilson. Petaling Jaya, Malaysia: Maya Press, 2003. 313–331.

Witke, Roxane. *Comrade Chiang Ching*. London: Weidenfeld and Nicolson, 1977.
Yahya, Zawiah. *Resisting Colonialist Discourse*. 2nd ed. Selangor, Malaysia: Pernerbit Universiti Kebangsaan, 2003.
Yeo, Kim Wah and Albert Lau. "From Colonialism to Independence, 1945–1965". *A History of Singapore*. Eds. Ernest C. T. Chew and Edwin Lee. Singapore: Oxford University Press, 1991. 117–153.
Yeoh, Brenda S. A. and T. C. Chang. "'The Rise of the Merlion': Monument and Myth in the Making of the Singapore Story". *Theorizing the Southeast Asian City as Text: Urban Landscapes, Cultural Documents, and Interpretative Experiences*. Eds. Robbie B. H. Goh and Brenda S. H. Yeoh. Singapore: World Scientific, 2003. 29–50.
Yeow, Agnes. "Conrad and the Straits Chinese: The Politics of Chinese Enterprise and Identity in the Colonial State". *The Conradian* 29.1 (2004): 84–98.
———. "'Here comes the Nazarene': Conrad's Treatment of the Serani and the Racial Politics of Empire". *Conradiana* 39.3 (2007): 273–290.
Young, Robert J. C. *Colonial Desire: Hybridity in Theory, Culture and Race*. London: Routledge, 1995.
———. *White Mythologies: Writing History and the West*. 2nd ed. London: Routledge, 2004.
Zamora, Lois Parkinson and Wendy B. Faris. "Introduction: Daiquiri Birds and Flaubertian Parrot(ie)s". *Magical Realism: Theory, History, Community*. Eds. Zamora and Faris. Durham: Duke University Press, 1995. 1–11.

Index

Achebe, Chinua, 25
Afonso de Albuquerque, 34
Ahmad, Aijaz, 6, 119
Alatas, S. H., 87
Alfian bin Sa'at, 8, 10, 11, 77, 78, 82–84, 94
amok, 8, 11, 15, 16, 22–29, 43, 50, 65, 87, 115, 151
Anderson, Benedict, 49, 94
Ang, Ien, 88, 129
annexation, 39–40
anxiety of influence, 45–46, 47, 54, 81
Appadurai, Arjun, 122, 132
Ashcroft, Bill, 6, 65, 72, 74
Aw, Tash, 4, 9, 12, 133–138, 144

Bakhtin, Mikhail Mikhailovich, 147
Baratham, Gopal, 8, 11, 12, 93, 94, 101–106, 134, 152
Barthes, Roland, 97
Bhabha, Homi, 5–6, 23, 46, 51, 53
Birch, James. W. W., 24–25, 26–28, 32–33
Bird, Isabella Lucy, 2, 8, 11, 20–21, 31–37, 40, 42, 43, 45, 54, 60, 151
Bloom, Harold, 45
Brennan, Timothy, 94, 105
Brewster, Anne, 10, 77
bumiputera, 3, 87–88
Burgess, Anthony, 2, 7, 8, 10, 11, 54–60, 63, 65, 151

Caddy, Florence, 8, 11, 29, 31, 32, 40–43, 45, 49, 60, 135, 151
Chatterjee, Partha, 94
Cheong, Colin, 7
Cheong, Felix, 82
Chineseness, 70, 141–143, 146, 148–149
Chow, Rey, 110
Chua, Beng-Huat, 3, 95
Clifford, Hugh, 2, 7, 15, 28
Clifford, James, 110
colonialist historiography, 15–16
Commonwealth literary studies, 5–7, 8, 10
"Confucian" (or "Asian") values, 4, 79, 100
Conrad, Joseph, 10, 25, 46–47, 54, 57, 59, 65
contact zone, 64
Cromwell, Oliver, 21
cultural imperialism, 4, 59, 152
Cultural Revolution, 134, 147–149

decolonisation, 1, 7, 54–56, 65
diaspora, 7, 8, 9, 10, 12, 110, 109–119, 133, 149
dis-identification, 6, 64–66
Douglas, William Bloomfield, 32, 36–37
Dutch East India Company, 21, 34

East India Company, 18, 21
Ee, Tiang Hong, 3, 9, 10, 80, 93, 109
Englishness, 11, 46, 48, 56–57, 60
Engmalchin, 77
essentialism, 27, 112, 125, 129, 132, 133, 146, 148–150

ethnicity, 5, 20,110, 125, 126, 129
    and authors, 9–10, 82, 133
    and Malay(sian) nationalism, 3, 12, 75, 84, 87–88, 91–92, 110, 119, 121, 151
    and Singapore's nationalism, 78–79, 146
    and representation, 58, 63, 68, 112–113, 116–118, 126, 128–130, 141

Fauconnier, Henri, 15
Fernando, Lloyd, 109
Foucault, Michel, 141
Frantz Fanon, 5, 6, 24, 25–26, 28, 29
Fukuyama, Francis, 79

Gellner, Ernest, 96
Gikandi, Simon, 48
Gilroy, Paul, 110
Goh, Robbie B. H., 4, 8, 80

Harper, T. N., 2, 77, 87
Haskell, Dennis, 99
hegemony, 46, 79, 86, 112–114, 118, 119, 143, 152
Hikayat Abdullah (The Story of Abdullah), 19–20, 22
Hikayat Hang Tuah (The Adventures of Hang Tuah), 22, 23
Holden, Philip, 15, 28, 51, 52, 101, 141, 143, 146
homeland, 71, 110, 116, 118
Huggan, Graham, 145
Hutcheon, Linda, 134, 146, 148
    and historiographic metafiction, 134, 152
hybridity, 51, 73, 122

ideological state apparatus, 81, 117
imagined community, 49, 96, 132
    and *Abraham's Promise*, 98, 105
    and *A Candle or the Sun*, 103
    and *Between Lives*, 117
    and *Breaking the Tongue*, 140
    and British Malaya, 16
    and Malayan Union, 57
    and Partha Chatterjee, 94
    and Singapore, 96
Indian "Mutiny", 2, 25, 36
Innes, Emily, 8, 11, 31, 32, 37–40, 43, 45, 60, 151

Jameson, Fredric, 6, 139
Jeyaretnam, Joshua Benjamin, 98
Jeyaretnam, Philip, 8, 11, 12, 94, 97–101, 152
Joyce, James, 56–57, 59

Karim Raslan, 3, 9, 11, 77, 78, 88–92, 151
Kipling, Rudyard, 54
Klein, Ronald D., 102
Khoo, Boo Teik, 86, 87
Kon, Stella, 7
Kuo, Pao Kun, 10–11
Kwa, Chong Guan, 20

language policy, 9, 10, 65, 84, 86, 109, 133, 143
Lau, Siew Mei, 3, 9, 12, 94, 133–134, 145–149
Lee, Kok Liang, 2, 6, 8, 9, 11, 63–75, 77, 151
Lee Kuan Yew, 3, 20, 134, 143–144, 147–150
    and English language, 143–144
    and Malayan Forum, 55
    and nationalism, 84, 96
    and People's Action Party, 78
    Battle for Merger, 78
    From Third World to First, 79, 80, 94–95
Lee, Tzu Pheng, 8
Leong, Liew Geok, 81, 106
Lim, Catherine, 95–96
Lim, David C. L., 112, 114
Lim, Shirley Geok-lin, 3, 8, 9, 10, 86, 93, 109, 133
Lim, Suchen Christine, 7
Loh, Vyvyane, 9, 12, 134, 138–145

magic realism, 111–112, 115, 119
Mahathir bin Mohamad, 86–88, 89
Malayan Emergency, 54, 104
Malayan Union, 54, 78
Maniam, K. S., 3, 9, 12, 64, 92, 109–119, 121, 133, 151
Manicheanism, 15, 23, 26, 51, 65
Mao, 3, 134, 146, 147–149
Marx, Karl, 126
Marxist "Conspiracy", 101, 134, 146
Mathews, Gordon, 130–131
Maugham, Somerset W., 7, 8, 10, 11, 45, 46, 63, 65, 151
    "German Harry", 48

"Masterson", 48–49
"Mirage", 48
"Neil MacAdam", 46–47
"The Book-Bag", 50–51
"The Letter", 51–53
"The Outstation", 49–50
McClintock, Anne, 65
Merlion, 8, 80–84, 92, 93, 128–129
Morgan, Susan, 16, 31, 35–36
Mills, Sara, 8, 11, 32, 40
Milton, John, 20–21
mimicry, 51–53, 141
"money politics", 88, 115, 117
Mukherjee, Arun P., 5, 65
Mukherjee, Meenakshi, 5, 109
multiculturalism, 58, 84, 88, 117, 151

National Arts Council (Singapore), 98, 122
nationalism, 3, 6, 8–9, 12, 56, 59, 151, 152
    and Malaya, 55, 58, 60
    and Malaysia, 75, 77–78, 84–92, 109–119, 121
    and Singapore, 77–84, 92, 93–106, 141, 144, 146, 148
New Economic Policy (NEP), 3, 12, 87–88, 90–91, 117

Occidentalism, 53, 69–70
Orientalism, 5, 27, 53, 56, 73, 130, 137, 138, 149
Orwell, George, 54, 101

Pang, Alvin, 10, 82
Pangkor Treaty, 2, 16, 24, 32–33
People's Action Party (PAP), 78–79, 93, 95–96, 146
Poon, Angelia, 82
postcolonialism, 5–7, 8, 11, 65, 79
post-diasporic condition, 3, 9, 12, 109–119, 121
postmodernism, 6, 146
Pratt, Mary Louise, 64
Press, John, 5

race riots, 86–87, 90–92, 116–117, 119
Raffles, Stamford, 16, 18–19, 20
Reid, Anthony, 15
Rodan, Garry, 3, 95
Rushdie, Salman, 5, 110, 119

Said, Edward, 5–6
Salleh Ben Joned, 92
Sang Nila Utama, 17, 19, 128
Scarry, Elaine, 139–140
Sejarah Melayu (*Malay Annals*), 17, 19, 22
Shakespeare, William, 56–57
Shiau, Daren, 82
Shohat, Ella, 65
Singapore Stone, 19–20
Slemon, Stephen, 112
Spivak, Gayatri Chakravorty, 5–6, 33, 125
Spores, John C., 23
Swettenham, Frank Athelstane, 2, 6, 7, 8, 11, 15–29, 32, 33, 43, 45, 54, 60, 65, 151
    British Malaya, 16, 17–18, 22, 33
    Footprints in the Jungle, 16, 27–28
    Malay Sketches, 16, 22–25, 27
    The Real Malay, 16, 24–25, 27

Talib, Ismail S., 7
Tan, Hwee Hwee, 3–4, 9, 12, 121–123, 126–132, 133, 152
Tay, Simon S. C., 9, 12, 121–126, 132, 152
Tennyson, Alfred Lord, 55, 56
The Empire Writes Back, 65–66, 72
Thio, Eunice, 140
Thomas, Nicholas, 18
Thumboo, Edwin, 8, 10, 11, 77–78, 80–84, 93, 152
Toh, Hsien Min, 10
Trivedi, Harish, 5
Turnbull, C. M., 17, 18, 54, 55, 84
transnationalism, 7, 12, 121–122

Viswanathan, Gauri, 46

Wagner, Tamara S., 4, 145
Wang, Gungwu, 10
Wee, C. J. W.-L, 4, 96
Wilson, Bernard, 63, 66, 68, 69, 72, 112
Wong, Cyril, 10
Wong, Phui Nam, 10

Yahya, Zawiah, 65
Yeow, Agnes, 10
Young, Robert J. C. 6, 19, 27, 73

www.ingramcontent.com/pod-product-compliance
Ingram Content Group UK Ltd.
Pitfield, Milton Keynes, MK11 3LW, UK
UKHW041428180426
11947UKWH00007B/347